LEGAL VALIDITY

Critical human interests are affected on a daily basis by appeal to past decisions deemed to be 'legally valid'. They include statutes, deportation orders, judgments, mortgage contracts, patents and wills. Through the technique of validity, lawyerly reasoning settles morally pressing matters in a way that largely bypasses moral argument. Legal philosophy has paid considerable attention to validity criteria, but it has neglected to explore validity's point: whether, and if so how, the pervasive technique of validity can contribute to a legal system's ability to realise justice and human rights. This book shows that validity can help a political community to foster justice precisely because validity does not primarily turn on moral considerations. Validity serves to both allocate, and limit, a distinct kind of power, a power that is key to forging valuable forms of enterprise and commitment in pursuit of individual and collective self-direction. By entrusting the capacity to decide to those who, in justice, ought to bear it, validity can enable persons and institutions to rally the resources and opportunities that only large-scale behavioural convergence can afford, thereby weaving a fabric of just relationships within the systemic framework of law.

European Academy of Legal Theory Monograph Series: Volume 15

EUROPEAN ACADEMY OF LEGAL THEORY MONOGRAPH SERIES

General Editors

Professor Mark Van Hoecke

Professor François Ost

Titles in this Series

Moral Conflict and Legal Reasoning
Scott Veitch

The Harmonisation of European Private Law
Edited by Mark Van Hoecke & Francois Ost

On Law and Legal Reasoning
Fernando Atria

Law as Communication
Mark Van Hoecke

Legisprudence
Edited by Luc Wintgens

Epistemology and Methodology of Comparative Law
Edited by Mark van Hoecke

Making the Law Explicit
The Normativity of Legal Argumentation
Matthias Klatt

The Policy of Law
A Legal Theoretical Framework
Mauro Zamboni

Methodologies of Legal Research
Which Kind of Method for What Kind of Discipline?
Edited by Mark van Hoecke

Objectivity in Law and Legal Reasoning
Edited by Jaakko Husa & Mark van Hoecke

An Introduction to Comparative Law Theory and Method
Geoffrey Samuel

The Tapestry of Reason
An Inquiry into the Nature of Coherence and its Role in Legal Argument
Amalia Amaya

Democracy and Ontology
Agonism between Political Liberalism, Foucault and Psychoanalysis
Irena Rosenthal

Global Constitutionalism and Its Challenges to Westphalian Constitutional Law
Martin Belov

Legal Validity
The Fabric of Justice
Maris Köpcke

Legal Validity

The Fabric of Justice

Maris Köpcke

•HART•

OXFORD • LONDON • NEW YORK • NEW DELHI • SYDNEY

HART PUBLISHING
Bloomsbury Publishing Plc
Kemp House, Chawley Park, Cumnor Hill, Oxford, OX2 9PH, UK

HART PUBLISHING, the Hart/Stag logo, BLOOMSBURY and the Diana
logo are trademarks of Bloomsbury Publishing Plc

First published in Great Britain 2019
First published in hardback, 2019
Paperback edition, 2020

A catalogue record for this book is available from the British Library.

Library of Congress Cataloging-in-Publication data
Names: Köpcke, Maris, 1978-author.
Title: Legal validity: the fabric of justice / Maris Köpcke.
Description: Oxford [UK]; Portland, Oregon: Hart Publishing, 2019. |
Series: European academy of legal theory series
Identifiers: LCCN 2018038297 (print) | LCCN 2018038553 (ebook) |
ISBN 9781509904297 (Epub) | ISBN 9781849466868 (hardback)
Subjects: LCSH: Effectiveness and validity of law. | Law—Methodology. | Rule of law. |
Jurisprudence. | Law—Philosophy.
Classification: LCC K260 (ebook) | LCC K260.T56 2018 (print) | DDC 340/.114—dc23
LC record available at https://lccn.loc.gov/2018038297

ISBN: HB: 978-1-84946-686-8
PB: 978-1-50994-524-5
ePDF: 978-1-50990-428-0
ePub: 978-1-50990-429-7

Typeset by Compuscript Ltd, Shannon

To find out more about our authors and books visit www.hartpublishing.co.uk.
Here you will find extracts, author information, details of forthcoming events and
the option to sign up for our newsletters.

For Pasqual R

And for my students, past, present and future

LEGAL VALIDITY IS A WINNER OF THE EUROPEAN AWARD FOR LEGAL THEORY. PAST WINNERS INCLUDE:

Michel Paroussis (1994),
Theorie des juristischen Diskurses

Emilios Christodoulidis (1996),
Law and Reflexive Politics (Kluwer 1998)

Scott Veitch (1998),
Moral Conflict and Legal Reasoning (Hart 1999)

Fernando Atria (2000),
On Law and Legal Reasoning (Hart 2001)

Matthias Klatt (2002),
Making the Law Explicit (Hart 2008)

Mauro Zamboni (2005),
The Policy of Law (Hart 2007)

Amalia Amaya (2008),
The Tapestry of Reason (Hart 2015)

Maris Köpcke (2011),
Legal Validity (Hart 2019)

Irena Rosenthal (2015),
Democracy and Ontology (Hart 2018)

Andrej Kristan (2015),
Law & Other Enigmas

Acknowledgements

THE CENTRAL IDEAS of this book took shape in the course of my teaching and research at the University of Oxford, where I was a Fellow and Tutor in Law until 2014 and had previously completed my doctorate, the earliest forebear of the present work. The masterfully inspiring joint supervision of John Finnis and John Gardner helped to steer and mould the original project, which reflected concerns I had incubated during my prior studies at Harvard Law School, the European Academy of Legal Theory (Brussels) and ESADE (Barcelona). Colleagues who also left an imprint on the following pages greater than footnoting can acknowledge, having made insightful comments on earlier drafts, include Timothy Endicott, Richard Ekins, Leslie Green, Nigel Simmonds, Nick Barber, Grégoire Webber, Dori Kimel and Donal Nolan. Paul Yowell provided help and encouragement during the closing stages, going over the entire manuscript and prompting countless improvements. Andrea Dolcetti suggested the cover design. The image shows the traffic light that is right across my street, in my beautiful hometown.

The writing of this book was facilitated at different stages by the financial support of the Oxford Law Faculty, the Arts and Humanities Research Council, the Oxford Centre for Ethics and Philosophy of Law, and University College Oxford. The professional environments in which I have been fortunate enough to work have provided far more than logistic support: both in my time at Oxford's unique Worcester College, and more recently at the University of Barcelona, where flexible arrangements enabled me to combine university life with the handling of grave family misfortune. Richard Hart, Bill Asquith, Kate Whetter and their colleagues at Hart Publishing were gracefully accommodating and set a high standard of professionalism. Catherine Minahan was a careful copy-editor. Perhaps the most pervasive, if subtle, contribution to the final guise of this work has been made by my students over the years – some of them (especially Emily Goddard, Sulman Iqbal, Harriet Owens, Gil-Ad Schwartz and Evan Whittal-Williams) by critically reading earlier drafts, and all of them by being a most empowering source of wisdom and irreverent common sense. This book is dedicated to them.

MKT
May 2018

Contents

Notes

ENDNOTES APPENDED TO each substantive chapter point to background literature and further reading in relation to propositions and ideas discussed in the main text. The main text is devised to be self-sufficient in its argumentative import.

1

Introduction: Why Legal Validity?

I. AN INTRIGUING FACT

EVERY DAY, IN many parts of our world, human beings are deprived of their freedom and denied assistance, their plans and expectations are thwarted, their belongings are seized, they are forcefully torn out of their homes and separated from their loved ones, by appeal to one or more past decisions deemed to be *legally valid*: for example, a legally valid deportation order, a legally valid contract, or a legally valid criminal statute. Even when we are not thus subject to exertions of legal force, our lives are shaped in far-reaching ways by our own and other people's reliance on the fact that certain things are legally valid, including job appointments, pension grants, passports, marriages, tax returns, or airline tickets. Many important matters turn on what is and what is not valid. Correctly pinpointing valid decisions is a fundamental lawyerly skill, and much argument in courtrooms and legal scholarship turns precisely on this question.

There is something deeply intriguing about this reality. Despite the central place that the idea of validity occupies in these familiar forms of reasoning, they rarely engage with the question of what legal validity *is*. Plainly they need not. The fact that an English will must have three rather than two signatures, for example, does not follow from anybody's understanding of the English phrase 'legally valid'. It follows from relevant statutory provisions that provide, amongst other things, requirements of procedure and form. So if I have to assess whether the document in front of me is a legally valid will, I have to check what other persons have decided in the past on the question of what makes a will valid. And the way in which I identify their decisions as being relevant to my enquiry, in turn, is in virtue of the fact that those decisions, too, are legally valid. They, too, were made in accordance with criteria, including requirements of procedure and form, set out in yet further decisions. In an important sense, therefore, my judgement – here and now – that this is a legally valid will is a judgement at several steps' remove. And the steps it builds on, those past judgements I have not witnessed, by persons I do not even know, do not settle what validity is either. They only specify how to tell *whether* something is valid.

Most of us, however, intuitively feel that we *do* have a firm grasp of what 'legal validity' stands for. This adds to the puzzle. Try asking people – lawyers, laypeople, theorists – what it means to say that a contract, a statute, a will, a passport or a bus-ticket is legally valid. Chances are that you will be told that it is pretty obvious, but you will be given quite a range of different ('obvious') responses. You may be told, for example, that it was done 'according to law'. Now, it is true as a general matter that all that is legally valid has been done according to law. But we do not think of all that is according to law as being legally valid. When I stop at a red light, I act according to law (lawfully). And likewise when I refrain from stealing. Yet it would normally be contrived to describe these kinds of act or omission as 'legally valid' – or 'invalid', for that matter. Of course, those who operate cameras at traffic lights, for example, might employ jargon by which a stop completely behind the white line is 'legally valid', but this would be a highly context-specific use of the expression. Stoppings-at-red and omissions to steal are not legally valid in quite the same stable, widely acknowledged sense as are contracts, passports and wills. This is partly because, when I issue a valid passport or make a valid contract or will, unlike when I stop at red, I bring something into existence: I create an entity – the passport, the contract, the will – that somehow lives on beyond the moment of its creation, and sometimes for generations. Perhaps this is why, for many legal professionals, 'legally valid' stands for 'created by following the relevant steps'. But again, although this is true of all that is legally valid, it is similarly true of many other things, for example brownies baked according to a recipe. To be sure, contracts, unlike brownies, have legal consequences. This yields another popular explanation of 'legally valid', as whatever 'has the consequences established by law'. The problem, here as well, is that not only do contracts have consequences established by law, but so do thefts, childbirths, floods and earthquakes. And none of these sorts of action or event is for most purposes thought of as being legally valid.

Validity is elusive, *and yet* critical aspects of human well-being pervasively hang on whether something is or is not valid. We individually and collectively let valid decisions occupy a place in our arrangements and deliberations, in our plans, vindications, justifications and hopes, that, in the final analysis, only *just* decisions deserve to occupy. In the name of validity, human interests are affected in ways that would only be justifiable if warranted by a morally compelling reason. But a valid decision at best reflects somebody else's past *view* of what it would be morally appropriate to do in certain circumstances. It need not even be that person's present view, if it was an honestly held view in the first place. At any rate, the view may be wrong. In short: not only do we settle questions of justice by reference to something *other* than a fresh reflection on what justice demands, but the idea we replace justice with, the property we treat almost *as if* it were a mark of justice, is one on which we hardly have a grip – though we seem deceived into treating it as self-explanatory. Are we under a collective spell?

II. THE CODE IDEA

In a sense, we are under a spell. The purpose of this book is to explore the moral need for this spell, and in so doing unravel how it operates. The book explains how, and within what general limits, legal validity can help a large community to foster justice precisely by helping it *bypass* concerns about justice and other concomitant matters. It shows that a fascinating legal technique is associated with the idea of legal validity, spanning the domains of private and public law. And it demonstrates that this technique is a valuable, in some ways an irreplaceable, tool for individuals and groups, for persons and institutions, to forge commitments and allocate responsibilities in pursuit of reasonable self-direction, by rallying the resources and opportunities that only large-scale patterns of behavioural convergence can afford, thereby weaving a fabric of just relations between persons within the framework of the law.

In thus probing the *point* of legal validity, the book exposes and explains some remarkable puzzles this everyday notion harbours. These puzzles may be grouped into three broad sets, each of which follows on from the previous one.

One first set of puzzles concerns the very sort of thing validity is. We routinely refer to certain things as legally valid, but is there anything common to the things we thus refer to – something other than the fact that we so refer to them? Is there more to our accustomed appeal to legal validity than a haphazard or random linguistic habit? We shall not unravel validity's point by pondering what the *term* 'validity' means. Its use appears to preclude the very kind of enquiry we are pursuing. One does not crack the workings of a magical trick by looking up the words 'hocus pocus'. Therefore the book's initial task is to look beyond the way we speak, in search of an underlying similarity amongst the miscellaneous things we habitually call legally valid. The way we speak is, for our purposes, no more, though no less, than a potential clue. It is a potential clue to the existence of a deeper similarity amongst certain kinds of things, a similarity that might begin to explain why we are justified in assigning them such a central place in our dealings.

The quest for this similarity occupies chapters 2 and 3. It is a revealing task. Valid things accompany us in the most diverse walks of life. Some valid things can be touched; some cannot. A valid 30-page deed may record an investment company's valid incorporation. One may validly trade a minute share in the risk involved in a transaction that itself occurs in a global financial market. Valid ID cards increasingly give way to valid codes. Valid things originating in the past may seal the fate of individuals in the present. Valid action may occur under the auspices of state law or of an ever-growing set of supranational regulations. Despite these variegated manifestations, it is common to valid things that they are *made* and, crucially, that they are made through a distinct kind of *technique*: in essence, by someone saying so. Valid things, the book shows, embody choices to change legal duties, rights and powers incumbent on the agent himself or on others. Valid choices are choices of a special kind. They become true in being expressed. Valid choices are self-fulfilling. One brings about what one says one intends to bring about – a feature rendered particularly conspicuous by the lawyerly 'hereby'. The technique of legal validity is a powerful tool to shape one's own and other people's legal relations. It is power exercised through a datable say-so. It is a technique fit to be deployed intentionally, but which may also curb the agent's intentions. It is a technique that manifests a present choice, but its binding force lasts over time. It is the technique whereby we exert what jurisprudential literature has insistently but imprecisely described as 'legal power'.

A second set of puzzles concerns the *moral* import of such *legal* power. Can the use of the legal technique of validity justify compromising sensitive human interests *as if* warranted by a compelling moral reason? In other words: Can validity bestow on one the power to change not only legal but also moral duties and rights, by so saying? In some respects it can. The basic logic that makes this possible is explained in chapter 4. It is the logic of *specific convergence*. Specific convergence is what it takes, across countless domains of social life, to foster human well-being as resources permit and justice demands. Many aspects of a person's well-being depend, for their protection and development, on the cooperation of other persons. In many regards, each of us is only able to make an effective contribution to the well-being of others when acting as part of a collective scheme. Only in the context of a fair redistributive system, for example, can my payment of a specified tax sum by a specified date make a duly apt and proportionate, and therefore necessary, contribution to the healthcare of others. Only in the context of an operative traffic order does my stopping here and now amount to a uniquely appropriate, and therefore necessary, means to safeguard the physical integrity of other drivers and pedestrians, compatibly with sustaining the amenities of swift transport. In each case, it is the presence of a scheme of *convergent* conduct that makes a difference to my own ability to foster justice, and thus to what it is necessary and morally obligatory for me to do. This is so even though the particulars of this scheme – eg how much to pay, when to stop – are *specific* enough that they could reasonably have been otherwise. In the absence of the relevant collective scheme, the same kind of conduct on my part would probably be ineffective to the same end, if not counterproductive. Specific convergence makes a standing difference to what persons ought in justice to do.

The kind of specific convergence required to foster justice, however, does not arise out of the blue. Valid choices are key to *generating* and sustaining it. Generating convergence involves publicly settling on determinate patterns of conduct, and seeing to their general compliance. The book speaks respectively of *marking* and *enforcing*. Marking and enforcing go, hand in hand, to ensure that specific provisions are convergently followed. It takes specific convergence to realise justice, and it takes marking and enforcing to realise specific convergence. Legal systems have a privileged tool for marking. It is the technique of legal validity. Valid choices are distinctly salient. They can stand out to a potentially wide range of people, given the characteristics of validity's technique. It is a technique for expressing choices through a specified process, often recorded on a lasting physical support. Criteria for identifying valid decisions make central considerations of procedure and form, that is to say, features of the choosing act or its record that even persons with different skills and clashing ideological outlooks can convergently identify: signatures, stamps, seals, registry entries. Validity serves to mark specific conduct as due, even in the face of moral controversy. It serves to mark specific conduct as due, also in the face of rational under-determination of general requirements of justice. Valid choices provide a stable focus for expectations because they are able to circulate as deliberately introduced normative changes and yet also as entities in their own right, which one can refer to and rely on, for many purposes, relatively independently of their originating circumstances and of shifting views about their merits. Valid choices, in being able to generate needed convergence, can *render* conduct due by marking it as due. The technique of legal validity can bestow a power to craft requirements of justice.

But this power is not unlimited. In fact, justice requires that we *lack* an unconstrained power to shape legal duties and rights as we happen to choose. Herein lies the third set of puzzles about validity. The book shows that legal power can be all the greater precisely in being limited. Even as a matter of law, legal power is limited power. It cannot be other than limited. It is only by acting in accordance with what is provided in the relevant legal regime that one's say-so can succeed in changing legal relations. If you try to marry a person who is already married, to convey land on tissue paper, or to issue a resolution that is deeply ultra vires, you fail. You fail, no matter how clearly you express your intention to thereby change legal relations. Your say-so only succeeds if it is expressed in the legally specified way, and if the law otherwise provides for this possibility. Only by complying with these limits will your say-so become part of the legal fabric. Ultra vires acts are loose, indeed lost threads. Chapter 3 accounts for these legal limitations on legal power in canvassing validity's technique. Later chapters are able to spell out the moral point of these limitations.

This requires understanding that the legal regime that places these constraints is itself the result of valid decisions of other persons and institutions, typically including legislatures and judges. There are stringent considerations of justice, as chapter 5 explains, why the many social affairs that fall to be settled through law ought to be settled by the valid decisions of a variety of agents acting at different times – rather than by a small set of agents choosing once and for all. These considerations speak to the need for, amongst other things, a separation of powers, institutional deference, relative freedom of contract, prosecutorial discretion, democratic self-government, and an appropriate balance between common law and legislative modes of law-making. In other words: the question of *who* should take the lead in generating specific convergence is itself a question of justice. In a just political community, the responsibility to bring about specific convergence will be shared. It will be shared amongst those who are in the best position to decide on each relevant matter, in light of requirements of expertise, impartiality, proximity, self-direction and the Rule of Law. Across private and public law, across the fields of official acts and individual arrangements, persons and institutions will have a correspondingly circumscribed decision-making power. Decisions may justifiably be ultra vires, in law, if someone else ought, in justice, to have pronounced instead. Bargained clauses may justifiably be superseded by statutory terms if the latter can better protect weaker parties to the relevant kind of deal. Legal limits on legal power are devices to allocate the responsibility to choose to those who, in justice, ought to bear it. Those legal limits are what we call criteria of legal validity.

It follows that the technique of legal validity can confer on persons an ability to craft moral duties and rights precisely by delimiting who can validly decide about what, and how. Validity's delimiting role has a familiar manifestation in legal reasoning. It is portrayed in chapter 6, through a contrast with the domain of ordinary communication. Valid choices are focally the agent's, but they have a crucial *systemic* dimension that ordinary communication lacks. The *legal meaning* of your valid choice – the legal relations it changes – may be co-determined by the valid choices of others. This happens, for instance, when statutes 'imply' clauses into your agreement, or judicial interpretation elaborates key statutory terms. Law students quickly learn to figure out 'what the law is' on some matter by reading together a miscellaneous range of legal materials. The technique of validity makes it possible *both* for valid decisions jointly to weave a relatively coherent normative fabric, *and* to focus on individual contributions to that fabric, isolated for some purposes as discrete valid contracts, statutes, passports, licences and so forth. Properly deployed, the technique of validity can empower persons to valuably exercise their autonomy in a way compatible with, and responsive to, the autonomy and well-being of others. To properly deploy this technique is to subject it to such limits as justice demands.

This is why, in the final analysis, it is paramount to use this technique with keen awareness of its point. Hence the importance of probing the moral need for, and lure of, its looming spell.

III. A NEGLECTED QUESTION

Legal philosophy has all but neglected this important task. It has certainly not neglected legal validity. But, bafflingly, it has neglected the enquiry about validity that this book vindicates and pursues. Largely mirroring ordinary legal thought, in recent years legal philosophy has focused on the strategy for establishing *whether* something is legally valid. It has sought to generalise about the nature of *criteria* of legal validity. And the things of which validity is at issue it has assumed to be primarily legal *rules* or *norms*.[1] Legal rules or norms, however, are units into which we divide up the content of legal materials to aid our reasoning.[2] There is no theory-independent individuation of legal rules or norms. Legal rules or norms do not enter legal reasoning complete with labels attached. Understandably, therefore, on the few occasions on which recent legal theorists have turned their minds to the question of *what* validity is, their answers have not substantially added to the theory's own conception of what legal rules or norms are in the first place.

For Kelsen, for example, a norm 'is the expression of the idea that something ought to occur'.[3] And in turn, to say that norms are valid is to say that 'men ought to behave as the … norms prescribe'.[4] Kelsen adds that 'validity' is 'the specific existence of norms',[5] and that valid legal norms exist as part of a legal system.[6] This latter consideration partly matches Hart's understanding of legal validity, chiefly as a rule's membership in a system of law. 'To say that a given rule is valid', Hart writes, 'is to recognize it as passing all the tests provided by the rule of recognition and so as a rule of the system'.[7] Raz's account echoes other aspects of Kelsen's. That a rule is valid, says Raz, means that it has the 'normative consequences' it 'purports' to have.[8] And '[a] rule which is not legally valid is not a legal rule at all'.[9]

For all their significance in contributing to pioneering accounts of law, these conceptions of validity consistently pass over the question that is the object of this book: the question *why*, if at all, it can be sound to settle questions of justice by pointing to a miscellaneous range of 'valid' artefacts, including legal norms. Contemporary jurisprudence errs in treating the validity of wills, licences, marriages, appointments or mortgage assignments as a matter of residual theoretical concern. It is worth noting, in this connection, that the present theoretical focus on the validity of norms is a relatively novel phenomenon in the nearly 2,000-year-old history of the technique of legal validity. When the

[1] In this book I speak interchangeably of 'rules' and 'norms' (and 'provisions', 'standards' …), except when focusing on the generality of rules (ie the fact that they apply to more than one person on more than one occasion: ch 5.IV–VI); cf Hart's specialised conception of a (social) rule: HLA Hart, *The Concept of Law*, 2nd edn (Oxford, Clarendon Press, 1994) 54–57.

[2] As Raz puts it, talk of norms 'facilitate[s] reference to considerations guiding human behaviour' (J Raz, *Practical Reason and Norms* (London, Hutchinson, 1975) 104).

[3] H Kelsen, *General Theory of Law and State*, A Wedberg (tr) (New York, Russell, 1945) 36.

[4] ibid 39, 30.

[5] ibid 30; in the same vein, H Kelsen, *General Theory of Norms*, M Hartney (tr) (Oxford, Clarendon Press, 1991) 28.

[6] Kelsen, *General Theory of Law and State*, n 3, 110ff.

[7] Hart, *The Concept of Law*, n 1, 103. This passage appears in the course of a discussion (102–09) which otherwise interdefines the ideas 'internal statement' and 'legal validity'.

[8] Or 'claims' to have, Raz says synonymously (!): J Raz, *The Authority of Law: Essays on Law and Morality* (Oxford, Oxford University Press, 1979) 149–50, 153.

[9] ibid 146.

technique of validity begins to be forged, to be devised as a tool to effect far-reaching social and political transformations, validity is first and foremost a property of *acts*, chiefly of acts arranging personal relations in the sphere of private life and business, such as contracts, wills, marriages or gifts. Eventually, in the Middle Ages, validity comes to be predicated, by extension, of particular official acts such as appointments or judgments, until, around 200 years ago, it starts to gain currency as a property of *general* enactments and their abstracted products, legal norms – once, that is, juristic consciousness has embraced the possibility that even the legislature's say-so may be legally constrained by a legally binding body of constitutional law. In an important sense, focus on valid norms and their criteria of validity is an offshoot, perhaps a creature, of modern constitutionalism.[10]

Although the question of validity's point has not been the focus of jurisprudential writings, at some junctures such writings provide reflections that inchoately broach this enquiry while falling short of doing so. We consider some of Hart's insights in chapter 2. From their different standpoints, Kelsen, Dworkin and Raz are further telling instances.

Kelsen's portrait of the systemic structure of legal orders vividly illustrates the *bypassing* role that legal validity discharges in legal reasoning. Kelsen appreciates, perhaps better than any other theorist, that the ability to make law, the power to act validly, is inherently vicarious: it is conferred on one by someone or something else. And he appreciates that legal reasoning systematically postpones or holds off the answer to the question about the ultimate basis of that power. I can act validly *if* A, who sought to empower me, could validly do so; and A could validly empower me *if* B, who sought to empower A, could validly do so; and so on. Logically speaking, the chain of conditionals must have a beginning. Someone or something must hold the master power, the power from which everyone else's power derives. Otherwise the chain collapses into an infinite regress. But, as Kelsen sees, legal thought does not articulate an answer. Rather it *presupposes* that there is one. It *assumes* that the chain has a beginning. Inasmuch as one engages in legal reasoning, says Kelsen, one acts *as if* the makers of the first positive link in the chain – the 'historically first' constitution – had the power to make it.[11] That is the content of the 'basic norm'.[12] It is the master conditional. *If* the makers of the first constitution had power (to make it), then so did everyone empowered by them. *If* one ought to obey the first constitution, then one ought to obey any norms made in accordance with it. Kelsen's stated 'basic norm' captures and formalises the assumption that

[10] For a historical journey tracing validity's roots in Western legal thought, see M Köpcke, *A Short History of Validity and Invalidity: Foundations of Private and Public Law* (Cambridge, Intersentia, forthcoming).

[11] Kelsen, *General Theory of Law and State*, n 3, 115–19 (the 'historically first' constitution is the first constitution after the last revolution).

[12] ibid 110ff, 115ff, 395–96.

legal reasoning leaves unstated. It closes the chain of 'ifs' by bracketing out the answer. The 'basic norm' does, in essence, what legal validity does.

Ironically, Kelsen's narrow view about the proper remit of legal theory bars him from searching for a non-question-begging answer to the question that legal reasoning so relentlessly postpones. Kelsen himself, like the legal reasoning he describes, pictures an upward-looking explanatory need but does not supply the needed explanation. His self-imposed methodological restrictions hinder him, in particular, from querying what it would take for the makers of the first constitution (and those acting under it) to have the power to craft, by so saying, what anyone *morally* ought to do. All this is ironic because, as this book shows, a key part of the answer lies in the very systematic bypassing that his 'basic norm' doctrine brings out. The currency of legal validity is largely undiscussed, and therefore robust. It can serve as a common denominator wherein to cast and vindicate clashing and incommensurable concerns – not unlike a currency, which facilitates trade, including fierce competition, in terms of a shared magnitude. Validity's grammar is able to render salient specific conduct descriptions – do's and don'ts – that, in a context of operative enforcement, can become appropriate strategies to meet just demands. Morally speaking, the master power, as it were, is held by the community whose legal system it is, and by those able to act on its behalf and in other ways within the framework of a sustained, large-scale effort of specific convergence that can help persons realise justice in ways otherwise beyond their reach. The book's defence of the moral need for positive law, given moral under-determination, moral disagreement and the moral value of self-directing choice, is articulated in the first section of chapter 6.

In contrast to Kelsen, Dworkin does resolutely enquire about the point of legal practice. His is a body of work comprehensively geared towards answering why it can be warranted, in justice, to settle questions of justice through legal technique. Dworkin's primary theoretical perspective is that of an appellate judge. Adjudication of controversial cases, which may require courts to revisit and reconsider principled foundations of whole areas of legal practice, engages modes of legal reasoning that openly grapple with law's systemic character. Dworkin's adjudicative focus sharply brings to light the systemic dimension of legal reasoning. The 'interpretive judgement', Dworkin's recommended strategy for identifying law, closely mirrors central features of adjudicative argument.[13] Judicial reasoning will typically, and not unsoundly, read down legal gaps, especially in jurisdictions whose legal culture expects judges not to 'make law'. And higher judges with legal power to review and even change settled law on moral grounds will often find themselves, for good reason, engaging head-on with the very kinds of moral consideration that, for most ordinary purposes, legal reasoning sidesteps. Even our normally useful, because simplifying, talk of discrete legal norms or rules, not to mention of discrete transactions

[13] R Dworkin, *Law's Empire* (Oxford, Hart Publishing, 1998) especially ch 7.

or proofs thereof, may well remain in an unfocused background as appellate judges enquire about the moral credentials of legal requirements in the process of reshaping them.

But just this judge-centred approach steers attention away from the pervasive need for law outside the courtroom. Dworkin's work on the whole underplays the extent to which legally valid decisions need to be able to circulate as such, that is, as bundles of legal duties and rights deliberately introduced by agents empowered to do so. It underplays the extent to which even *after* competent and conscientious lawyers have worked out legal requirements, the law may evince extant conflicts, injustices and gaps. Valid decisions are next to dissolved within the pool of miscellaneous facts – attitudes, events, 'past political decisions' – that provide the raw input for Dworkin's 'interpretive judgement'.[14] This not only obscures validity's remarkable contribution to legal reasoning, including judicial reasoning, by facilitating an alternative focus on datable choices and propositions of law. It also fails to do justice to the idea of legal power, a power exercised by validly crafting duties and rights that are legal and so far forth not moral – and which *therefore* can morally warrant what they claim in law.

That law is *made* or 'source-based', and that this is critical to law's ability to realise justice, is a central tenet of Raz's work.[15] Law can have authority over us, Raz argues, because legal requirements are presented as someone's view on how we ought to act, a view capable of being identified without revisiting the moral questions the authority is there to settle. For the job of an authority, says Raz, is to improve the subject's compliance with right reason. A legitimate authority can change, through its say-so, what the subject morally ought to do. Because law is source-based, it is in principle capable of holding legitimate authority.

Raz's account, however, pays comparatively little heed to what *else* it takes for a legal system to hold legitimate authority. Raz's beneficially simple and abstract model is chiefly concerned with the nature of authorities in general, and with the nature of law's claims to be one. Other than through generic appeals to law's 'expertise' and ability to 'coordinate',[16] Raz does not purport to show whether, and if so why, law may be *better* than other source-based standards at addressing problems of community-wide concern, given some distinct characteristics of law and legal technique.[17] Raz's account envisages an *individual*

[14] He jointly dubs these 'law in the preinterpretive sense' (ibid 65ff, 91ff).

[15] eg J Raz, *Ethics in the Public Domain: Essays in the Morality of Law and Politics*, rev edn (Oxford, Clarendon Press, 1995) ch 10; Raz, *The Authority of Law*, n 8, chs 2–4.

[16] eg J Raz, 'Introduction' in J Raz (ed), *Authority*, Readings in Social and Political Theory (New York, New York University Press, 1990) 6ff; J Raz, *The Morality of Freedom* (Oxford, Clarendon Press, 1986) 30–31, 74–76; Raz, *Ethics in the Public Domain*, n 14, 347ff.

[17] Some elaborations of the Razian apparatus, eg by Marmor (*Social Conventions: From Language to Law* (Princeton, NJ, Princeton University Press, 2009) especially chs 6 and 7) or Shapiro (*Legality* (Cambridge, MA, Harvard University Press, 2009) especially chs 5 et seq), place greater emphasis on the *manner* in which law can go about solving problems of community-wide concern, but remain circumspect on what these problems are and how the technique of validity helps address them; for an argument, see M Köpcke, 'Positive Law's Moral Purpose(s): Towards a New Consensus?' (2011) 56 *American Journal of Jurisprudence* 186.

person as the holder of authority, as opposed to a set of institutions sharing limited power in the framework of a legal system. It envisages authoritative directives as *communications* addressed by that one person to its subjects, as opposed to canvassing the irreducibly systemic character of legal meaning. It portrays the authority of legal requirements as inherently *fading with time*, hand in hand with the authority of their human author, as opposed to seeing in the continued relevance of valid choices an expression of their ability to generate salience through time amongst members of a subsisting group. And it insists that law cannot perform its morally needed task unless legal requirements can be discerned *thoroughly* without resort to moral argument, thereby overstating the important truth that law can only forge and sustain patterns of convergence if validity does not *predominantly* turn on moral considerations. These arguments are developed in chapter 6.

Pursuing a neglected concern, therefore, this book shows why, and subject to what limits, the valid say-so of countless different persons and institutions can craft moral duties and rights precisely because expressed in the grammar of legal validity. Key to the law's capacity to realise justice, in other words, is not only that law is something made, but that it is made, invoked and brought to bear on our lives *through the technique of legal validity*, even though there is more to law than validity, and even though there is more to justice than law.

NOTES

Section III: A Neglected Question

Kelsen on Legal Validity

On Kelsen's interdefinition of validity, existence and/or binding force, see, eg, E Garzón Valdés, 'Two Models of Legal Validity: Hans Kelsen and Francisco Suárez' in SL Paulson and B Litschewski-Paulson (eds), *Normativity and Norms: Critical Perspectives on Kelsenian Themes* (Oxford, Clarendon Press, 1998) 263–66; A Ross, 'Book Review: Kelsen, "What is Justice?"' (1957) 45 *California Law Review* 564, 567. Kelsen not only interdefines validity and ought, but also ought and norm: 'The norm is the expression of the idea that something ought to occur'; 'the "ought" simply expresses the specific sense in which human behaviour is determined by a norm' (Kelsen, *General Theory of Law and State*, n 3, 36–37). In later work, Kelsen defines 'ought' to encompass command, permission and empowerment (H Kelsen, *The Pure Theory of Law*, 2nd edn, Max Knight (tr) (Berkeley, CA, University of California Press, 1967) 4–5).

Hart on Legal Validity

On Hart's interdefinition of legal validity and (derivability from the) 'rule of recognition', NE Simmonds, *Law as a Moral Idea* (Oxford, Oxford University Press, 2007) 126ff.

Raz on Legal Validity

Raz rejects validity as membership on grounds of a stipulative understanding (i) of contracts, regulations of associations, etc, as not being 'part of the legal system' (Raz, *Practical Reason and Norms*, n 2, 152–54), and (ii) of 'legally valid rule' as including legally recognised standards of foreign law (ibid 152–54; Raz, *The Authority of Law*, n 8, 148–49).

Other Accounts of Legal Validity

Most other accounts of the validity of legal norms are essentially variations of Kelsen's, Hart's and/or Raz's: see, eg, S Munzer, *Legal Validity* (The Hague, Martinus Nijhoff, 1972); JW Harris, *Legal Philosophies* (London, Butterworths, 1980) ch 6; CS Nino, *Introducción al Análisis del Derecho* (Barcelona, Ariel, 1983) 132ff; J Finnis, *Natural Law and Natural Rights*, 2nd edn (Oxford, Oxford University Press, 2011) 25ff and 266ff; E Bulygin, 'Tiempo y Validez' in CE Alchourrón and E Bulygin, *Análisis lógico y Derecho* (Madrid, Centro de Estudios Constitucionales, 1991) 195ff; N MacCormick, *Institutions of Law: An Essay in Legal Theory* (Oxford, Oxford University Press, 2007) 161; G Sartor, 'Legal Validity: An Inferential Analysis' (2008) 21 *Ratio Juris* 212; but cf an inchoate concern with validity's point in D von der Pfordten, 'Validity in Positive Law – A Mere Summary Concept' in P Westerman et al (eds), *Legal Validity and Soft Law* (Dortrecht, Springer, 2018); P Sandro, 'Unlocking Legal Validity: Some Remarks on the Artificial Ontology of Law' in P Westerman et al (eds), *Legal Validity and Soft Law* (Dortrecht, Springer, 2018).

Contemporary Jurisprudence Treats the Validity of Transactions as a Matter of Residual Theoretical Concern

On validity as being primarily a property of norms, see, eg, Raz, *The Authority of Law*, n 8, 150; T Spaak, *The Concept of Legal Competence: An Essay in Conceptual Analysis*, R Carroll (tr) (Brookfield, VT, Dartmouth, 1994) 50; J Ferrer, *Las normas de competencia: Un aspecto de la dinámica jurídica* (Madrid, BOE/Centro de Estudios Políticos y Constitucionales, 2000) 155. Exceptions to this trend include DWP Ruiter, *Institutional Legal Facts: Legal Powers and Their Effects* (Dortrecht, Kluwer, 1993); R Guastini, 'Rules, Validity and Statutory Construction' in A Pintore and M Jori (eds), *Law and Language: The Italian Analytical School*, S Stirling, A Pirrie and Z Bankowski (tr) (Liverpool, Deborah Charles Publications, 1997); and RS Summers, 'Toward a Better General Theory of Legal Validity' (1985) 16 *Rechtstheorie* 65, 67–68. Ross goes as far as to deny the intelligibility of predicating validity of norms, which he says can only be 'in force' (*gœldende*, in Danish; *geltend*, in German; *vigentes*, in Spanish): see A Ross, 'Validity and the Conflict between Legal Positivism and Natural Law' in SL Paulson and B Litschewski-Paulson (eds), *Normativity and Norms: Critical Perspectives on Kelsenian Themes* (Oxford, Clarendon Press, 1998) 158–63; A Ross, *On Law and Justice* (London, Stevens & Sons Limited, 1958) 29–50.

2

Legal Power

I. THE TASK AHEAD

RELYING ON AND reasoning with what is *legally valid* is a fundamental and intriguing feature of legal practice. It is fundamental not only in that it is pervasive, but also in that critical human interests are affected in the name of what bears legal validity's seal – a valid contract, a valid judgment, a valid statute, a valid residence permit, a valid patent and countless other things. But our recurrent appeal to validity is intriguing in that, as the previous chapter has canvassed, it appears to systematically sidestep reflection on the moral merits of treating validity as a sufficient warrant for settling morally sensitive matters. Engagement with legal validity, by laypersons, professional lawyers and legal theorists alike, focuses on the question *whether* something is legally valid, that is, it focuses on criteria of legal validity. Such criteria characteristically do not make reference to the fairness or justice of the relevant act. They primarily make reference to its originating procedure, formal source and wider consistency with other legal provisions – provisions that are legally valid themselves. Engagement with legal validity, in short, treats the idea of validity as a currency of almost undiscussed value. In so doing it avoids querying the merits of this practice, a practice that discourages raising questions about merits. Engagement with legal validity omits to ask *why*, if at all, it can be justified to assign legal validity such a central place. This question is the object of this book.

We shall not arrive at an answer to this question by investigating the sheer language of legal validity, as it leaves this very question outside debate. If we are to grasp the point of appealing to validity, we must begin by determining whether there is something common to the things we recurrently call 'legally valid', something other than the fact that we so call them. Here, as elsewhere, legal thought can gather weighty clues from legal language but must never accord it the final word. It particularly matters to our judgement about the point of this practice whether our accustomed appeal to validity is more than just a random or haphazard linguistic habit. The fact that we can think of more or less focal uses of the term 'validity' is in itself a promising indication that an underlying similarity may be lurking in this vicinity. Thus, on the one hand, we recognise *extended* uses of the term. We would understand, for example, if someone spoke of a 'valid' fish to refer to a kind of fish that is not too small to keep under existing fishing regulations. But we appreciate that fish are not legally valid in quite the same sense as passports, software licences and credits cards. Conversely, we are well acquainted with terminology that is *alternative* to 'legal validity'. Lawyers sometimes frame enquiries in specialised language that could in principle be translated into 'validity' talk. They ask, for example, whether a council has acted 'ultra vires', whether a promise is 'enforceable', or whether a statute is 'constitutional' or remains 'good' law. Still none of this is conclusive. Indeed, it is only by reference to an underlying similarity that both extended and alternative uses of language may be pinpointed as such.

This chapter and the next search for this similarity. Their job is to figure out whether 'validity' language is a surface manifestation of a distinct mode of reasoning or operating in law, *of which* we can eventually probe the moral point.

Jurisprudential accounts of legal validity can barely assist us in this task. As chapter 1 explained, the focus of these accounts has almost exclusively been on the validity of legal rules or norms. This is a narrow, abstract focus that pays little heed to the richness of our ordinary attribution of validity to variegated things such as job appointments, cheques, marriages or fines – as well as rules. There is a different respect, however, in which jurisprudential thought holds out a potentially fruitful starting point for our enquiry. Over the last couple of centuries, jurisprudential writings have gradually given shape to an idea that seems broadly to match the practical realities we are looking to make sense of. It is the idea of *legal power*. It was introduced into the English-speaking world chiefly through the work of Bentham, Hohfeld, Kelsen and, especially, Hart, and has long had a likewise solid implant in Continental legal scholarship, especially in some private law traditions. Discounting differences of emphasis amongst conceptions, an exercise of legal power is the same thing as a legally valid act. Put differently: all that is legally valid has been brought about through the exercise of legal power, and every exercise of legal power yields a legally valid result.

The idea of legal power, unlike the idea of legal validity, is a theoretical device. It has been developed by scholars, as Raz notes, to 'draw attention to important similarities between otherwise heterogeneous phenomena',[1] phenomena that in legal practice often do not go under that name. That there is a close connection between the idea of legal power and the language of legal validity is not always made conspicuous in these writings, but it is widely presupposed. The idea of legal power therefore has the potential to supply what we seek. If the literature on legal power spells out what is distinctive of an exercise of legal power, it may thereby point us to validity's distinctive mark. This preliminary chapter puts to the test central elements of the received idea of legal power to this end.

[1] J Raz, 'Voluntary Obligations and Normative Powers' in SL Paulson and B Litschewski-Paulson (eds), *Normativity and Norms: Critical Perspectives on Kelsenian Themes* (Oxford, Clarendon Press, 1998) 451.

II. FACILITIES TO CHANGE LEGAL POSITIONS

The most prominent source of the received account of legal power is probably Hart's work.[2] Central to *The Concept of Law* is the proposition that law regulates human conduct not only through the imposition of duties,[3] but also through the conferral of powers.[4] Like other theorists, Hart explains legal power by explaining what legal rules do when they confer legal power. Hart dubs the rules in question 'power-conferring rules'. He chiefly characterises them by appeal to their 'social function'.[5] Power-conferring rules 'provide individuals with *facilities* for realizing their wishes'[6] – to realise their wishes not by any means whatsoever, but specifically by altering the legal duties, rights, and powers incumbent on themselves or others.[7] The set of legal duties, rights and powers incumbent on a person at a particular point Hart sometimes calls the person's normative or legal situation.[8] In line with much of the ensuing literature, I speak of the person's normative or legal position. What is distinctive of power-conferring rules, on Hart's account, is that they provide individuals with facilities to realise their wishes by changing legal positions.

It certainly seems sound to describe in this fashion the rules that determine how to make valid contracts, marriages, wills, enactments or rulings, which are Hart's recurrent examples. More fundamentally, talk of *power* conferred on persons, apt to be *exercised* in achieving certain results, draws attention to the fact that legally valid things are *made*. This is one significant characteristic of valid things, if the received idea of legal power is anything to go by. Legally valid things are artefacts. They are brought about through intentional human action, namely the kind of action meant to be guided by the corresponding *rules*.

And yet Hart's above description of such rules does not bring out features sufficiently distinctive of them. There are numerous kinds of legal rule that may be said to provide individuals with facilities to realise their wishes by changing

[2] Hart's ideas on legal power find an earlier and in some ways more nuanced articulation in Suarez in the 17th century (see M Köpcke, *A Short History of Validity and Invalidity: Foundations of Private and Public Law* (Cambridge, Intersentia, forthcoming), ch 8). Hohfeld's well-known scheme of 'jural opposites' and 'jural correlatives' (WN Hohfeld, 'Some Fundamental Legal Conceptions as Applied in Judicial Reasoning' (1913) 23 *Yale Law Journal* 16), in turn, *relies* on a master distinction equivalent to Hart's contrast between duties and powers (although Hohfeld, unlike Hart, is chiefly concerned with private law and relatively particular, rather than general, normative changes).

[3] I treat 'duty' and 'obligation' as coextensive.

[4] HLA Hart, *The Concept of Law*, 2nd edn (Oxford, Clarendon Press, 1994) 27ff.

[5] ibid 27, 32, 38, 39, 40; the ambiguities in Hart's idea of 'social function' need not concern us.

[6] ibid 27 *et passim*.

[7] For simplicity I chiefly list rights, duties and powers as normative modalities; this does not imply that they are jointly exhaustive or in every way mutually exclusive. This book does not take on the problem of norm individuation (see section III of this chapter).

[8] Hart, *The Concept of Law*, n 4, 27–28, 41. Hart (and much of the ensuing literature) speaks indistinctly of changes in normative situations (HLA Hart, *Essays on Bentham*, Studies in Jurisprudence and Political Theory (Oxford, Clarendon Press, 2001) 218), of normative effects or consequences (ibid 217), of changes in legal situations (ibid 219), of changes in the parties' rights and duties (ibid 212), of the creation of (structures of) legal rights and duties (Hart, *The Concept of Law*, n 4, 27–28, 31, 41) and of determining the course of the law (ibid 41).

legal positions. Legal rules establishing access to government loans, legal aid programmes or crash-courses for the unemployed, for example, facilitate people to change legal positions by embarking on legally valid ventures, such as purchasing their first home, filing a lawsuit or setting up a business. Plainly these are not the kinds of rule Hart has in mind. So in order to spell out what, if anything, is distinctive of power-conferring rules, and thus of legal power, Hart would need to tell us more about what the relevant kind of *facility* consists in. But Hart is surprisingly circumspect on point.

He comes closest to pinning down the nature of the facility involved when he notes, almost in passing, that power-conferring rules are 'recipes for creating duties';[9] that they resemble '*instructions* how to bring about certain results'.[10] The analogy with recipes or technical instructions helpfully brings out the fact that doing what the rule says is, in itself, producing the legal change. One may be given numerous facilities to purchase one's first home, including financial support and professional advice, but one will not purchase and come to own it unless and until one concludes the appropriate conveyancing process. Following the rules on conveyancing and real property (amongst others) yields the normative change ipso facto. It is *these* rules that confer legal power, on Hart's account. These rules do not facilitate the change in legal positions by equipping one with resources to perform it. They facilitate it because following them *is* effecting the change. They govern the production of a valid result in the way that brownie recipes govern the production of brownies. A recipe does not merely seek to provide hints or resources for better attaining a certain result. It facilitates the result by setting out a formula the use of which is sufficient in principle for succeeding in that endeavour, without further acts or events having to occur.

But there is more to the facility provided by power-conferring rules. This is brought out not by comparing them to recipes but by *contrasting* them – a step that Hart does not undertake. If you wish to bake brownies, having a brownie recipe empowers you to realise that wish in the sense that it outlines all that needs to be done in order to make it happen. The rules on wills in a given jurisdiction empower you to make a valid will in this very sense.[11] But they also empower you in a crucial additional sense. In the absence of these rules, you would not be able to make a legally valid will. You might make informal arrangements for distributing your estate after your death, but they would not yield the change in legal positions that we refer to as a valid will. One could, however, bake brownies even if there were no such things as brownie recipes. What it takes to bake brownies is mixing certain ingredients and heating them in an oven. A good brownie recipe *reflects* the steps to be undertaken. But it is

[9] Hart, *The Concept of Law*, n 4, 33.

[10] Hart, *Essays on Bentham*, n 8, 219.

[11] There are typically several ways to make valid wills in any jurisdiction (just as there are several – many! – different ways to make brownies). For simplicity, we may think of all the different variants as forming one disjunctive set. My discussion is compatible with the relevant formulae being vague and thus calling for supplementing decisions.

not what renders it possible to bake brownies. What turns the batter into brownies is, ultimately, what we might call the 'laws' of physics and chemistry. It is an empirical, causal process that unfolds independently of the recipe itself. The legal rules on wills, by contrast, do not reflect or describe a possibility to make wills that exists independently of these rules. They are not mere summaries or reminders. It is not a physical or chemical process that transforms the signature of a paper into a valid will. When the rules say 'this is how to make a valid will', they create a possibility that did not exist before. They somehow constitute the very thing they describe.

This is a fascinating feature of such rules, which is only latent in Hart's discussion. As the reader may be aware, some writers have sought to pin down this constitutive feature of power-conferring rules by drawing on the idea of 'constitutive rules' developed in a body of mostly non-legal literature, most famously by Searle.[12] But in so proceeding little progress has been made that is relevant to us, not least because that body of literature is marked by a deep, unexplained scepticism towards the very ideas of duty, right and thus normative position.[13] Accordingly the literature pervasively equivocates on just *what* it is that the rules in question 'constitute'. It barely leaves room for recognising that what is constituted is a normative change (and remains otherwise elusive on what is meant by 'constitution').

III. SUPER-TRAMP

It will of course not be enough for us, by way of capturing the puzzling constitutive facet of power-conferring rules, to note that what they constitute is a

[12] J Searle, *Speech Acts: An Essay in the Philosophy of Language* (Cambridge, Cambridge University Press, 1969) 33ff; J Searle, *The Construction of Social Reality* (New York, Free Press, 1995) 27ff, 43ff; see also A Ross, *Directives and Norms* (London, Routledge, 1968) 53ff; GH von Wright, *Norm and Action: A Logical Enquiry* (London, Routledge & Kegan Paul, 1963) 6–7. The jurisprudential literature includes: R Alexy, *Theorie der Grundrechte* (Frankfurt, Suhrkamp, 1986) 211ff, especially 214–17; E Bulygin, 'Sobre las normas de competencia' in CE Alchourrón and E Bulygin, *Análisis lógico y Derecho* (Madrid, Centro de Estudios Constitucionales, 1991); J Ferrer, *Las normas de competencia: Un aspecto de la dinámica jurídica* (Madrid, BOE/Centro de Estudios Políticos y Constitucionales, 2000) especially ch 4; M Atienza and J Ruiz Manero, *Las piezas del Derecho: Teoría de los enunciados jurídicos* (Barcelona, Ariel, 1996) ch 2; DWP Ruiter, *Institutional Legal Facts: Legal Powers and Their Effects* (Dortrecht, Kluwer, 1993).

[13] Along with an overriding commitment to an 'empirical' analysis of 'speech': see, eg, Searle, *Speech Acts*, n 12, 15, 50–51 ('ethics and esthetics … are controversial areas' that deal with 'matters of opinion or sentiment or emotion' as opposed to 'objective facts'); J Searle, *Expression and Meaning: Studies in the Theory of Speech Acts* (Cambridge, Cambridge University Press, 1979) viii; Searle, *The Construction of Social Reality*, n 12, 1–2; even promises are characterised as primarily linguistic phenomena (J Searle, 'How to Derive "Ought" from "Is"' (1964) 73 *The Philosophical Review* 43; Searle, *Speech Acts*, n 12, ch 3; Searle, *Expression and Meaning*, 14). Ross's effort, in *Directives and Norms*, n 12, to analyse norms by analysing 'speech' wherein they are expressed, is in keeping with his general denial of the intelligibility of normative ideas as anything other than handy presentational tools (A Ross, 'Tû-Tû' (1958) 70 *Harvard Law Review* 812; A Ross, *On Law and Justice* (London, Stevens & Sons Limited, 1958) 158ff, 170ff).

change in legal positions. That is also true of the rules that Hart calls 'duty-imposing' and wishes to distinguish from power-conferring rules. Indeed it is true of any legal rule that associates certain normative consequences with (avoidable) human conduct. It would not be possible to commit first-degree murder, and incur the associated legal liabilities, but for the relevant regime of criminal law. The kind of possibility created by such rules may even be used in the spirit of a facility. MacCormick, for example, recollects the case of 'Super-Tramp', a literary character who commits arrestable offences in early winter in order to steadily secure a convenient shelter in his local jail[14] – a predicament by no means unheard of in the real world.[15]

It might seem tempting, at this point, to seek to isolate power-conferring rules by exclusion, that is, as any legal rules that are *not* duty-imposing. Hart sometimes appears to invoke this strategy in the course of his well-known attack on Austin. But this strategy would be of no avail either. It presupposes not only a robust understanding of duty-imposing rules, but also, crucially, a fully-fledged account of rule individuation, that is: an answer to the question how to exhaustively divide up normative material in law, including what counts as a 'complete' rule as opposed to a fragment thereof. But an account of rule individuation, as most writers nowadays recognise, can only be developed *after* clarity has been gained about the distinctness of legal power as a mode of regulation – which is our present task.[16] The strategy, in other words, presupposes the answer it is meant to supply. It is question begging.

Kelsen is more sensitive than Hart to the need for a positive articulation of the rules that confer legal power, as opposed to a characterisation by exclusion. Perhaps this is because legal powers come into view in Kelsen's 'dynamic' account of law, which is a part of his theory detached from the 'static' account wherein the problem of complete (non-dependent) legal norms is broached.[17] The idea of acts that yield *valid* results is central to Kelsen's 'dynamic' portrayal of the layered structure of legal orders. He regards a legal order as being made

[14] WH Davies, *The Autobiography of a Super-Tramp* (London, Fifield, 1908), referred to in N MacCormick, *H.L.A. Hart*, Jurists: Profiles in Legal Theory (London, Edward Arnold, 1981) 75. Similarly, O Henry tells the story of Soapy, who repeatedly tries but fails to commit a minor offence in order to 'accompli[sh] his desire' to spend the night in a warm jail rather than to sleep out on the street: see O Henry, 'The Cop and the Anthem' in O Henry, *100 Selected Stories* (Ware, Wordsworth Editions, 1995) 32–36. Soapy might even comment on his failed attempts by saying, intelligibly, 'that wasn't a *valid* crime either!'

[15] See, eg, Shiho Fukada, 'Japan's Prisons Are a Haven for Elderly Women', Bloomberg Newsweek, 19 March 2018, at https://www.bloomberg.com/news/features/2018-03-16/japan-s-prisons-are-a-haven-for-elderly-women.

[16] See, eg, Raz's sound principles of norm individuation: J Raz, *The Concept of a Legal System*, 2nd edn (Oxford, Oxford University Press, 1980) 141ff; J Raz, *Practical Reason and Norms* (London, Hutchinson, 1975) 104–06.

[17] eg H Kelsen, *The Pure Theory of Law*, 2nd edn, Max Knight (tr) (Berkeley, CA, University of California Press, 1967) 54ff, 70–71, 238; H Kelsen, *General Theory of Law and State*, A Wedberg (tr) (New York, Russell, 1945) 60–61, 122–23, 143–44.

up of acts creating valid enactments, judgments, decrees, contracts and so forth.[18] Throughout his career Kelsen makes several attempts to articulate the idea of legal power (*Rechtsmacht*) in a way that is sufficiently narrow to match such valid acts, and only them. It is particularly instructive to see how Kelsen wrestles with the problem of explaining the difference between performing a legally valid act and committing an offence, and thus between the way guest-house lodgers form a valid transaction to achieve their goal of a warm bed and the way Super-Tramp achieves the same goal.

In the second edition of his *Pure Theory of Law*, perhaps the most considered statement of his legal theory, Kelsen distinguishes between a narrow and a broad sense of legal power. The broad sense, says Kelsen, includes the 'capacity' to commit a delict:

> [A]ny human behaviour, determined by the legal order as a condition or consequence, may be regarded as being 'empowered' by the legal order. The man who can exhibit such a behaviour is enabled by the legal order to behave in this way. He has a capacity conferred upon him by the legal order ... Even the capacity of committing a delict is a capacity conferred by the legal order ...[19]

But Kelsen's effort to offer a contrasting, narrow idea of legal power is prematurely truncated. By way of showing why enactments and transactions involve 'true legal power' (*echte Rechtsmacht*), but delicts do not, all he has to say is that the former, unlike the latter, 'imply approval' by the legal order.[20] Kelsen does not elaborate on the vague notion of the law's 'implied approval'. As it stands, the notion is plainly insufficient for both his and our purposes. As Kelsen himself reluctantly implies at the end of his discussion, according to the test he is proposing, 'the capacity of fulfilling legal obligations' is a 'true legal power' as well.[21] For one may change legal positions by *complying with* rather than breaching one's legal duties, notably where compliance extinguishes a duty altogether (as in completing military service) or a particular instance thereof (as in paying this year's income tax). Surely, if the law 'implicitly approves' of our entering ordinary transactions, a fortiori it 'implicitly approves' of our complying with our legal duties.

Kelsen is right to be reluctant to reach this conclusion. Kelsen's test for 'true legal power' not only catches the fulfilment of legal duties. It also catches any form of legally permitted conduct that alters legal positions – such as moving one's residence from one district to another. This kind of conduct typically renders one subject to new entitlements and liabilities in matters of municipal

[18] Kelsen, *General Theory of Law and State*, n 17, 110ff; Kelsen, *Pure Theory*, n 17, 193ff.

[19] Kelsen, *Pure Theory*, n 17, 146 (the quotation follows the translation in the English edition, but replaces 'authorized' with 'empowered', in line with the German edition, H Kelsen, *Reine Rechtslehre*, 2nd edn (Vienna, Österreichische Staatsdruckerei, 1960) 150–51).

[20] Kelsen, *Pure Theory*, n 17, 146–47.

[21] ibid 148; the implication is unambiguous in the English edition (at 147–48), but most obvious in the German one (Kelsen, *Reine Rechtslehre*, n 19, 151–52).

services or local tax. It is a voluntary act that changes one's legal positions. One may even perform it for the sake of changing them. Or take a more colourful example. In eighteenth-century England, before genuine income tax was introduced, the so-called 'window tax' made the tax liability of landowners depend on the number of windows on their buildings, supposed to be a proxy for their wealth. Many owners were led to block up their windows in an effort to minimise tax, with effects still visible today. Blocking up one's window, like moving residence, is a legally permitted act that changes one's legal positions.

Neither Hart nor Kelsen wants to say that the mere act of moving from one house to another, or the mere act of blocking up one's window, is an exercise of legal power. These acts are no more exercises of legal power than is the fulfilment of a legal duty or the commission of an offence. But, as our discussion shows, Hart and Kelsen do not sufficiently spell out what an exercise of legal power is, such that it follows that those acts are not exercises of legal power. We still do not know whether power-conferring rules involve a distinct facility, and if so what that facility consists in.

IV. RAZ'S TAKE

But we may be close to finding out. The comparison of transactions and enactments with the kinds of act just mentioned – changes of residence, window-blockings – is particularly revealing. Both kinds of act are legally permitted, in the standard case. They are neither prohibited nor obligatory. Both of them trigger changes in legal positions ipso facto, upon being performed. And it is not unusual for both to be performed for the sake of producing those changes. What is more, it is true of both broad kinds of act that they may produce much the same kinds of normative consequence even when they are prohibited or obligatory. In many legal systems, for instance, although it is a crime to sell property known to have been stolen, in certain circumstances even the thief will be able to validly effect a prohibited sale.[22] Analogously, one's home move may yield the associated shifts in local charges and entitlements quite independently of the normative changes it may *additionally* yield if it is also, say, a breach of a restraining order or the fulfilment of binding professional arrangements. All this suggests that we may be able to discern what we are looking for by homing in on the difference between valid contracts, enactments, wills, etc, on the one hand,

[22] Hart uses this example in arguing, *contra* Bentham, that legal powers are not permissions (Hart, *Essays on Bentham*, n 8, 212). Further examples abound, including agents validly concluding transactions in excess of their mandate, valid enactments in breach of mandatory constitutional terms, and marriages validly celebrated in breach of certain kinds of prohibition. On the emergence and development of the distinction between validity and prohibition in Western legal thought, see M Köpcke, *A Short History of Validity and Invalidity*, n 2, chs 3, 5 and 8.

and changes of residence, window-blockings and other tax-avoiding or forum-shopping conduct, on the other.

Raz proposes a way to explain the differences at hand. He offers what in effect is an elaboration of Kelsen's test of the law's 'implied approval'. Raz argues that changes of residence altering local liabilities or entitlements do not amount to exercises of legal power, even though '[o]ne's position changes in such cases in a *way* very similar to the changes produced by the sale of a car or a house'.[23] For Raz, the distinction we are looking for does not depend on the *way* the legal change is effected. Instead, he says, 'it *depends entirely* on the *justification* for regarding such acts as effecting these normative changes'.[24] He goes on to formulate the justification, and thus the test, as follows:

> An act is the exercise of a power only if the reason for recognizing it as affecting norms and their application is that it is desirable to enable people to affect norms and their application in such a way if they desire to do so for this purpose.[25]

It emerges from other passages of Raz's work that the relevant question of desirability, according to him, falls to be assessed in the law's eyes. The 'reason for recognizing' the relevant act, says Raz, is the '*law's* reaso[n]'.[26] This means that Raz's test turns not on whether it *is* desirable that persons can thus alter legal relations, but on whether the law so deems it. Raz does not specify how to determine the law's reasons, but let us assume that we can, for argument's sake.[27]

Raz's test can then be recast as follows. An act is an exercise of legal power if the reason why the law recognises it as effecting a legal change is that the law deems it desirable to enable people to thus effect this change if they wish to do so for this purpose.

Now this proposition is a plausible articulation of at least one important difference between changing residence to minimise tax and striking a contractual deal. The test is more refined than Kelsen's generic talk of 'approval' by the legal order. The law's 'approval' of our entering into transactions is different from its 'approval' of our fulfilling our legal duties. From the law's point of view, we are to fulfil our duties whether we wish to or not. But the law deems it desirable that we can enter contractual relations *if* we wish to do so. Indeed, the law deems it desirable that we can enter contractual relations if we wish to do so *for the purpose of* altering duties and rights. It is this last point that shows how the law's 'approval' of our entering transactions differs from its 'approval' of our minimising tax. The law does not deem it desirable that we move residence

[23] Raz, *Practical Reason and Norms*, n 16, 102 (emphasis added).

[24] ibid (emphasis added).

[25] ibid.

[26] Raz, 'Voluntary Obligations and Normative Powers', n 1, 453, also 465. (Here Raz specifically discusses legal powers, not normative powers in general as in the quoted sentence.)

[27] He only says, 'Lawyers have established procedures for determining what are the law's intentions or reasons. These need not be discussed here' (ibid fn 6 at 453).

for the purpose of minimising tax. Legally we may.[28] But that is not, plausibly, what the law seeks to enable us to do in recognising our move as effecting a normative change.

But Raz's test has an important shortcoming. The shortcoming lies in the claimed comprehensiveness of the test. Raz presents the test as the consideration that makes the *entire* difference between acts that exercise legal power and acts that do not. On Raz's view, recall, acts that exercise legal power do not involve a distinct *way* of changing legal positions. The difference between them and tax-minimising home moves 'depends entirely' on the law's *justification* for recognising the respective change. It depends not on *how* the change is performed, but on whether the law deems it *desirable* to enable persons to perform it. There is something unsettling about this position. Taken at face value, it entails that, for example, home moves and construction works sometimes amount to exercises of legal power and sometimes they do not. They amount to exercises of legal power insofar as they fit with policies or goals deemed by the law – by the powers that be – to be socially desirable. It is not uncommon, after all, for governments to attach legal incentives, such as tax breaks or subsidies, to certain forms of conduct in order to encourage their performance. The law may link incentives, for example, to moving to an underpopulated area, or to renovating historic sites. Plausibly, in such cases, particularly where incentives are significant, the law deems it desirable that people move home or conduct construction works for the purpose of securing those entitlements, and this is the law's reason for – indeed the point of – recognising such conduct as qualifying under the incentive scheme. But even in these scenarios it is contrived to regard the relevant acts as exercises of legal power.[29]

The root of the difficulty is not hard to see. It is the supposition that exercises of legal power are not characterised by a distinct way of changing legal positions. Raz's test turns on the justification for recognising the change, not on the means by which the change is effected. The mark of legal power, on Raz's test, is the desirability that a legal change is made deliberately. It is not a method for deliberately making it. But if this is true, it means that power-conferring rules bestow on us the power – the *ability* – to deliberately change legal positions only in the generic sense that they make it *possible* for us to do so, as do other kinds of rule as well. It means, in other words, that although the law deems it desirable to *enable* us to change certain legal positions on purpose, in making such things as transactions or enactments, the law does not provide a distinct method

[28] But compare, for example, the 'general anti-abuse rule' in pt 5 of the Finance Act 2013 (UK), imposing duties to 'counteract' certain kinds of 'abusive' tax advantage (and so far forth not permitting the advantage-securing conduct).

[29] Unless, of course, the incentive involves opting into some kind of government-sponsored programme, rendering the act nearly or actually contractual. I am likewise disregarding the possible need to validly apply for the relevant incentive, and so to make an ancillary exercise of legal power in addition to satisfying the qualifying conditions, on which I focus. On official rulings validly awarding benefits that subjects legally qualify for, see ch 5.IV.

of changing legal positions *by way of enabling us* to do so, indeed by way of *facilitating* that we do. Given the richness of resources of legal reasoning and technique, the countless shapes that legal regulation can adopt, this diagnosis cannot but look suspicious.

It looks suspicious even on Raz's own terms. For Raz shares Hart's view that power-conferring rules provide individuals with facilities to realise their wishes by moulding legal relationships.[30] In a sense, both Hart and Raz characterise legal power by considering what it is *for*. Hart speaks of its 'social function'; Raz speaks of the law's 'justification' for recognising a legal change. Neither Hart nor Raz pronounces on what legal power *looks like*, on what the facility *consists in*. It is significant that, towards the end of his career, Hart notes that his account of legal powers leaves much 'unfinished business', including an analysis of 'the structure of the rules by which [legal powers] [are] conferred'.[31] Hart in that connection points the reader to an early work of Raz that sketches different ways in which power-conferring and duty-imposing rules 'guide conduct'.[32] But it is an account that Raz soon enough takes back.[33] The account wrongly makes central the subject's capacity to eschew state coercion. Raz eventually develops a sophisticated account of the structure of duty-imposing rules. It replaces the coercion-based analysis with an understanding of protected reasons for action.[34] But Raz shows no comparable interest in the general structure of the rules that confer legal power.[35] He never pronounces on the facility they provide.

It is likely that that business remains unfinished. Something important about legal power is still eluding us.

V. FACILITIES REVISITED, OR ROBERT'S HOME MOVE

As often in legal thought, insight can be gained by considering the predicaments we are seeking to disentangle from the point of view of the individuals involved in them. So take the case of Robert, who lives with his wife and their small children in a house that falls within a certain catchment area for local public healthcare services. He wishes to be treated at a health institution that falls outside that catchment area, but the services of that institution are accessible exclusively to those residing in the relevant part of town. One cannot procure the services by hiring them or by otherwise applying for them. Robert's wish to secure those services being firm enough, he persuades his family to

[30] Raz, *The Concept of a Legal System*, n 16, 158.

[31] Hart, *Essays on Bentham*, n 8, 196.

[32] ibid fn 58 at 219. The account is in Raz, *The Concept of a Legal System*, n 16, 156–66.

[33] Postscript to Raz, *The Concept of a Legal System*, n 16, fn 19 at 224.

[34] eg Raz, *Practical Reason and Norms*, n 16, chs 2 and 5.

[35] Except for insisting that they constitute 'a distinct type of norm' and do not purport to provide complete reasons for action (ibid 106). Both characteristics, however, are also true of permissive norms, as Raz conceives them (ibid 95–97, 106).

move. By moving residence, Robert and his family become legally entitled to the services.

That Robert's method for procuring the services is not a *facility* will be plain to him at the very latest by the time he feels his legs yield under the weight of the eleventh round of boxes, amidst a sea of bubble wrap and packaging tape, and children struggling to come to terms with new domestic arrangements. The legal rules on the eligibility to local health services have made it possible for Robert to choose an institution. To the extent the eligibility requirement is residence, rather than (say) birthplace or age, one can (in principle) bring oneself within the scope of the rules. One is even legally permitted to do so. But the rules hardly provide one with a facility to that end. Wiping off his sweat, and feeling anything but empowered by law, Robert may well wish to himself that local regulations had devised a somewhat less unwieldy method for him to prove his interest in the new health institution.

Of course, as Robert understands, local regulations do not envisage his home move as a proof or expression of his interest. That is because public health institutions in his jurisdiction are not assigned on the basis of patients' choices but on the basis of their residence. There may be good reasons for the public healthcare system to be set up in this way. The reasons may have to do with facilitating universal access to healthcare by distributing patients evenly and so avoiding delays and resource waste. Someone speaking on behalf of the healthcare system might truthfully claim that its design facilitates the realisation of many people's wishes in providing them with adequate and prompt medical care. Good government, at the end of the day, involves trading some facilities for certain others, and also in this sense spawning winners and losers. Not all facilities that law can and should provide are legal powers. But legal powers are facilities of a distinct kind.

Robert's case furnishes a backdrop against which we can begin to discern it. The home move costs Robert energy and time. It is likely more arduous for him than filing a valid application or concluding a valid contract would have been. But that is not the important difference. Intricate application requirements, never mind financial constraints, can render an exercise of legal power a painstaking task. The important difference is not in degree but in kind. It concerns the very nature of the acts involved in moving home or blocking up a window, on the one hand, and filing a valid application or concluding a valid contract, on the other. The latter, *but not* the former, are strategies specifically devised for changing legal positions on purpose. They are methods for changing legal positions *with the aim of changing them*. It is that which the law deems it desirable to enable us to do, according to Raz. But if the law means to enable us to do so, indeed to facilitate that we do, it is only natural that the law recognises as the act that effects this legal change an act that manifests the person's purpose as unequivocally as possible. The manifestation of one's purpose being the primary point of the act in this respect, there is in principle no need for the act to do anything other than that. Human beings have a privileged vehicle to manifest and convey to each other their purposes, relatively simply and unmistakably. This vehicle is language. If the law means to facilitate that Robert can pick a particular institution, it can ask him to *say so*.

Saying so, saying that he wishes to become entitled to treatment at a certain institution, is what, in essence, Robert would have done in filing an application or concluding a contract. We can imagine a form, presented to him for signature, containing an operative clause such as 'I hereby register at this practice …' or 'I hereby engage the services of …'. 'Hereby' is an habitual lawyerly phrase. If our suppositions are correct, that short phrase may capture, indeed harbour, the missing element we have been looking for throughout this chapter. To say that 'I *hereby* marry' is to say that I marry *by* doing the very thing I am doing *here* and now – namely, saying that I marry. Traces of this method of changing legal positions can be found across public and private law. And they come in close association with legally valid results. Thus enactments, decrees, judgments and other kinds of official pronouncement, characteristically involve an expression of the maker's intention to thereby introduce a legal change. Sometimes this occurs in set formulae ('be it enacted', 'we … hereby proclaim'), or through an emphasis on operative words, which are verbs that describe a legal change in the process of making it ('appeal dismissed', 'decision reversed'). Analogous forms of language are also used in private transactions ('I hereby authorise', 'Mrs Smith accepts the inheritance').[36]

Moreover, this method for changing legal positions seems to be absent from the predicaments that we have sought to *contrast* with exercises of legal power. For one thing, saying so is not the means by which Super-Tramp secures his entitlement to lodging. To be sure, some legal wrongs can be committed through the use of language, including libel, harassment and fraud. But the relevant utterances, to qualify as wrongful, must fulfil characteristics that do not include the speaker's statement that he thereby wishes to commit a wrong. 'I hereby slander Tom' is not a tort. Nor, for another thing, does tax-avoiding conduct change the relevant legal positions by so saying. Of course it may take an exercise of legal power to bring oneself within the scope of the relevant regulations. If Robert or his family do not already have a place in the new neighbourhood, they may need to buy or rent one. Likewise, a business may need to hire a certain number of employees to qualify for a certain tax break. In all these and similar cases one becomes entitled to the legal benefits by making the relevant transaction. But one does not become entitled to the benefits by making a transaction the

[36] There are echoes of this kind of language even in informal settings. The operative clause of the Spanish tenancy agreement I was presented for signature reads: 'The tenant is interested in leasing the described flat, and the landlord is likewise interested in leasing it to the tenant'. It does not say that the parties are interested in *hereby* leasing it, still less that the flat hereby *is leased*, but it implicitly conveys all of this in referring to the parties by the names that will result from the legal change having taken place.

content of which is one's becoming entitled. One does not become entitled to the benefits by manifesting one's wish to thereby so become.[37]

At this stage we may venture to formulate a hypothesis. The hypothesis is that acts that yield legally valid results involve a common and distinct method of changing legal positions. The method amounts to changing legal positions by manifesting one's wish to change them – by saying so. Henceforth I refer to this method as a legal *technique*. The hypothesis is, in short, that there is a distinct legal technique associated with legal validity. If the hypothesis is true, it means that our broadly stable language of 'validity' is a surface manifestation of a genuine underlying similarity amongst the variegated things we call 'legally valid'. It means that the acts that exercise legal power, on the received understanding of this idea, do share a distinct modus operandi. It means that there is a distinct kind of facility that power-conferring rules provide.

Indeed it means that there is a special plausibility to regarding these rules as conferring *power*. We think of a person's power as his capacity or ability to bring about certain states of affairs, and of this power as being all the greater the easier it is for this person to do so – easier, that is, in light of the significance or magnitude of what he accomplishes. Truly powerful people may just need to pick up the phone to influence the policy of national banks, whereas I myself, through this same kind of means, might at best manage to persuade the local bank clerk to swap my bonus alarm clock for a bonus pan. And even so I might not get precisely the pan I wanted by the time I wanted it. For power has to do not only with relative ease of performance, but also with targeted control over the particulars or contours of the result. Power is a matter of how much one can accomplish, how easily and in how targeted a way. If our hypothesis is correct, the technique of legal validity confers a power, constitutes an ability, in this most focal sense: it not only creates the possibility to alter the legal duties, rights and powers incumbent on oneself and others, possibly on many persons, but it also entrusts the capacity to pull off and steer this normative feat to something as simple yet forceful, as candid yet mighty, as one's datable, individual, intentional say-so.

Confirming the hypothesis is the remit of the next chapter.

NOTES

Section I: The Task Ahead

Legal Thought Must not Accord Legal Language the Final Word

The early Hart, at the time of his 1953 Oxford inaugural lecture (published as HLA Hart, *Essays in Jurisprudence and Philosophy* (Oxford, Oxford University Press, 1983)

[37] Again I am disregarding the possible need to validly apply for the benefits by way of ancillary exercise of legal power (see n 29).

ch 1), had toyed with the idea that progress could be made in legal theory by elucidating the meaning of legal terms in the spirit of 'ordinary language philosophy'; but he soon came to realise that there is more to the central categories of legal thought than patterns of linguistic practice (see eg ibid 5–6). This has since been a standard position amongst legal theorists: useful articulations include J Raz, *Ethics in the Public Domain: Essays in the Morality of Law and Politics*, rev edn (Oxford, Clarendon Press, 1995) 194–98; T Endicott, 'Adjudication and the Law' (2007) 27 *Oxford Journal of Legal Studies* 311, 324–25.

Legal Powers May not Go under that Name in Legal Practice

In this spirit, Raz, 'Voluntary Obligations and Normative Powers', n 1, 451; Hart, *Essays on Bentham*, n 8, 194; T Spaak, *The Concept of Legal Competence: An Essay in Conceptual Analysis*, R Carroll (tr) (Brookfield, VT, Dartmouth, 1994) 20–21; see further LJ Cohen, 'Critical Notice' (1962) 71 *Mind* 395, 396–99 (noting that in colloquial parlance, 'powers', unlike 'capacities', are primarily wielded by specified individuals or narrow classes thereof, eg powers of attorney, judicial powers). In particular, we often speak of 'powers' in connection with permissions or liberties to exert force on the part of public officials (eg powers of search, police powers): on the important distinction between such executive acts and exercises of legal power, see eg Hart, *Essays on Bentham*, n 8, 194–219 (discussing the distinction in Bentham); A Halpin, 'The Concept of a Legal Power' (1996) 16 *Oxford Journal of Legal Studies* 129, 129–39; A Ross, 'On the Concepts "State" and "State Organs" in Constitutional Law' (1961) 5 *Scandinavian Studies in Law* 111, 119–21; G Lamond, 'The Coerciveness of Law' (2000) 20 *Oxford Journal of Legal Studies* 39, 41–42. Conversely, we often say of persons who have the legal power to enter contracts, make wills or issue judgments that they have the 'capacity', 'competence' or 'jurisdiction' to do so, which terms name at least part of what is included in the theoretical idea of legal power. It is worth noting that some writings on legal power nominally explore the (narrower) idea of competence: eg Spaak, *The Concept of Legal Competence*, 51ff; Ferrer, *Las normas de competencia*, n 12; R Guastini, 'Invalidity' (1994) 7 *Ratio Juris* 212. The idea of competence abstracts an agent's quality or condition of 'being competent' from procedural requirements for 'actualizing' that competence (to use the phrasing in Ferrer, *Las normas de competencia*, n 12, 124ff, 137ff). Given that abstraction, 'competence' becomes a rather undifferentiated condition as applied to, especially, many areas of private law. In our terminology, actualising one's legal competence is exercising one's legal power.

Section II: Facilities to Change Legal Positions

Hohfeld on Legal Power

Hohfeld's seminal essay ('Some Fundamental Legal Conceptions as Applied in Judicial Reasoning' (1913) 23 *Yale Law Journal* 16) decisively maps different kinds of normative position in law, amongst them legal powers. However, by way of *characterising* these positions Hohfeld chiefly relies on examples. His one attempt to provide an 'approximate explanation' of 'the intrinsic nature of legal power as such' (ibid 44) is both convoluted and uninformative: he says that where 'a change in a given legal relation … result[s] … from some superadded fact or group of facts which are under the volitional control of one or more human beings …, the person (or persons) whose volitional control is paramount may be said to have the (legal) power to effect the particular change of legal relations' (ibid 44). In short: one exercises legal power when one's voluntary act results in a change in legal relations. The insufficiency of this kind of understanding is discussed in section III of this chapter.

Hart on Power-conferring Rules

In making sense of Hart's idea of power-conferring rules we cannot draw on his cognate idea of secondary rules. Notwithstanding Hart's insinuations to the contrary (eg in Hart, *The Concept of Law*, n 4, 81), his contrast between duty-imposing and power-conferring rules does not match his contrast between primary and secondary rules (ibid ch 5). Hart's repeated equation of the category of secondary rules with the kind of rules that enable the transition 'from the pre-legal into the legal world' (ibid 41–42, 94), along with his characterisation of the latter as conferring official powers (ibid 94) and his admission that primitive communities typically recognise private powers (ibid 93), suggests that Hart's notion of secondary rules may be best understood as referring to a subclass of power-conferring rules, namely, rules conferring public powers. Then again, there is some evidence, notably Hart's claim that secondary rules are *about* primary rules (ibid 94), for thinking that a secondary rule is a rule about other rules, ie a meta-rule, so that rules imposing duties to exercise (official) powers would be Hartian secondary rules as well.

Hart on the 'Social Function' of Rules

It is unclear whether Hart's idea of the '(social) function' of rules (Hart, *The Concept of Law*, n 4, 27, 32, 38, 39, 40) tracks the rules' *frequency* of use, the point they are *deemed to* have by the relevant community, or the point they *truly* have; compare Hart's reference to how rules are 'thought of, spoken of, and used in social life' (ibid 41) to his acclaim of power-conferring rules as 'valuable to society' (ibid 41), indeed as 'one of the great contributions of law to social life' (ibid 28) and a 'huge and distinctive amenity' (ibid 41). Raz instead speaks of 'normative function' (Raz, *The Concept of a Legal System*, n 16, 158); on Raz's different use of 'social function', see ibid 158; Raz, *The Authority of Law: Essays on Law and Morality* (Oxford, Oxford University Press, 1979) 165 (he is wrong to attribute this use to Hart's enterprise of norm individuation: ibid 178–79).

Changing Legal Positions

The literature sometimes distinguishes between exercises of legal power that create (modify, repeal) norms, and exercises of legal power that determine the incidence of pre-existing norms. See, eg, Hart, *The Concept of Law*, n 4, 41, 81 *et passim*; more explicitly Hart, *Essays on Bentham*, n 8, 212ff. Raz (*The Concept of a Legal System*, n 16, 162ff; 'Voluntary Obligations and Normative Powers', n 1, 454; *Practical Reason and Norms*, n 16, 103ff) speaks respectively of 'legislative' (or 'norm-creating') and 'regulative' powers; there are also echoes of this distinction in Kelsen's work (compare Kelsen, *General Theory of Law and State*, n 17, 123ff, on the creation of legal norms, with 136ff on 'legal transactions'). Seeing as this distinction presupposes an account of norm individuation, which this book does not develop (see ch 2.III and corresponding endnote), the idea of a change in legal positions offers an appropriate common ground for our purposes.

'Constitutive Rules'

Searle (*Speech Acts*, n 12, 33–34) portrays 'constitutive rules' as rules that 'create or define new forms of behaviour', and contrasts them with 'regulative rules', which 'regulate antecedently or independently existing forms of behaviour' (characteristically in imperative mode). An effectively identical distinction is developed also by Alf Ross in his later work, it seems in parallel to Searle (Ross, *Directives and Norms*, n 12, 53ff; see fn 1 at 53). Both Searle and Ross insist that behaviour which is governed by 'constitutive rules' is 'logically dependent' on these rules. In Ross's words, the rules endow the behaviour with its 'specific meaning' (ibid 53–54). In Searle's words, the behaviour 'can receive specifications or descriptions which it could not receive if the rule or rules did not exist' (*Speech Acts*, n 12, 35); accordingly, Searle's formulation of the rules is 'X counts as Y in context C' (ibid 36; Searle, *The Construction of Social Reality*, n 12, 28). Although both Searle and Ross insist that 'constitutive rules' are not mere labels or definitions (*Speech Acts*, n 12, 36; *The Construction of Social Reality*, n 12, 44; *Directives and Norms*, n 12, 56), they only tenuously chart what the rules' constitutive character *does* entail. Searle vaguely speaks of 'consequences' (*Speech Acts*, n 12, 36) and of 'linguistic' and 'nonlinguistic' powers (*The Construction of Social Reality*, n 12, 110), having at one point taken the step, eventually aborted, to dub at least some of the relevant powers 'deontic' (ibid 109, also 100–01; on Searle's account, 'powers' are conferred not only on persons but also on events and objects such as walls: ibid 95–96 *et passim*). Ross, in turn, refers to 'legal effects' (*Directives and Norms*, n 12, 56) that he elsewhere describes as 'releas[ing] ... the forces that move the legal machinery' (A Ross, 'Rise and Fall of the Doctrine of Performatives' in RE Olson and AM Paul (eds), *Contemporary Philosophy in Scandinavia* (Baltimore, MD, The Johns Hopkins Press, 1972) 211). For further refinements of the idea(s) of 'constitutive rules' that do not bear on our concerns, see AG Conte, 'Eidetic-Constitutive Rules' in A Pintore and M Jori (eds), *Law and Language: The Italian Analytical School*, S Stirling, A Pirrie and Z Bankowski (tr) (Liverpool, Deborah Charles Publications, 1997). An idea similar to 'constitutive rules' can be found in von Wright's treatise on the logic of norms, where he speaks of a class of norms that 'determine something' (von Wright, *Norm and Action: A Logical Enquiry*, n 12, 6–7 (emphasis omitted)); he calls them 'rules'. His only examples are the rules of games, the rules of grammar, and the rules of logic and mathematics. He contrasts this class of norms with, inter alia, 'technical norms' such as recipes (ibid ch 1), but does not explain how the two classes of norms differ. Crucially, he does not identify the 'something' that is 'determined' by norms of the former class, or indeed what 'determination' means. But 'determination' is ambiguous: one can say of recipes, too, that they determine – clarify, enumerate, set out – the steps necessary to bake a cake.

Power-conferring Rules as 'Constitutive Rules'

In an effort to build on von Wright, Searle and Ross, Bulygin portrays legal power-conferring rules as rules that 'define concepts' (Bulygin, 'Sobre las normas de competencia', n 12, 493, emphasis omitted). Ferrer (*Las normas de competencia*, n 12, ch 4) characterises power-conferring rules as rules 'constitutive' of the 'dispositional property' of 'being competent' to realise certain valid juridical acts. But that which one brings about in realising valid acts is referred to merely as 'institutional results', not as normative changes. Indeed Ferrer goes as far as to deny that exercising normative power entails changing normative positions (ibid 156–57), because he understands the latter, narrowly, as 'producing or applying norms'. Ruiter, in turn, in *Institutional Legal Facts*, explains legal power-conferring rules ('norms of competence', n 12, 91) as Searlean constitutive rules that set the conditions for the successful performance of ('declarative') speech acts the results of which are 'legally valid presentations', rather than normative changes; underlying the account is an untenable understanding of legal obligations that reduces them to mere 'images of persons ordered to carry out some course of action' who 'count as coerced to fulfil it' (ibid 70, emphasis omitted). In contrast to the preceding authors, both Alexy, on the one hand, and Atienza and Ruiz Manero, on the other, explain power-conferring rules as 'constitutive rules' that enable normative changes, and, unlike Searle, they also confront the difficulty, noted in section III of this chapter, that this description is also true of rules of other kinds, including duty-imposing ones. Whereas Alexy (*Theorie der Grundrechte* (Frankfurt, Suhrkamp, 1986) 214–17) offers no plausible solution to this problem (neither does Ferrer, *Las normas de competencia*, n 12, 149–50), Atienza and Ruiz Manero (*Las piezas del Derecho: Teoría de los enunciados jurídicos*, n 12, 61–62) point to the ideas that I discuss and deem insufficient in section IV of this chapter. Although MacCormick's legal theory is sympathetic to Searlean ideas, it does not normally build on this apparatus when explaining power-conferring rules (eg MacCormick, *H.L.A. Hart*, n 14, ch 6; N MacCormick, 'Powers and Power-Conferring Norms' in SL Paulson and B Litschewski-Paulson (eds), *Normativity and Norms: Critical Perspectives on Kelsenian Themes* (Oxford, Clarendon Press, 1998); N MacCormick, *Institutions of Law: An Essay in Legal Theory* (Oxford, Oxford University Press, 2007) ch 9); when it does, in N MacCormick and Z Bankowski, 'Speech Acts, Legal Institutions and Real Laws' in P Birks and N MacCormick (eds), *The Legal Mind: Essays for Tony Honoré* (Oxford, Clarendon Press, 1986), it uncharacteristically loses sight of the idea of normative changes.

Section III: Super-Tramp

Rule Individuation

The question of rule individuation is usually and soundly regarded as independent of, and secondary to, an understanding of the idea of legal power. Sometimes this is made explicit, as by MacCormick (*H.L.A. Hart*, n 14, 76ff), Raz (*Practical Reason and Norms*, n 16, 104) or Spaak (*The Concept of Legal Competence*, 154); sometimes it is implicit, as when Ross characterises power-conferring norms (*Directives and Norms*, n 12, 53ff) before arguing that they are reducible to duty-imposing norms (ibid 118, 199), or when Ferrer (*Las normas de competencia*, n 12, 1) and Atienza and Ruiz Manero (*Las piezas del Derecho*, n 12, 45) begin their studies of power-conferring norms, in which the question of individuation figures prominently, with the assumption that there *are* such things as norms that confer legal power. Although in *The Concept of Law* Hart merges these two questions (n 4, 35ff), in *Essays on Bentham* he shows some awareness of the distinction (n 8, 218–19). I agree with most of the preceding authors that power-conferring and duty-imposing norms fall to be individuated as distinct kinds of norms. An account of norm individuation must not be confused with a *typology* or classification of kinds of norms thus individuated. The typology I find most useful distinguishes norms that establish *how* to bring about something from norms that establish *whether* we ought, ought not or are permitted to bring it about. Hence permissions are normally included in my generic references, throughout the book, to duties and rights as normative positions. One can of course think of alternative typologies of norms, such as whether or not they give reasons: this would place (strong) permissions (Raz, *Practical Reason and Norms*, n 16, ch 3.1) alongside power-conferring norms. Spaak (*The Concept of Legal Competence*, ch 7; T Spaak, 'Norms that Confer Competence' (2003) 16 *Ratio Juris* 89) unhelpfully treats this latter criterion not as a classificatory device but as the main test for norm individuation, concluding that power-conferring norms are fragments of duty-imposing norms.

Kelsen on Legal Power

Kelsen's idea of empowerment in its 'broadest sense', discussed in the main text, corresponds to what in earlier work Kelsen simply calls 'legal capacity' (*General Theory of Law and State*, n 17, 90–91); in this earlier work 'empowerment' is narrowly understood as *delegation* of norm-creating power from higher-order to lower-order authorities (ibid 113, 270). There are further ways in which Kelsen fails to narrow down the idea of legal power at various stages of his career. He sometimes seeks to pin it down simply by invoking the *contrast* with the ideas of permission or command (eg *Pure Theory*, n 17, 4–5, 15–16). But this strategy falters because, for one thing, he himself does not keep permission and power wholly separate (eg ibid 15–16; H Kelsen, *General Theory of Norms*, M Hartney (tr) (Oxford, Clarendon Press, 1991) 104–05) and, for another thing, the strategy presupposes an account of norm individuation, and Kelsen's own account of norm individuation only has room for *one* type of complete (non-dependent) norm (*Pure Theory*, n 17, 54ff, 238; *General Theory of Law and State*, n 17, 60–01, 143–44). This is also why his explication of legal power as the capacity to (participate in the) creation of legal norms (*Pure Theory*, n 17, 146–47; *General Theory of Norms*, 96ff) only compounds the vagueness on point. For an argument that the idea of legal power becomes more important as Kelsen's career progresses, see N Bobbio, 'Kelsen and Legal Power' in SL Paulson and B Litschewski-Paulson (eds), *Normativity and Norms: Critical Perspectives on Kelsenian Themes* (Oxford, Clarendon Press, 1998). For an interpretation of Kelsen's later work as portraying power-conferring norms as the fundamental type of norms, S Paulson, 'An Empowerment Theory of Norms' (1988) 1 *Ratio Juris* 58.

Section IV: Raz's Take

Acts That are Prohibited Yet Valid

The fact that familiar kinds of act can be *both* prohibited *and* legally valid is recurrently brought up in arguments for the distinctness of legal powers: see, eg, Hart, *Essays on*

Bentham, n 8, 212–13; Spaak, *The Concept of Legal Competence*, 83ff; Alexy, *Theorie der Grundrechte*, n 12, 213, especially fn 160; Bulygin, 'Sobre las normas de competencia', n 12, 489; Atienza and Ruiz Manero, *Las piezas del Derecho*, n 12, 46ff; Ferrer, *Las normas de competencia*, n 12, 65ff. The examples invoked by these discussions include, in addition to a thief's valid sale of stolen goods, an agent's transaction with a good faith third party in excess of the terms of the principal's authorisation (Spaak, *The Concept of Legal Competence*, 83–84; also in Ross, *Directives and Norms*, n 12, 131), a claim filed by a lawyer appointed judge and therefore prohibited from practising law (Bulygin, 'Sobre las normas de competencia', n 12, 489), a contract in breach of a prohibition to distribute a given pharmaceutical substance (Alexy, *Theorie der Grundrechte*, n 12, fn 160 at 213), marriages celebrated against certain legal prohibitions (in German law: ibid; in old Swedish law: Spaak, *The Concept of Legal Competence*, 84), and indeed enactments and other official decisions violating the terms of higher-order laws (Hart, *Essays on Bentham*, n 8, 214; Ferrer, *Las normas de competencia*, n 12, 66; Atienza and Ruiz Manero, *Las piezas del Derecho*, n 12, 46ff), especially when the decisions are legally final. A danger inherent in these arguments is that the sheer existence of prohibited but valid acts is taken to prove too much. The reasoning of these authors tends to be: because the acts in question change legal positions even when they are prohibited, (i) those changes cannot spring from a permission, and so (ii) they must spring from a legal power. But (ii) does not follow from (i): as the main text shows, there are other kinds of act, such as moving residence, that change legal positions whether or not they are prohibited, but that are not for that reason appropriately regarded as exercises of power. In fact, even (i) is questionable. It affirms that legal powers are not permissions on the premise that, if they were, the legal system would contain as many normative contradictions as prohibitions to perform valid acts, because it would be prohibiting and permitting conduct at the same time. But it is by no means obvious that a legal system cannot be thought of as exhibiting this degree of contradiction. Legally final yet mistaken decisions, for example, carry an accustomed sense of contradiction that legal theorists have not generally sought to dispel, with the possible exception of Kelsen's chimerical suggestion that legal systems here implicitly empower decision-makers to produce *either* legal *or* illegal law (Kelsen, *General Theory of Law and State*, n 17, 153ff; Kelsen, *Pure Theory*, n 17, 267ff; Kelsen, *General Theory of Norms*, 248–49) – a construction that dissolves the possibility of legal reasoning. See further ch 5.V and corresponding endnote.

Bentham on Legal Power

Bentham is probably the first scholar explicitly to map different kinds of exercises of legal power, both general and particular, in both public and private law, all of them associated with the idea of legal validity: see J Bentham, *Of Laws in General*, HLA Hart (ed) (London, The Athlone Press, 1970) chs 2 and 9. But when it comes to spelling out the idea of legal power, and the nature of the rules that confer it, Bentham vaguely speaks of the sovereign 'allowing' certain persons to participate in the task of 'imperation', a task that is tantamount to changing legal positions. 'Imperation', in Bentham's view, is a task privy to the sovereign, which others may therefore discharge only by sovereign concession. Even adding oneself to the class of persons henceforth subject to existing 'mandates' (such as contractual or marriage duties), because it involves supplementing those 'mandates', requires sovereign permission. Legal powers are therefore permissions, according to Bentham; for sound criticism, see Hart, *Essays on Bentham*, n 8, 212–13. The view that power-conferring norms are permissions has also been defended by von Wright, who discusses 'norms of higher order' in these terms (*Norm and Action*, n 12, ch 10) (accordingly von Wright only conceives of physical, not normative abilities: ibid 48ff, 121ff). See further CE Alchourrón and E Bulygin, *Normative Systems* (New York, Springer, 1971) 73, 151; Guastini, 'Invalidity', 223–24.

Raz's Test

The main text sidesteps an ambiguity in Raz's test. He offers two formulations thereof. According to the first formulation, reproduced in the main text, 'An act is the exercise of a power only if the reason for recognizing it as affecting norms and their application is that it is desirable to enable people to affect norms and their application in such a way if they desire to do so for this purpose' (Raz, *Practical Reason and Norms*, n 16, 102). According to the second formulation, 'An act is the exercise of a normative power if, and only if, it is recognized as effecting a normative change because, amongst other possible justifications, it is an act of a type such that it is reasonable to expect that, if recognized as effecting a normative change, acts of this type will be generally performed only if the persons concerned want to secure this normative change' (ibid 103). In short, the first formulation concerns the *desirability* and the second formulation concerns the *likelihood* of a certain kind of act's being performed for the sake of producing a normative change. But the second test cannot be made sense of independently of the first. The sheer likelihood that people will generally perform some conduct for the sake of securing a legal change can only supply a *justification* for recognising that change if it is desirable that they should do so. After all, the very same kind of prediction will often justify *refusing* to recognise a putative legal change (eg financial compensation for the provision of bodily organs). Hence the second formulation collapses into the first. Invocations of Raz's test in the literature are not stable either. For example, Atienza and Ruiz Manero (*Las piezas del Derecho*, n 12, 62) wrongly present as 'the same idea' a test based on 'the purpose generally attributed' to each norm; Spaak (T Spaak, 'Explicating the Concept of Legal Competence' in JC Hage and D von der Pfordten (eds), *Concepts in Law* (Dortrecht, Springer, 2009),76) proposes a criterion equivalent to the Raz's first test ('the reasons … *we can rationally attribute to the legislature*'); Halpin ('The Concept of a Legal Power', 143) speaks of what is 'normally done'; and Klass (G Klass, 'Three Pictures of Contract: Duty, Power and Compound Rule' (2008) 83 *New York University Law Review* 1726, 1739–41) interchangeably uses the first and the second versions of the test.

The Early Raz on How Power-conferring Rules 'Guide Conduct'

On his early account (Raz, *The Concept of a Legal System*, n 16, 156–66), both duty-imposing and power-conferring norms confer on the subject a 'power' to control certain consequences of his conduct, consequences defined essentially in terms of state coercion. The difference is that in the case of duty-imposing norms the consequences are always disadvantageous for the subject, whereas in the case of power-conferring norms the consequences are advantageous or disadvantageous depending on the subject's wishes. Plainly this is both a poor characterisation of the idea of legal duty, effectively indistinguishable from the 'gunman situation writ large' (Hart, *Essays in Jurisprudence and Philosophy*, 58), and a poor characterisation of the 'facility' (Raz, *The Concept of a Legal System*, n 16, 158) involved in legal power, effectively indistinguishable from that provided by the weather forecast.

Technique and Point of Legal Power

Theorists who, like Hart, show some awareness of the relation between the point of legal power and its technique, or normative structure, include Atienza and Ruiz Manero (*Las piezas del Derecho*, n 12, 58ff), Ross (*On Law and Justice*, n 13, 203–04, 216–23; 'On the Concepts "State" and "State Organs"', 116ff; 'Rise and Fall of the Doctrine of Performatives', 209–11), MacCormick (*H.L.A. Hart*, n 14, ch 6) and, especially, Spaak ('Explicating the Concept of Legal Competence', 77–78; also 'Norms that Confer Competence', 91; *The Concept of Legal Competence*, 102–03, 124). See also Raz on the relation between the way promises are made ('by communicating an intention to undertake, by that very communication, an obligation', J Raz, 'Promises in Morality and Law' (1982) 95 *Harvard Law Review* 916, 927) and the 'justification' why they are binding ('because it is desirable to give effect to the intentions of the promisor': ibid 929–30).

3

Intention in Valid Acts

I. FOUR PECULIAR TRAITS

SUPPOSE YOU HAD the power to make something happen simply by expressing your wish to make it happen – simply, as it were, by saying so. Not even lamp genies in fairy tales bestow on persons such a power. A lamp genie, after all, invites a person to manifest a wish, which he, the genie, will take care to realise. The wish comes true if and as the genie awards or grants it. But if you have the power to make your wish come true simply by expressing it, your utterance itself has magic import. Your wish comes true not in being granted, but in being uttered. Your power is mightier still than King Midas' capacity to turn whatever he touches into gold. Unlike King Midas, you can choose both *which* things to transform, and what to change them *into*.

According to our surmises at the end of the previous chapter, the ability to enter into valid contracts, make valid wills, enact valid statutes, issue valid rulings and create other kinds of valid results involves a power of this kind. On our provisional hypothesis, all these forms of acting are exercises of a distinct kind of power we call legal power. It is characterised by the fact that it involves a distinct *technique* for changing legal positions (which I indistinctly call the technique of legal validity or the technique of legal power). The technique is a matter of changing legal positions by expressing one's wish to change them. It is a matter, in essence, of changing legal positions by saying so. What Hart famously describes as a facility for realising one's wishes, on this view, amounts to the possibility to forge legal relationships and otherwise shape social arrangements and allocate responsibilities by means of a self-fulfilling expression of intent: 'I *hereby* …'.

The purpose of this chapter is to test this hypothesis. This requires paying closer heed to some familiar aspects of legal practice, aspects which suggest that the power of the valid say-so is in some ways more perplexing than we have canvassed so far. Four aspects of legal practice deserve consideration.

First, *a valid say-so can invoke a legal regime beyond what is ostensibly in the mind of the sayer*. Valid utterances often yield normative changes well beyond those that the agent describes and ostensibly purports to introduce. The point is not merely that we may sometimes legally *say* things in relatively inexplicit ways, for example by placing a bunch of carrots on the shop counter. This kind of act expresses the agent's intention to purchase the goods, but it does not in the same way express or convey the complex set of changes in the parties' legal duties, rights and powers that are effected by a valid transaction, which are substantially determined by legislation and case law. Just as an incantation may beseech and rally the forces of nature, so a valid utterance, it seems, can invoke and harness the power of the valid utterances of *others*, for example the past utterance(s) of a legislature enacting consumer legislation that is now said, cryptically, to 'imply terms' into the parties' agreement.

Secondly, *a valid say-so can endure through time and circulate as a relatively free-standing entity*. In *Casablanca*, Ugarte entrusts to Rick two 'letters of transit' signed by General De Gaulle: they 'cannot be rescinded; not even questioned'. The portability of the letters forms the essential backdrop to the story's plot. So, too, does the portability of valid passports, credit cards, vouchers or bills of exchange form the backdrop to countless modes of legal interaction. Valid utterances, it seems, have the capacity to become embodied in physical shape and be exhibited, reckoned with and relied on, for many purposes and by many hands, as entities fundamentally detached from the intentional act that originally gave rise to them, and sometimes even of the identity of their author, who may have long come to regret the legal motion he has thereby set in train, perhaps irreversibly so.

Thirdly, and more poignantly still, *a valid say-so may accomplish effects unintentionally*, by producing legal changes the author never wished to bring about, indeed wished *not* to bring about. Legal regimes on mistake, procedural safeguards such as witnessing, and many other forms of legal doctrine substantially go to reduce, but they cannot eliminate, the standing possibility that legally valid acts are performed wholly or partly by accident. Electronic or automated forms of transaction or voting magnify the chance of this occurring. One careless slip and the magic say-so may take over, to the point of thwarting rather than realising one's wishes.

And fourthly, *a say-so will not be valid unless it adopts the valid wording, requirements and form*. The importance of the valid say-so is such that one cannot wield legal power through alternative means, however intent one is on doing so. One may fail to exercise legal power if, for instance, one's purported resolution is ultra vires, if one's draft will lacks the requisite attestation, or if one seeks to conclude a transaction orally when it can only be made validly in writing. Having an intent and expressing it, however clearly, is sometimes not enough to rally the law's forces – just as it was not enough to open the mouth of the cave in which Ali Baba's brother tragically found himself trapped. Although he unambiguously manifested his wish to open the cave, he did not manifest it through the specific formula, 'Open Sesame!'

If there is a distinct technique associated with legal validity, it must be able to account for these traits. Some writers have recoiled in their search for a technique of legal validity precisely on stumbling upon these traits. Other writers have sought to explain them away as exceptions. But exceptions so widespread and prosaic call in question the existence of the corresponding standard.

If a distinct technique underlies valid action, we must be able to show how its workings are forcefully displayed, rather than anomalously distorted, in each of these four scenarios.

To that end, our provisional hypothesis may require some adjustment or supplementation. We should therefore consider the hypothesis more closely. Central to it is the idea of *saying something*. It appears to be an ingredient of the technique of validity, and for that reason easier to study than the whole of which it is part. Philosophers of language have shed useful light on what is involved in saying something to someone else in ordinary communication. They have contributed to spelling out what we might call the technique of ordinary communication. Understanding this, in sections II–IV, will equip us to tackle the peculiar traits of the technique of legal validity from section V onwards. This will dispel a number of misconceptions in which philosophers of law remain stuck. As we shall see, there is something to be learned by appreciating both the similarities and the differences that lie between the technique of validity and the technique of ordinary communication.

II. THE TECHNIQUE OF COMMUNICATION

Take everyday conversation. What is involved in saying something to someone else? In the mid-twentieth century, JL Austin's influential work *How To Do Things With Words*[1] changes how philosophers go about answering this question. In fact he makes them raise it. Austin makes a plea for studying utterances as acts. Philosophy of language, he complains, has exceedingly focused on *what* is said. It has neglected the very *act* of saying something: the 'total speech act in the total speech situation'.[2] Thus traditional philosophy of language has studied, for example, the truth and falsity of assertions. But Austin insists that even false assertions are 'speech acts'. So are questions, warnings, complaints and so forth. Austin's interest lies in the technique that is common to all these communicative acts. He devotes much of the book to determining the parallel amongst them. Austin expresses the parallel by saying that one *does* things with words whenever one marshals the conventions of language to make a meaningful utterance; that the acts involved in asserting, asking, warning, complaining and so on, viewed precisely as acts, have similar criteria of success and failure.

Austin's work is more circumspect about just what the *success* involves, just what one *does* in saying something to someone else, than is the work of other writers, notably Grice and Strawson.[3] Austin's insights can therefore be valuably

[1] JL Austin, *How To Do Things With Words*, 2nd edn, JO Urmson and M Sbisà (eds) (Cambridge, MA, Harvard University Press, 1975).

[2] ibid 148.

[3] PF Strawson, 'Intention and Convention in Speech Acts' (1964) 73 *The Philosophical Review* 439; P Grice, 'Meaning' (1957) 66 *The Philosophical Review* 377.

complemented by theirs. Taken together, these contributions yield a perceptive understanding of communication.

The core of that understanding is this. In making a communicative act – in saying something meaningful – I achieve something through a special method: namely, by manifesting an intention to thereby achieve it. This is best appreciated with an example. Suppose I am deciding whether to join the dinner after the seminar session. The restaurant is not cheap and I am not very hungry, so it matters to my decision how the dinner will be paid for (splitting bills evenly, from the seminar budget, etc). You are the organiser – you know the answer to this question. But I am too embarrassed to ask it. I wish to be told, but I would rather not go about attaining this wish through the method of asking. What could I do instead? I might, of course, do nothing and entertain my wish in silence. Call this scenario 1:

> *Scenario 1 (wishing in silence)*:
>
> I wish to be told.

But suppose I move to action. I devise some indirect strategy to make you aware of my wish to be told how the dinner will be paid for. I ensure, for instance, that you overhear my remarking to a colleague that I really wish I knew. What I am doing in this second scenario can be described as follows:

> *Scenario 2 (being overheard)*:
>
> I wish to be told, and I am trying to realise this wish by making you aware that: I wish to be told.

The important difference from scenario 1 is that in scenario 2 I do not only have a wish, I have a strategy. I am doing something in order to realise my wish: I am deploying some means to that end. My strategy, my means, involves making you aware that I have the wish.

Now imagine that I actually ask you. What is different? In this third scenario, I also have (and implement) a strategy. I am doing something for the sake of realising my wish of finding out. My strategy again involves making you aware of something. But the thing I am making you aware of is not merely that I wish to be told, as in scenario 2. At the point of asking, I not only have a strategy but I also disclose to you that strategy. In scenario 2, by contrast, I had a strategy but I only disclosed a wish. In scenario 3, my strategy involves sharing with you that very strategy. So, when I say to you 'How will the dinner be paid for?', I am trying to be told by making you aware *not only* that I wish to be told, *but also* that I am trying to realise this wish thus – 'thus', that is: through this very effort, *hereby*.

> *Scenario 3 (asking)*:
>
> I wish to be told, and I am trying to realise this wish by making you aware that: I wish to be told, and I am trying to realise it thus.

This analysis explains why the conduct in scenario 3 is both easier and more embarrassing than the conduct in scenario 2. It is more embarrassing because it involves a direct and transparent disclosure to you of my relevant train of thought, a second-person engagement with you as my interlocutor. But it is easier because I no longer need to resort to laborious machinations to calibrate which bits of my strategy you should become aware of. My success in realising my wish is far less dependent on happenstance. It is in my power to make a relatively simple and targeted attempt at finding out. The attempt is targeted in being unambiguously directed at you and precise in its import.

I have so far spoken of wishes and strategies to realise them. The time has come to cast the discussion in the more accurate language of intention. When a person self-consciously deploys some means to attaining a wish, the object of that wish becomes the end or goal the person is *intentionally* engaged in pursuing. In scenario 1, I only have a wish; but from scenario 2 onwards I have an intention. In scenario 2, I have an intention but I only disclose a wish. It is not until scenario 3 that I have an intention and disclose that very intention. Because that intention concerns itself, because it is realised in being expressed, the literature calls it a *reflexive* intention. The strategy of asking involves manifesting a reflexive intention. It involves, in other words, achieving something by means of manifesting an intention to thereby achieve it.

Manifesting a reflexive intention is the method whereby we go about asking, asserting, complaining, warning or performing any other kind of communicative act. It is the core of the technique of communication. The technique is much easier to use than to explain. You learned to use it at a very early age, probably before you began using words, never mind reading about philosophers of language and the reflexive intention analysis. The art of communicating is set apart from other forms of intentional action by the fact that the agent's intention is relevant not only to *why* the action is performed, but also to *how* it is. Grabbing three piled boxes normally manifests my intention to hold them all. However, whether or not I manage to hold them all does not depend on anyone's identifying my intention. The manifestation of intent is not the means whereby I succeed, and expect to succeed, in holding the boxes. My act has no communicative meaning.

The idea of communicative meaning falls to be explained in the context of what counts as success in performing a communicative act. There are a number of stages of success involved in a communicative act, which are not always appropriately disentangled in the literature. At a very basic level there is success involved in the sheer act of uttering some noises (or making some written marks) that amount to words used with a certain sense and reference.[4]

[4] Austin characterises these three sub-stages as respectively a 'phonetic act', a 'phatic act' and a 'rhetic act', jointly making up a 'locutionary act' (Austin, *How To Do Things With Words*, n 1, 92ff: 'The act of "saying something" … I dub the performance of a locutionary act', ibid 94).

We may consider this a first stage of success. But as Austin well appreciates, this kind of act, which he dubs an act *of* 'saying something', can for many purposes not be usefully considered, let alone understood, in isolation from the act that is performed *in* saying something: namely, the act of asking, asserting, complaining, warning, etc.[5] One may be performing any of these latter acts in uttering one and the same string of sounds ('h e i s l e a v i n g'). The meaning of what one says varies accordingly. Saying something meaningful is therefore a second stage of success. It is the key stage for our purposes.

One succeeds in making a communicative act, we shall say, if one's act has communicative meaning.[6] An act has communicative meaning if the speaker's communicative intention can be reasonably understood – reasonably, that is, in the circumstances in which the utterance is made, including the level of background noise, the audience's language competence, and any other facts that are common knowledge between speaker and audience. Success in performing a communicative act, therefore, involves *reasonably manifesting* a reflexive intent. A communicative act means what a reasonable interlocutor, in the circumstances, would understand it to mean. The meaning of a communicative act is the message it expresses.

It follows that a communicative act is successful regardless of whether the message it expresses is actually understood. The audience's actual understanding is a third stage of success.[7] Of course when utterances are meaningful, reasonably understanda*ble*, they are normally understood. But they remain meaningful even if they are not. Note that this is the standard of success we implicitly invoke when saying, for example, 'I *did* tell you but you didn't pay attention', or 'I *did* greet him but he looked away'. One succeeds in performing

[5] ibid 99–100. Austin calls these 'illocutionary acts': 'to perform a locutionary act is … *eo ipso* to perform an *illocutionary* act' (ibid 98).

[6] Communicative meaning, in this sense, corresponds to the *conjunction* of what Austin misleadingly calls ('locutionary') 'meaning' and ('illocutionary') 'force' (ibid 121, 148 *et passim*; but cf 149). For a powerful argument that 'force' is an aspect of (communicative) meaning, see LJ Cohen, 'Do Illocutionary Forces Exist?' (1964) 14 *The Philosophical Quarterly* 118.

[7] Although Austin treats actual understanding by the audience ('uptake') as the primary condition of success ('felicity') of utterances (Austin, *How To Do Things With Words*, n 1, 116–17), he implies that it is relevantly different from the conditions that go to ensure that something is an utterance in the first place (and so is successful in our second sense) as opposed to being a mere attempt (ibid 22–23, 16). Strawson follows Austin in associating communicative success to 'uptake' (Strawson, 'Intention and Convention', n 3,458–59; so does Searle in J Searle, *Speech Acts: An Essay in the Philosophy of Language* (Cambridge, Cambridge University Press, 1969) 47), but he also toys with the idea that 'at least *the aim, if not the achievement*, of securing "uptake" is an essential element in the performance of the illocutionary act' (Strawson, 'Intention and Convention', n 3, 448), and stresses the necessary 'overtness' or 'avowability' of the speaker's intentions (ibid 454). Cohen, for his part, explicitly links communicative success to the reasonable possibility of being understood: an utterance is 'happy', he says, if it is 'of a kind that [the speaker] could reasonably expect to secure uptake' (Cohen, 'Do Illocutionary Forces Exist?', n 6, 129, emphasis omitted). Searle is wrong to claim that Grice's account does not leave space for the idea of understanding (Searle, *Speech Acts*, 46ff; cf P Grice, *Studies in the Way of Words* (Cambridge, MA, Harvard University Press, 1989) 351–52).

a communicative act as soon as one does all that is in one's power (as a speaker), as opposed to the audience's.

Now it is all very well for you to understand my question after the seminar. But my aim is to obtain a reply, not only to be understood. Obtaining a reply is a fourth stage of success. It has an analogue in other kinds of communicative action. In (sincerely) making an assertion, my goal is not only to be understood, but also to be believed. In (sincerely) issuing a warning, my goal is not only to be understood, but also to make the audience consider responding appropriately to the supposed danger. Communicating involves addressing someone with the aim of eliciting some kind of reaction from him – which reaction is primarily a matter of affecting his beliefs and attitudes, and possibly courses of action. The literature calls this reaction a communicative *response*.[8]

No doubt the speaker may have further goals still. I want to obtain your reply in order to decide on a course of action that will save me money, and I want to save money in order to ... We normally act with a whole nested sequence of goals in mind, and our communicative action is no exception to this. But there is a difference between my goal to elicit your response and any further goals I may have in speaking.[9] Only the former goal I seek to attain by manifesting an intention to thereby attain it, and hence through the technique of communication. I shall not save money by manifesting an intention to thereby save money, any more than I shall hold three piled boxes by manifesting an intention to hold them. We shall therefore reserve the term 'response' to name your communicative reaction that determines the fourth stage of success.

These considerations about communicative response help us to round the picture of the technique of communication. They reveal the specific kind of reflexive intention that we manifest in communicating. What we *do* in making a communicative act is to express a message (the second stage of success). But we do this *by* manifesting an intention to thereby elicit a response (the fourth stage of success). When we communicate, in other words, we aim at a success that lies beyond what our act necessarily succeeds in doing. That is an accustomed experience. Understanding that you (sincerely) ask a question is inseparable from understanding that you thereby aim to obtain an answer – which may or may not be forthcoming. Understanding that you (sincerely) make an assertion is inseparable from understanding that you thereby aim to be believed – which may or may not occur. Understanding that you (sincerely) issue a warning is inseparable

[8] Both Strawson and Grice appreciate that making a communicative act involves (manifesting) an intention to elicit a certain response, a response they call 'primary' ('primary response': Strawson, 'Intention and Convention', n 3, 452; 'primary intention': Grice, 'Meaning', n 3, 386) to distinguish it from further effects the speaker may purport to bring about; this distinction is only implicit in Austin's contrast between 'perlocutionary object' and 'perlocutionary sequel' (Austin, *How To Do Things With Words*, n 1, 118).

[9] I may also have parallel, rather than further, goals: eg, to highlight to a bystander that the seminar needs better sponsorship. Again, this is not a goal I seek to achieve by manifesting an intention to thereby achieve it.

from understanding that you thereby aim to make someone consider responding to a danger – which he may or may not do. Your aim of eliciting a response is part of the very meaning of your utterance. It is part of the message it expresses. It follows that a successful communicative act reasonably manifests a reflexive intention, specifically: an intention to thereby *elicit a response*.

We can articulate the technique of communication as follows:

> The technique of communication: We express a message by reasonably manifesting an intention thereby to elicit a response.

III. CODES, OR HOW TO SPEAK YOUR MIND

Communicating involves manifesting one's intentions, directly and transparently disclosing one's relevant thoughts.[10] But just this idea of *disclosing one's own thoughts* invites closer scrutiny. It is by no means obvious how one goes about speaking one's mind, as it were, and so transforming what de Saussure called the 'indefinite plane of jumbled ideas'[11] into externally recognisable shape. We should briefly pause to enquire about the tools we use in implementing the technique. The better the tools we have at our disposal, the more expediently and reliably we are able to communicate. An overview of tools of communication, in this section, will bring us ever closer to appreciating, from the next section onwards, the legal counterpart to communication's technique.

Very rudimentary tools of communication may not be culture-relative. How would you greet a native you encounter upon arriving in a remote island? You may try reaching out your hand or bending forward, but be careful: for all you know, in the native's culture these gestures might count as threats or admissions of guilt. Perhaps your best bet is to smile and look relaxed. That should effect some reassurance. Indeed, even if you just smile, but do so in a way that the native can understand as amounting to a greeting (or to something akin to a greeting), you will have already made an elementary sort of communicative act. The tool you will have deployed in doing so will be similar, as it happens, to that which many millions of users of electronic devices reportedly used during 2015, to the point that Oxford Dictionaries proclaimed it as 'word of the year': a smiling *emoji*, a pictograph of a smiling face – that raw contemporary embodiment of the idea of a reflexive intention.

Of course, the range of messages you can express with the help of such rudimentary tools of communication is very limited, especially where your interlocutor cannot see you close up. If you are to convey a message at some

[10] Even lying involves a transparent disclosure of my aim to induce in you a certain belief by making you aware that I thereby aim to induce it (except that the belief is false).

[11] F de Saussure, *Course in General Linguistics*, C Bally and A Sechehaye (eds), W Baskin (tr) (New York, McGraw Hill, 1960) 112.

distance, you may need something like a code. Smoke signals function in this fashion. Under certain conditions, such-and-such a size and frequency of smoke puffs is code for a certain message, for example 'storm approaching' or 'we capitulate'. Ships have long been using single-message flags to a similar end, not least in order to circumvent the risk of interception of radio messages. The pattern and colour of a certain flag stands for a certain message. It is almost as if the message travelled from the sender to the receiver packaged in a code. But that is only a metaphorical way of talking. What really goes on when your interlocutor understands you is that he understands that your act of making that particular sequence of smoke-puffs, or of hoisting that particular flag, is your way of conveying to him the message that the particular act stands for, according to the code that both of you knowingly share. For you need to share a code in order to communicate in an encoded fashion. Codes enable you to communicate across distance, and in relatively private ways, because they presuppose some kind of standing arrangement amongst the persons who use them.

But codes are not only needed in situations where communication in a natural language such as English is unfeasible or unsafe or impossible. Codes are not merely a *substitute* for communicating in English or a *complement* to such communication, as, for instance, is Morse. In an important sense, a natural language is *itself* to some extent a matter of codes, albeit very complex ones as compared to smoke signals or ship flags.[12] When you orally address me in English, you emit a combination of vocal sounds. When I read, I decode a message on the basis of a pattern of traces with certain shapes. Someone not familiar with the rules of English grammar, syntax, semantics, spelling, etc, would probably be unable to decipher the message.

What I am loosely calling 'codes',[13] diverse as they may be, share two important features. First, what codes associate with certain (parts of) messages are *perceptible physical changes in the world* resulting from intentional human action. This is true of hoisted flags, smoke-puffs, sounds and traces on paper. These kinds of physical change are perceptible in that they have a visibility or salience appropriate to their identification (and attribution to the speaker) in the relevant circumstances. The second important feature of codes is that the association they effect between physical changes and units of meaning is *arbitrary* in the sense that it could have reasonably been otherwise. There is nothing about two short smoke-puffs or the shapes 'd a n g e r' that specifically relates to the idea of danger. Three short smoke-puffs, or 'G e f a h r', would have done as well. But given the code, *this* is what making those changes now *means* in the relevant context. The idea of arbitrariness at issue here has no pejorative connotation. We sometimes speak of arbitrary acts or decisions to convey that

[12] A natural language is substantially coded but by no means *wholly* so. There is certainly less arbitrariness in onomatopoeias, ideographic characters (eg in Chinese) and certain deep aspects of a language's grammar, for example, than there is generally in sound–sense relations.

[13] Technically, only a subset of the cases I discuss involves codes (eg Morse).

they are unreasonable, that they were taken in wrongful neglect of applicable standards. But here, as elsewhere in the book, I use the idea of arbitrariness in the well-known sense in which we speak of the arbitrariness of a symbol or sign.

Ferdinand de Saussure said that 'no one disputes the principle of the arbitrary nature of the sign, but it is often easier to discover a truth than to assign to it its proper place'.[14] What is the proper place of codes in communication? There is a sense in which codes create the possibility to express and share the relevant ideas – to express and share them, that is, in ways vastly more precise, subtle and expedient than would be in our reach in the absence of a code. Consider, for example, the incalculable amenity involved in speaking and understanding a natural language. In this sense, codes are not mere recipes for communication. Recall a distinction made in chapter 2 (section II). A recipe tells us how to go about achieving a result, but it remains possible to achieve that result, by taking the same (or similar) steps as the recipe describes, even in the absence of a recipe. Codes of communication, by contrast, do not merely describe the means to express certain ideas in the relevant language. They also create these means. The marks on this page would not mean what they mean but for the relevant rules of English grammar, syntax, semantics and spelling. Note that codes forge avenues of communication precisely in being arbitrary. Especially where the range of messages liable to be expressed exceeds by far the palette of available and distinguishable marks or sounds, it is their arbitrary combination that yields supple means to manifest one's thoughts.[15]

But it would be a mistake to conclude that communication is essentially or even exclusively a matter of codes, as is sometimes too rashly assumed. For one thing, there are uncoded tools of communication. They include tone of voice, facial expressions and countless forms of bodily gesture.[16] Sometimes uncoded tools alone will embody a message, as in the case of your smile on the island (or its *emoji* equivalent); often they will co-determine the meaning of a message otherwise expressed in coded fashion. For another thing, even coded and uncoded tools of communication, taken together, do not exhaust the range of considerations that determine what an utterance means. An utterance means what a reasonable interlocutor would understand it to mean in the circumstances, and thus in a certain context. The relevance of context to meaning can be vast. The words 'hello Lynn' take on a special meaning when written on a dirty window pane, where Lynn is your house mate who was in charge of cleaning it. Context may even reveal that a certain sound or mark is an utterance in the first place: but for the context, for instance, the groan some US immigration

[14] de Saussure, *Course in General Linguistics*, n 11, 68.

[15] de Saussure (ibid 117–18) suggests that linguistic signs are primarily characterised by their contrast with one another.

[16] Bodily gestures must not be confused with 'body-language', which is not a tool of communication. You may fake a tremble to make us believe you are scared, but not to make us believe that you want to make us believe you are scared. It is worth noting, too, that not all non-verbal tools of communication are uncoded: there may be coded elements in, eg, nodding or bending forward.

officers emit to call the next non-resident in line might reasonably be attributed to a bout of food poisoning.

Still there is this difference between context and tools of communication (coded or uncoded). The latter are the devices we resort to in speaking our mind. They are the things *to which* any context must relate. They are the physical changes in the world that stand for a certain message. They make up what I am calling an 'utterance'. The notion 'utterance', as Grice reminds us, has an act–object ambiguity.[17] It can refer to the act of making the physical changes in the world, or to the changes made. We use the term in either sense interchangeably, depending on whether we want to draw attention to the act of formulation or rather to the utterance's content in relative isolation from that datable act, perhaps even of the speaker's identity.

So codes have a central, enabling role in communication, but there is more to communication than codes. Ironically, Austin errs in suggesting that communication is coded ('conventional') through and through.[18] This is ironic, because the very perspective of analysis he advocates, the study of the 'total speech act in the total speech situation', crisply brings to light that to make a communicative act is not to passively put in circulation units of meaning previously and independently bundled, but to form, then and there, a message which partly results from the interplay of factors tied more or less closely to the performance of the datable utterance. Codes are at the service of, and secondary to, intentions. The proper place of codes is to serve as facilities for communication. As Strawson saw more clearly than Austin, it is because communication essentially involves reflexive intentions that communication often and usefully involves codes.[19]

IV. BACK TO LAW

We made a passage through the philosophy of language, in the last three sections, in the hope of making sense of the ordinary idea of saying something to someone else. This idea appeared to be an ingredient of the technique of legal power, on our provisional hypothesis about it, the hypothesis that in exercising legal power we change legal positions by saying so.

But the preceding sections reveal that the form of intentional action we call communication itself involves a self-fulfilling intent. In an important sense, even the making of a simple communicative act involves doing by saying. This becomes most obvious when we render our communicative intent as explicit

[17] Grice, 'Meaning', n 3, 380; also called 'product/process ambiguity' (K Korta and J Perry, 'Pragmatics' in EN Zalta (ed), *The Stanford Encyclopedia of Philosophy*, Winter 2015 Edition (online) section 5; more generally, J Searle, 'Austin on Locutionary and Illocutionary Acts' (1968) 77 *The Philosophical Review* 405, 422).

[18] Austin, *How To Do Things With Words*, n 1, 14, 105, 119, 121–22 *et passim*.

[19] Strawson, 'Intention and Convention in Speech Acts', n 3, 449ff.

as can be, through the vehicle of a natural language.[20] Thus I may warn you through a pointed glance. Or by shouting 'Watch out!'. Or by uttering 'I am warning you that …'. In this last case, I am being so explicit about my state of mind that I am naming the very thing I do, namely warning. I am not only doing it but I am also saying it. Indeed I am doing it by saying it. And I can get even more explicit. I can stress that my utterance is the *means* that I use to warn you: 'I am *hereby* warning you that …'. The more explicit the utterance gets, the more crisply the underlying technique of communication is brought to the surface. Very explicit forms of utterance are rare in everyday exchanges, except for emphasis or clarification. But they remain possible, and are intelligible. It therefore appears as though the technique of communication is not so much an ingredient of the technique of legal power, as a *parallel* technique.

Austin, in fact, famously insinuates this in *How To Do Things With Words*. Austin's argumentative strategy in the book begins by drawing a contrast between utterances of a kind he calls 'constatives' or statements of fact ('the cat is on the mat'), and utterances of a kind he calls 'performatives' ('I acquit you'). It is remarkable that most of his initial examples of 'performatives' are legally valid acts. He discusses marrying, bequeathing, betting, appointing, acquitting and selling, amongst others. He even notes that jurists may be better equipped than he is to tackle the issues he purports to discuss.[21] But halfway through the book, Austin comes to acknowledge that even 'constative' utterances involve some kind of doing by saying, along the lines our previous sections have portrayed. At this point Austin gives up the label 'performatives' to refer to just one group of utterances, and devotes the remainder of his book to working out the similarities amongst the criteria of success of all of them. In so proceeding, Austin effectively abandons his initial contrast between ordinary saying and legal (or law-like) saying. He never returns to that contrast, not even to try to reformulate it in the context of his final tentative typology of 'speech acts'.[22] Part of the reason for Austin's neglect of legally valid acts may well lie in his unwarranted scepticism about the idea of a normative position as something fundamentally different from empirical fact.[23]

There is much plausibility to Austin's suggestion that the technique of communication and the technique of legal validity have a parallel structure.

[20] This is not to suggest that communicative meaning can be exhaustively represented in language; on this difficult question, see eg Searle's 'principle of expressibility' (Searle, *Speech Acts*, n 7, 17ff).

[21] Austin, *How To Do Things With Words*, n 1, fn 2 at 4, 19; there is juristic terminology, he says, on the conditions of 'felicity' (success) of 'performative' utterances (ibid 24).

[22] ibid 151ff, 163.

[23] eg ibid 149 ('the familiar contrast of "normative or evaluative" as opposed to factual is in need, like so many dichotomies, of elimination'). Interestingly, Hart, who does not share Austin's scepticism, at least with respect to normative positions *in law*, suggests in his mature work that the idea of legal power may be usefully clarified in light of the developments in the philosophy of language fuelled by Austin (HLA Hart, *Essays on Bentham*, Studies in Jurisprudence and Political Theory (Oxford, Clarendon Press, 2001) fn 55 at 217, 244). But Hart does not pursue this line of enquiry either.

Our argument so far has unearthed a number of similarities, worth spelling out briefly. Quite apart from the use of 'hereby', exercises of legal power appear to match our above conception of an utterance. They also primarily involve, and are identified by, sets of physical changes in the world, such as sounds or written marks, often alongside specific supports or records thereof, including deeds, registry entries, stamps or seals. We refer to some of these as 'criteria of validity' of the act in question, although such primarily *procedural* criteria do not exhaust the considerations that determine what the act means in law. What an act means in law – its *legal meaning* – is the set of legal positions that it changes. And as lawyers well know, an act's legal meaning depends on matters of *substance* as well, such as what the act purports to decide about, and more generally on its wider fit with the context of legal doctrines and regimes into which it is to be inserted. Furthermore, criteria of legal validity, somewhat like codes of communication, are characteristically arbitrary to some extent. They could have reasonably been different. For example, they may reasonably vary from jurisdiction to jurisdiction. Complete with their arbitrariness, criteria of validity determine the avenues for manifesting one's intent successfully – for legal purposes. Just as codes of communication create avenues for manifesting one's intent successfully for the purposes of expressing a message, legal power-conferring rules, it seems, create avenues for manifesting one's intent successfully for the purposes of changing legal positions. A successful communicative act has communicative meaning. A successful valid act has legal meaning.

This parallel between the technique of communication and the technique of legal validity suggests that our study of the former has already brought to light some basic features of the latter. It suggests that we can model our understanding of the technique of validity on our understanding of the technique of communication. This equips us with a robust basis to go about tackling the four peculiar traits of valid acting flagged up at the start of the chapter. As we shall see in the following sections, although these traits are by no means unknown to the domain of communication, in the domain of legal power they acquire a special bite. The reasons why they do help explain how the technique of legal validity differs from the technique of ordinary communication – and hence why an exercise of legal power is a distinct form of intentional action.

V. VALID ACTS THAT INVOKE A LEGAL REGIME

One can manifest one's intent other than by putting it into words. Many everyday exercises of legal power are inexplicit in this sense. Picking up a newspaper in a newsagent's and taking it to the counter unmistakably, if inexplicitly, conveys one's intent to purchase it. In ordinary communication it is frequent for messages not to be exhaustively articulated by verbal means. It can be invaluable for meaning to be left implied or presupposed – this is how much poetry is written. In law there is typically less opportunity for this kind of inexplicitness.

There is a greater need for certainty, and the subject-matters that valid acts concern do not lend themselves to inexplicit articulation in the same way as subject-matters in which feelings and emotions figure prominently. Still, inexplicit valid acts abound in informal settings. Sometimes apparently succinct valid utterances are accompanied by an explicit immediate context, as in the case of ballot papers or terms and conditions on display at box offices, rendering the relevant utterance nearly or actually explicit after all. None of these forms of inexplicitness poses a challenge to our hypothesis that valid acts change legal positions by saying so. It is no different from inexplicitness in ordinary communication.

But valid acts can be inexplicit in another, more troubling sense. The brief exchange at the newsagent's expresses something like 'I wish to purchase this'. But it does not in the same way express or convey the many particulars of the purchase contract determined by the applicable regime of contract law. These particulars go well beyond what is ostensibly in the mind of the parties concluding the transaction. These are not considerations the parties imply, in the ordinary sense of this term. Some jurisdictions therefore speak of terms 'implied in law' or of sources of 'integration' of the contract. Analogous phenomena occur all across the land of valid acting. Marriage ceremonies and oaths of office do not normally involve a comprehensive recitation of the legal regime to which one thereby subjects oneself. Nor do resolutions awarding residence status articulate the colossal set of normative changes they thereby introduce. Statutes, too, may invoke legal concepts and regimes substantially spelled out in other statutes or in the common law. And yet these particulars, these regimes, these terms 'implied in law', are part of the legal meaning of the respective valid acts. Acquiring duties, rights and powers relating to the disposal of common property, amongst other things, is part of what it legally means to 'marry' another. Bestowing powers and rights in relation to voting and employment, amongst other things, is part of what it legally means to confer on someone the status of 'resident'. So the legal meaning of an act, it seems, can extend beyond the content of the agent's manifested intention, to incorporate particulars of a regime that was in turn crafted by other persons or institutions, such as judges or legislatures, perhaps a long time ago. To that extent, it might be thought, it is not true that in performing a valid act one changes legal positions by saying *so*.

Alf Ross shares in this line of thinking. It leads him to largely give up his search for a distinct technique underlying all kinds of valid acting. His first take at understanding legal power had been broadly in line with our original hypothesis. On his initial view, legal power is exercised through 'a declaration that normally brings about legal effects in accordance with its content'.[24] The idea of 'declaration', and of its effects being 'in accordance with its content', matches

[24] A Ross, *On Law and Justice* (London, Stevens & Sons Limited, 1958) 166; also ibid 167, 217, 218.

the spirit of our argument. But Ross eventually backtracks. This understanding of legal power, he worries, does not adequately account for the kinds of valid acts captured by our examples. These are performed through what he calls 'truncated declarations', as if by 'pressing a button' to release consequences predetermined by law.[25] A 'truncated declaration', says Ross, does not bring about legal effects 'in accordance with its content'. So he revises his account of legal power. On his revised account, legal power is exercised through a declaration that produces 'legal effects which the [agent] desires to produce'.[26] Unfortunately this revised, watered-down account fails to capture something distinctive of legally valid acts. It no longer explains what sets valid acts apart from other 'declarations' that produce the legal effects the agent desires to produce. The account would even apply to Super-Tramp, were he to use defamation as his tactic to secure a warm lodging in jail (chapter 2.III).

Ross's move is unwarranted. He is wrong to give up his initial understanding of the technique of legal power. *Pace* Ross, the legal particulars involved in all the above examples are very much 'in accordance with' the 'content' of the relevant declaration, in the important sense that they bear a rational connection with what the agent says he intends to do. They are legal specifications of the result to which the agent's utterance invariably refers, if under a general description. One cannot fail to notice this as soon as one appreciates, as Ross does not, that the 'declaration' one hears or sees is not a mere string of words, or (as Ross thinks) a 'meaningless' 'formula' that 'functions as a directive to the judge',[27] but a manifestation of intent to bring about a normative result, a result that the applicable regime both renders possible and concretises. For instance, amongst the dozens of terms that sales contracts coming under the UK Consumer Rights Act are 'to be treated as including', is the term that 'the trader must deliver the goods … not more than 30 days after the day on which the contract is entered into'.[28] No doubt the 30-day limit could have reasonably been different, and perhaps could have reasonably *not* been set. But it shares a rational connection with, because it supplements, the parties' manifested purport in entering the relevant transaction. It relates to that manifested purport as the particular relates to the general.

The idea of a 'rational connection' between manifested intent and legal meaning is not empty. It tracks the loose criterion we intuitively use to distinguish legal changes that are part and parcel of a given transaction, from further legal changes *triggered* by it. A work contract, for example, may include expressly articulated terms, such as a term stating the wages, and terms 'implied' by a statute, such as the employer's duty not to endanger the employee's health. The contract's conclusion, however, may also, ipso facto, cause changes of legal

[25] ibid 166–67, 217–23 (especially 217–18).
[26] ibid 223, also 218.
[27] ibid 220.
[28] Consumer Rights Act 2015 (UK), s 28(3).

positions as varied as the employee's losing his unemployment benefits, and his former wife's becoming entitled to a higher amount of money by way of spousal support (in virtue of a valid judgment of divorce).[29] Legal language and reasoning buttress the rational connection between a manifested purport and the associated legal particulars, and between those particulars themselves, by portraying them as a distinct 'regime', as I have been doing. Such regime, in turn, is the reference of a myriad of placeholder terms such as 'marriage', 'lease contract' or 'limited company', which are the lawyer's tools of trade.

In truth, the reality that Ross banishes to the residual heading of 'truncated declarations' is the bread and butter of legal reasoning. Across the fields of private and public law, it is routine for lawyers to flip back and forth between a valid act's manifested content and its supplementation or qualification by, notably, statutory law or case law. It is a matter of law how articulate an utterance must be to exercise a legal power. Contract law may even exceptionally deem an agreement to be contractual even though it does not manifest the parties' intent to be bound *in law*, provided it does not manifest an intent *not* to be so bound. In the first weeks at law school students learn to treat different kinds of legal materials and sources as largely continuous, in a way ill-captured by Ross's term 'truncation', which conjures up the image of two or more juxtaposed utterances, cut and pasted. The ultimate cause of this familiar reality will be explained in chapter 6. It is the fact that legal meaning is *systemic*: unlike communicative meaning, legal meaning is a function of valid acts made by other persons and institutions, at earlier or later points in time, which jointly make up the legal regime that bestows on the relevant act its validity. We need not delve into this root cause here. Our concern is the technique whereby legal power is exercised. The argument in this section has reinforced, rather than challenged, our hypothesis that legal power is exercised by the agent's saying so – where 'so' has all the intelligibility yet vagueness of a general description of a normative result to which other elements of the act's legal meaning rationally connect.

Before closing this section we should, however, mention a set of scenarios that do not instantiate this technique, although in practice they may closely resemble some of the predicaments just discussed. Sometimes legal consequences akin or identical to those produced by a valid act can be produced by states of affairs that do not focally involve an utterance. This includes property acquired through adverse possession, 'common law marriage', 'tacit' amendments to a contract, or the approval of administrative requests through what Continental jurisdictions call 'administrative silence'. Here the legal changes are not brought about by a deliberately targeted act. The relevant conduct may

[29] This second set of normative changes is no more part of the contract's legal content than local healthcare entitlements are part of the legal meaning of the valid conveyance that Robert, whom we met in ch 2 (section V), might make in moving from one district to another in order to secure those entitlements.

even occur over a protracted period of time, rather than be a one-off event. And although the conduct may conceivably be performed with the intention of (eventually) producing the relevant normative change, it is not a manifestation of that intention, in and of itself, that produces the change. The change does not come about by someone saying so. Of course there can be and often are good reasons for so extending the scope of law-changing conduct, especially where the existence of an utterance is not essential to the justice of the relationship in question, or where questions of proof might be needlessly intricate (silence, for one, sometimes amounts to an utterance and sometimes does not).[30] But in so extending the scope of law-changing conduct, the law replaces rather than extends the technique of legal validity.

VI. VALID ACTS THAT CIRCULATE

The two 'letters of transit' signed by General De Gaulle spend much of the *Casablanca* movie concealed inside Sam's piano. They are coveted objects. They bestow important legal entitlements. They are something like a circulating bundle of normative positions. We are not told exactly when they were issued, but we understand that this is irrelevant to their enduring legal import. We happen to be told by whom they were issued, but a similar plot could be devised around 'letters of transit' simply said to be 'indefeasibly valid' in law. General De Gaulle's valid say-so has the capacity to circulate – not simply in the sense that what he said can be known and understood by persons at some later point in time, thanks to the fact that it was recorded on paper. It can circulate in the additional, critical sense that it remains a standing legal warrant, until cancelled. The 'letters of transit' are not just a testimony of what De Gaulle intended in the past. They confer rights on the holder in the present.

It is in the nature of a valid say-so that it has lasting normative relevance. This is because of the kind of meaning it has: legal meaning. A valid say-so changes legal positions. And normative changes last in time because normative positions last in time. Legal duties, rights and powers regulate the ongoing affairs of subsisting persons, unless and until otherwise delimited. This has no parallel in the domain of ordinary communication. Shortly after you have posed a question you cannot be said to be still *asking*, but you may remain bound by a valid pledge you signed years ago.

This section shows that the peculiar ability of valid objects such as deeds, PIN codes, passports or credit cards to circulate, even independently of the intentions of their maker, does not call into question that valid objects are brought

[30] For an interesting set of examples, see s 69 of the Restatement (Second) of Contract 1981 (US), which lists various circumstances in which an offeree's 'silence and inaction operate as an acceptance'.

about through a manifestation of intent. Rather it presupposes that they are. The fact that valid objects can circulate enhances the power the maker can intentionally wield by making them, because it buttresses the lasting relevance of what the valid say-so brings about: a normative change. It is a measure of my power deliberately to craft legal positions that these can be ascertained relatively independently of my deliberate act of crafting them.

There are three significant ways in which the circulation of valid things buttresses their normative relevance. They represent different degrees to which the valid thing can become detached from the originating act. Well-entrenched resources of legal reasoning and practice make these degrees of detachment possible.

At a first level of detachment we find valid objects such as contracts, wills, licences, enactments or resolutions. We often do not use these terms only to refer to past, datable acts. Instead we speak of such objects as subsisting entities bearing on our present legal positions ('the contract entitles me to …'). But these objects are not physical things either. To be sure, they may have physical representations in documentary supports, which representations may have such practical evidential value that we may call the inscribed piece of paper *itself* the 'contract', 'licence' or 'will' ('he wasn't carrying his licence', 'I keep the will in the drawer'). Still, in an important sense the paper only represents the valid contract, licence or will. The latter's validity may not be lost even if the document is destroyed or goes amiss.[31]

Contracts, licences, wills, resolutions and so on, in a sense central to legal reasoning, are neither acts nor physical things. The terms function as placeholders for normative configurations. They name sets of normative positions with an often well-understood core and diffuse boundaries. Legal reasoning uses plenty of placeholder terms (eg 'property', 'trustee', 'jurisdiction'). They are key to handling the systemic intertwinement of legal materials (chapter 6.VI). But the particular terms we are considering here are special in that they have a built-in reference to the *source* of the relevant normative configuration. A lease contract is not merely the name of a set of duties, rights and powers concerning somebody's use of a certain piece of land. It is a set of normative positions that came into being when and because someone *contracted*. A gun licence is not merely the name of a set of duties, rights and powers concerning somebody's possessing and carrying of a firearm. It is a set of normative positions that came into being when and because an agency *licensed* this person to do so. These terms refer to normative *changes*, not just to normative positions. At this first level of detachment, the very way in which we call valid objects denotes that their origin lies in a datable act.

[31] This may be so even where a given documentary support is a requirement of the transaction's validity (eg with respect to gifts of land in Spanish law, art 633 of the Spanish civil code).

This linguistic counterpart of the first level of detachment has a curious feature. It consists in pairs of verbs and matching nominalised verb forms that designate formation and product: to contract/contract, to license/licence, to enact/enactment, to judge/judgment, to appoint/appointment, to resolve/resolution … Interestingly, all verbs that designate the formation of legally valid things are verbs of a special kind, which we may call success verbs. Success verbs designate purposive actions that have succeeded in attaining their purpose, or are expected by the speaker to succeed when carried out. 'To purchase' and 'to enact' are success verbs; 'to paint' and 'to read' are not. Compare 'I am (right now) purchasing a car' with 'I am (right now) painting a car'. Taken literally, the first sentence sounds somewhat unusual because we do not think of purchasing as an activity stretched over a period of time. 'I am about to purchase a car (as soon as I have finished signing my name)' would seem more appropriate. The success in success verbs is instantaneous. It is also an all-or-nothing matter. The act is one of its kind inasmuch as it is *fully* successful. If I did not end up purchasing the car after all, I was wrong when I told you I was purchasing it, whereas it was right for me to say that I was painting the car even if I later ran out of paint before I finished. The accomplished result of a valid act is somehow built into the verb that designates its formation, just like the originating act is somehow built into the noun that designates the result.

At a second level of detachment we find valid passports, valid bus-tickets, valid vouchers and valid ID cards. These *are* physical entities. They are not names for the valid transactions or resolutions therein represented. And yet we call these entities *themselves* 'valid' (or 'invalid'). They even seem to have their own criteria of validity, such as shape, colour, texture or a printed date. Yet passports, bus-tickets, vouchers and ID cards do not float in a vacuum. When I show the bus-driver that I have a valid bus-ticket I am showing him that I am entitled to something. If he refuses to take me (when seats are available), he will be in breach of contract. His contract with the bus company binds him to execute *my* contract with the bus company. It is my prior contract with the bus company that entitles me to a bus ride. The ticket is the contract's proof.

Portable proofs of valid acts immensely facilitate social interaction. Negotiable instruments such as promissory notes, cheques or bills of exchange confer rights so closely embedded in the physical document that they may be transferred through the document's delivery. In German they are tellingly called 'value papers' (*Wertpapiere*). These instruments can facilitate the circulation of transactions in the special sense that involves *assignment*, and thus alteration of the parties to an otherwise constant set of contractual relationships. But even where assignment is not possible, a system of portable proofs can support the effectiveness of the underlying act in ways so decisive that, in their absence, the purpose of that act would be thwarted. The point of granting citizenship would largely be defeated if one could not produce an internationally recognised imprint to vindicate this condition vis-à-vis persons who might not understand the grounds or the language of the administrative resolution that gave rise to it.

Valid things open doors, and sometimes they do so without having to be checked by doorkeepers – increasingly nowadays. They do it automatically, because the checking is done by a machine. This takes us to the third group of valid objects. Sometimes when I try to sign into my email account the computer screen reads 'invalid password' and I do not get access to my email. When I try to withdraw money from the ATM I am asked to 'introduce a valid card' and then to 'enter a valid PIN number'. If I fail to do so, I do not get the money. Here it is a machine, not a bus-driver or a customs officer, that 'refuses' to grant me access. Of course it does not literally refuse to do so. It has been set up in such a way that it will not perform certain mechanical operations unless particular keys are pressed or a certain magnetic band is swiped through. Credit cards, PIN codes, passwords and the like have something in common with door keys: if you use the wrong one, the door will not open. Using an invalid password, or an expired credit card, makes the operation fail – both as a matter of law and as a matter of mechanics. A valid password not only is a proof that I am entitled to something, but it also gives me the physical ability to procure it. A valid password is halfway between a valid passport and the right door key. But in calling the password 'valid' we abstract from its mechanical properties and focus on its normative ones. (For we do not typically speak of valid door keys.) In this sense, calling a password 'valid' is like calling a bus-ticket 'valid'. Both are elliptical for the underlying contract, which itself is elliptical for the power-exercising *act*.

VII. UNINTENTIONAL VALID ACTS

Pick the wrong ballot paper and you may have supported a motion you meant to oppose. One mouse-click too many, and you may be bound by a transaction you did not wish to enter. There is a standing possibility that legally valid acts are performed wholly or partly unintentionally, and so in a way that does not give effect to, even subverts, the agent's intentions at the time of performing the act. Doctrines on mistake or other impediments of the will leave room, on the whole, for legally valid acts performed by accident. Procedural safeguards such as witnesses, ceremonies, notary attestation or the display of visible warnings at the time and place of performance, only go so far in reducing the incidence of unintentional valid acts.

Some writers have taken the reality of unintentional valid acts to be an indication that there is no uniform technique underlying valid action, or at least no technique definable in terms of intentions. Raz is amongst them. We saw in chapter 2 that, according to Raz, exercises of legal power do not involve a distinct *way* of changing legal positions, one that sets apart these kinds of act from other kinds of law-changing conduct such as moving residence to minimise tax. The difference, says Raz, 'depends entirely' on the law's reasons for recognising the respective conduct as producing a normative change.[32] Raz takes the following consideration to bolster his argument on point:

> Normally only acts done with the intention of producing relevant normative change are recognized as producing it. But this is not always the case, and there are many exceptions particularly in the law … One may make a contract without realising that one did, for example. For this reason the definition [of an exercise of normative power] turns, not on the intentions with which the act is performed, but rather on the reasons for regarding it as effecting a normative change.[33]

Raz soundly appreciates that unintentional valid acts are exercises of legal power. But he is wrong to infer from this that the definition of legal power cannot in any sense turn on the agent's intentions. Halpin makes the contrary move, in his critique of Raz. Halpin rightly insists that legal power is exercised in a distinct way. But he mischaracterises that way as involving the agent's 'decision' to bring about the legal change: 'decision,' he says, 'is the paramount practical feature, the first feature, of every legal power'.[34] This leads him to exclude unintentional valid acts from the scope of legal power. To the extent it is possible for someone to act validly without having 'decided' to do so, Halpin concludes, the regime is duty-imposing, not power-conferring.[35]

Raz and Halpin commit the same mistake. They both seek to explain away what in truth is a central feature of the nature of legal power and valid acting. This feature has been present in our discussion from the very start, but we have not yet drawn attention to it. It is true that legal power is not always exercised intentionally. It does not in any way follow, however, that intention is irrelevant to the way legal power is exercised. Legal power is exercised by *manifesting* an intention. And it does not take an intention to manifest an intention.

This feature of legal power is brought out particularly well by the idea of 'manifestation', more so than by ideas such as 'expression', 'disclosure', 'avowal' or 'acknowledgement'. Despite your best efforts to look fit, you may manifest signs of tiredness or disease. Indeed your skin may manifest them. You may likewise manifest a reflexive intention you do not actually have. When the law entitles your contractual partner to rely in good faith on what *looked like* an intentional proposal on your part, it entitles him to rely on the intentions you manifested, even if you manifested them unintentionally.

There is nothing contrived or unstable about this feature of legal power, although textbooks on contract law and other legal areas sometimes portray

[32] J Raz, *Practical Reason and Norms* (London, Hutchinson, 1975) 102.

[33] ibid 104. Similar argument in J Raz, 'Voluntary Obligations and Normative Powers' in SL Paulson and B Litschewski-Paulson (eds), *Normativity and Norms: Critical Perspectives on Kelsenian Themes* (Oxford, Clarendon Press, 1998) 452–53.

[34] A Halpin, 'The Concept of a Legal Power' (1996) 16 *Oxford Journal of Legal Studies* 129, 145.

[35] ibid fn 68 at 147.

it as resulting from a more or less ad hoc, haphazard compromise between two extreme positions, presented as the only fully coherent ones: on the one hand, a position that sees the source of legal liability in the agent's (internal) 'will', and on the other hand, a position that sees the source of legal liability in the agent's (external) 'declaration'. Real or genuine agreement, some well-known contract doctrines suggest, occurs inside the parties' minds, yet various kinds of policy reasons may justify the law's departing from this standard by holding persons to what they only *appeared* to agree to, for example because the law would otherwise be unfair to the other party who could not have reasonably recognised the mistake. As Endicott helpfully shows, this conception of agreements is false.[36] Minds do not meet in some ethereal or supra-sensorial sphere that the law can only imperfectly afford to reflect. Whether someone has entered an agreement with another is an objective question about what that person has done, because it is a question about the meaning of his conduct.[37] It is a question about what that person can reasonably be taken to have intended to do, in acting as he did. 'Reasonably', that is: including mistakes not reasonably apparent, but excluding obvious ones. For 'a reasonable person who knows of a blunder would treat it as a blunder'.[38] Lord Hoffmann makes this point at some length in the English contract case *Mannai Investment*:

> It is a matter of constant experience that people can convey their meaning unambiguously although they have used the wrong words … When … lawyers say that they are concerned, not with subjective meaning but with the meaning of the language which the speaker has used, what they mean is that they are concerned with what he would objectively have been understood to mean … [by] a reasonable recipient …[39]

In providing 'objective' tests for determining intent, and for assessing the relevance of mistakes and other impairments of the will, sound regimes of contract law, administrative law, succession law and others do not make a concession to evidentiary constraints or to the need to promote good faith reliance or avoid fraud. They acknowledge the basic technique for exercising legal power. Reasonably manifesting your reflexive intent is the thing to do if you are to perform a valid act. It is not a test we apply to accidental performances to mitigate the harshness of unfulfilled expectations. The voluntary contractor, too, has to deploy this technique in going about contracting. Minds cannot be read. It is beyond human reach to bring about changes in legal positions – and probably in any part of the empirical world outside one's own self – merely by forming the relevant intent, without expressing it. In the movie *Life is Beautiful*,

[36] T Endicott, 'Objectivity, Subjectivity, and Incomplete Agreements' in J Horder (ed) *Oxford Essays in Jurisprudence Fourth Series* (Oxford, Oxford University Press, 2000).

[37] ibid 152ff.

[38] ibid 159.

[39] *Mannai Investment Co Ltd v Eagle Star Life Assurance Co Ltd* [1997] AC 749, [1997] 3 All ER 352.

Roberto Benigni repeatedly tries and fails to steer the movement of persons and things simply by thinking really hard about it, having misunderstood Schopenhauer's claims about willpower's force. In many fields of life, law included, realising your wishes requires doing something about them that includes speaking your mind.

Of course this holds in ordinary communication as well. One tragic flip side of the elaborate linguistic tools through which we can convey subtle messages is that by an improper use of these tools we may reasonably manifest something we did not intend to manifest. Trust appearances and appearances may take hold. But in everyday conversation such slips are generally harmless. If I realise that I said something I did not intend to say, perhaps because I mixed up words in a foreign language or used the wrong intonation, I may be able to clarify this on the spot, to everyone's satisfaction. The stakes are higher in the legal domain, because the law's temporal logic may leave no room for a release from liabilities accrued. Hence the importance of procedural checks and safeguards that minimise the likelihood that certain valid acts are performed altogether by accident, especially those made through automated means, or that have a far-reaching import. Note, however, that the very presence of such procedural measures, which help secure deliberate and informed action, may often be part of the reason why others are entitled to rely on what, given those measures, reasonably looked like a deliberate and informed act even though it was not.

VIII. FAILED ATTEMPTS

Take now the converse scenario: you fail in your attempt to perform a valid act, notwithstanding your manifest intent to perform it. If you try to make a contract that fundamentally goes against public policy, you fail. You likewise fail if you try to convey land on tissue paper, to make a ruling that is deeply ultra vires, or to marry a person who is already married. Your intention to change legal positions may be obvious to a reasonable observer. It may be a deliberated and pondered choice, unambiguously manifested. But that is sometimes not enough to unleash the legal spell. It was not enough for Ali Baba's brother to clearly order the cave to 'open'.

This fourth trait of legal power, like the other three, has a parallel in ordinary communication. The parallel primarily concerns what do *not* count as failed attempts. Evident grammatical or spelling errors, for example, do not impede the successful performance of a communicative act as long as they do not obscure the agent's communicative intent. Someone who offers 'cheap *accomodation*', with one 'm', succeeds in expressing the message he seeks to express, even though he does not succeed in conforming to what, since roughly the seventeenth century, have come to be regarded as standards of proper spelling in English.[40] One's message is recognisable as long as one's errors are recognisable too, for reasons we touched on in the previous section. There we also noted how this logic, up to a point, applies to law. Where a reasonable manifestation of intent has the capacity to validly change legal positions, minor or transparent foul-ups need not stand in the way of the utterance having the legal meaning the agent purported it to have.

But not every reasonable manifestation of intent has the legal meaning it manifestly purports to have. There are many reasonable ways in which a person can manifest his intent, but not all of them may be legally appropriate for exercising legal power. Manifestations of intent, to be legally valid, may have to be made in a certain format, on a certain documentary support, by a certain agent, within a certain time or otherwise in compliance with procedural requirements (some of which are meant to ensure that the act is duly voluntary). There may additionally be legal restrictions concerning the substance or content of one's choice. You may legally fail, for example, if you try to make a will without witnesses, or to allocate assets without respecting statutory quotas. You may fail, in short, where your act, for reasons of procedure or substance, does not fulfil the requirements for being legally valid. You may fail where your act does not fulfil *criteria of legal validity*.[41]

The limiting role of criteria of validity at once confirms and helps to supplement our working hypothesis about the technique of legal validity. Criteria of validity ensure that we exercise legal power by reasonably manifesting an intent to do so. But they may place further conditions. They may determine through what procedure one's choice must be manifested, and what the choice may be about. There is, therefore, this important difference between the technique of communication and the technique of validity. A reasonable manifestation of intent is necessary to perform a valid act, but it may not be sufficient. Legal regimes do not bestow legal meaning on all recognisable attempts at securing it.

We can incorporate the limiting role of criteria of validity into our working hypothesis as follows. We can accommodate procedural criteria of validity by saying that one exercises legal power by *legally manifesting* an intent. An intent is legally manifested when it is manifested through the procedure legally determined. A will without witnesses manifests an intent, just not legally so. A legal manifestation is a reasonable manifestation, but not all reasonable manifestations are legal.

We can, in turn, accommodate substantive criteria of validity by saying that a manifestation of intent will only change legal positions *if and to the extent the law provides for this possibility*.[42]

[40] Some people may want to say that he is not speaking English. I take no stance on this classificatory question.

[41] On the possible validity of acts in (significant) breach of some criteria of validity, see ch 5.V.

[42] This second qualification could encompass the first. By stating the two separately, it is hoped that we make up in clarity what we lose in concision.

IX. THE TECHNIQUE OF LEGAL VALIDITY

Based on the argument in the preceding sections, the technique of legal validity falls to be articulated in these terms:

> The technique of legal validity: We change legal positions, if and to the extent legally provided, by legally manifesting an intention thereby to do so.

Each of the four peculiar traits of legal power finds expression in this formulation.

A valid say-so can invoke a legal regime beyond what is ostensibly in the mind of the sayer, which regime rationally connects to, because it specifies and supplements, the agent's manifested purport to change legal positions by saying *so*.

A valid say-so can endure through time and circulate as a relatively free-standing entity, given simplifying modes of reasoning and language that, along with physical or digital supports, buttress the enduring relevance of the valid act's result, which is a *change in legal positions*.

A valid say-so may accomplish effects unintentionally, because it does not take an intention to *manifest* an intention.

A say-so will not be valid unless it adopts the valid wording, requirements and form, because one will not secure the sought legal change if one does not *legally manifest* one's intent, or if the law otherwise does not *provide for the possibility* of one's making that change.

By comparing our formulation of the technique of legal validity with our earlier formulation of the technique of communication (on page 42), we can appreciate that they share a basic structure. They both involve a reflexive intention. That is: they both involve attaining something by manifesting an intention to thereby attain it. In this elementary sense, they both involve saying something. They both involve 'speech', a use of language. But communicating and exercising legal power are two focally different forms of intentional action. The agent aims to attain something different in each case. In making a communicative act, the agent aims to elicit a response from the interlocutor, which is primarily a matter of affecting his attitudes or thoughts. The speaker, for example, aims to be replied to or to be believed. In exercising legal power, the agent aims to change legal positions. A change in legal positions is not to an exercise of legal power what a response is to an act of communication. A communicative response may or may not come forth, but a valid act cannot but change legal positions. A change of legal positions is the result that the valid act attains automatically, on its own strength, without further interposition of any agent's will. It does not take a legal genie to *grant* one's wish once it has been legally expressed. A fortiori an exercise of legal power would be ill-conceived as a directive or command addressed to certain persons for the sake of eliciting their compliance. To take seriously the sound Hartian critique of sceptical lines of thought that reduce normative positions to the expected occurrence of empirical facts, is, in the final analysis, to appreciate that exercising legal power is a form of intentional action in which the aim necessarily manifested *cannot fail to succeed.* It is to appreciate that there is a distinct technique involved in exercising legal power.

No doubt one may use both techniques at one and the same time. It is not infrequent to do so. When we exercise legal power in front of other persons in certain settings, we often report to them the legal change we are making, in making it. This is what goes on when the judge utters the words 'I marry you', or when the chair of the panel tells the interviewee 'you are appointed'. We may say that these persons are performing a communicative act and an exercise of legal power at the same time. But note that the acts have different criteria of success. If the chair of the panel does not have the requisite legal power to make the appointment (there and then), his utterance lacks legal meaning (it is not an exercise of legal power) but it still has communicative meaning. It is a successful English assertion – though, much to the candidate's regret, a false one. Communicative acts and exercises of legal power may not just casually overlap, but it may be a legal requirement that they do. Some forms of legal power must be exercised *through a communicative act*, on pain of invalidity. Contract law is interwoven with this requirement. Still it remains possible, and in many fields of law it is routine, to exercise a legal power without in so doing trying to send a message to anyone or otherwise tell them something. Concluding a corporate merger or drafting a bequest do not characteristically involve addressing an interlocutor – unless, of course, the bequest happens to be cast in the form of a farewell letter to one's beloved, in which case its communicative meaning has (in principle) no bearing on its legal meaning.

In chapter 6 we shall explore the most profound difference between the exercise of legal power and communication. Unlike communicative meaning, legal meaning is systemic. An act's legal meaning has a continuous temporal relevance, and may be co-determined by the valid acts of other persons and institutions. The systemic character of legal meaning is the root cause, as I foreshadowed above, of the most significant differences we have spotted in this chapter between the two techniques. It is the law-making acts of other persons and institutions that read terms and particulars into our transactions – terms and particulars that, partly for this reason, we may end up endorsing unintentionally or be unable to untie ourselves from. It is the law-making acts of other persons and institutions that set criteria of validity that may thwart our attempts to craft normative changes. As we shall see in chapter 6 (sections III–V), the still widespread assumption that legal power is best characterised as an instance of communication has bred much confusion amongst legal theorists.[43]

---

[43] Not to mention amongst philosophers of language who seek to make sense of legal realities as sheer linguistic phenomena devoid of normative import: on the linguistic approaches of JL Austin and Searle, see respectively section IV of the present chapter, and ch 2.II and corresponding endnote.

Let us briefly recap to appreciate where we are in our argument. We have now vindicated the hypothesis advanced at the end of chapter 2. We have put our finger on the similarity we were looking for from the start of that chapter. There *is* something common to the miscellaneous range of things we habitually call 'legally valid'. The language of validity is the outward manifestation of a distinct and important legal technique. This is why our grasp of this technique, in turn, helps explain our sense that there are more central and less central uses of the term 'validity'. Thus one might speak of a 'valid' fish or a 'valid' auto exhaust system to convey that they conform to current environmental regulations. But those are *extended* uses of 'validity': a fish is not an artefact, and an exhaust system is not an artefact created by someone saying so. An extended use of 'validity' is involved, too, in the criminal lawyers' talk of 'valid' consent to what might otherwise be a sexual or bodily assault: in English law at least, consent is a state of mind, not its manifestation.[44] Our grasp of the technique of validity also helps explain *alternative* uses of language. It shows when and why, for instance, consideration of the 'constitutionality' of statutes, the 'legality' of administrative decrees, the 'bindingness' of contracts, or the 'diriment' nature of marriage impediments, amounts to a concern about the validity of a normative change introduced, or sought to be introduced, by so saying.

We have been steered towards the technique of legal validity by the literature on legal power. The literature itself, however, does not pinpoint validity's technique. It focuses on the question what legal power is *for*. Hart famously argues that the 'social function' of power-conferring rules is to provide individuals with facilities to realise their wishes. Raz, and even Kelsen in a faint way, emphasises the law's reason or justification for conferring legal power. Now that we understand what the *facility* consists in, now that we know *how* the law enables us to mould legal relationships at scales small and large, it is time to revisit the question *why* it does. It is time to probe whether it can ever be desirable to confer and to wield this kind of power – desirable *tout court*, not merely in the law's eyes. It is time to tackle this book's central concern: the moral point of legal validity.

NOTES

Section II: The Technique of Communication

Communicating Involves a Second-person Engagement with One's Interlocutor

On the loosely related, narrower idea of a 'second-personal reason', circumscribed to (the addressing of) certain kinds of demands or claims, see S Darwall, *The Second-Person Standpoint: Morality, Respect, and Accountability* (Cambridge, MA, Harvard University Press, 2006).

[44] See, eg, s 74 of the Sexual Offences Act 2003 (UK). Whether consent was reasonably manifested bears on the defendant's *mens rea*.

Communicative Meaning

What the main text calls 'communicative meaning' encompasses a range of different elements that need not be disambiguated for our purposes. They include the reference of words and phrases, 'implicatures' (Grice, *Studies in the Way of Words*, n 7, 22ff), whether the speaker 'subscribes' to the utterance (RM Hare, *The Language of Morals*, 2nd edn (Oxford, Oxford University Press, 1961) 18–19; RM Hare, 'Meaning and Speech Acts' (1970) 79 *The Philosophical Review* 3, 19ff), whether language is used 'non-literally', and both of what Austin misleadingly calls ('locutionary') 'meaning' and ('illocutionary') 'force' (Austin, *How To Do Things With Words*, n 1, 121, 148 *et passim*). Austin's distinction is misleading because he often suggests that the 'force' of an utterance, such as the fact that it is a question rather than a warning, is what the utterance *does* as opposed to what it *means*; at one point, however, he himself decisively qualifies the dichotomy between 'force' and 'meaning' in remarking that 'the theory of "meaning" as equivalent to "sense and reference" will certainly require some weeding-out and reformulating in terms of the distinction between locutionary and illocutionary acts' (ibid 149). On the basis of Austin's distinction, Searle ('Austin on Locutionary and Illocutionary Acts', n 17) somewhat less ambivalently distinguishes between an utterance's 'propositional content' and its 'force', although his discussion of 'meaning' is scattered and elusive (Searle, *Speech Acts*, n 3, 17–18, 42ff; J Searle, *The Construction of Social Reality* (New York, Free Press, 1995) 21). It is worth flagging up that the English idea of 'meaning' is ambiguous as between (a) what a person *means* (by an utterance), that is, the utterance he intends to make, and (b) the *meaning* of his utterance, that is, the utterance he does make (in reasonably manifesting an intention). In 'Meaning' (n 3), Grice is not unaware of the difference, but his analysis equivocates between the two. Grice's well-known focus on the speaker's intention to produce an effect in an audience by means of the recognition of that intention (ibid 385) naturally draws attention *to* (a), as well as to the audience's actual recognition of that intention, and *away* from (b). This ambiguity is not present in other languages. In German and Spanish, for instance, one speaks of what an utterance means ('*bedeutet*', '*significa*') very differently from how one speaks of what someone meant (by it) ('*wollte sagen*', '*quería decir*': equivalent to 'wanted to say'; and the German '*meinen*', related to '*Meinung*', opinion). The English 'S means by (an utterance)' strikes me as genuinely intermediate between 'S means to do (something)' and 'the utterance (or statement) means', in a way that would more often bear clarifying (eg in the spirit of A Marmor, *The Language of Law* (Oxford, Oxford University Press, 2014) 19–22).

Section IV: Back to Law

Austin Abandons the Contrast Between Ordinary Saying and Legal Saying

At the end of *How To Do Things With Words* (n 1, 151ff, 163), Austin tentatively proposes a five-fold classification of 'explicit performatives' into: veridictives ('exercise of judgement'), exercitives ('assertion of influence or exercising of power'), commissives ('assuming of an obligation or declaring of an intention'), behabitives ('adopting of an attitude') and expositives ('clarifying of reasons, arguments, and communications'). With the possible exception of 'behabitives', each of these categories, per his discussion and examples, cuts across the distinction between ordinary communicative acts and exercises of normative power. The closest Austin gets to pinpointing this distinction are some scant remarks on the possibility that expressions like 'I shall' do not merely announce an intention but 'inaugurate' 'a certain further action ... (whether making it obligatory or permissive)', for example by amounting to a promise (ibid 44–45). The difference between our general responsibility for our intentional acts, including our acts of communication, and any duties we may acquire specifically by saying so, is brought out somewhat more sharply in G Watson, 'Asserting and Promising' (2004) 117 *Philosophical Studies* 57, and in Austin's early paper 'Other Minds' in JL Austin, *Philosophical Papers*, JO Urmson and GJ Warnock (eds) (Oxford, Clarendon Press, 1961) 67–68; the difference is compatible with the existence of hybrid cases (J Ransdell, 'Constitutive Rules and Speech-Act Analysis' (1971) 68 *The Journal of Philosophy* 385, 398–99; TM Scanlon, *What We Owe to Each Other* (Cambridge, MA, Harvard University Press, 1998) 306–07). By contrast, Brandom (*Making it Explicit: Reasoning, Representing, and Discursive Commitment* (Cambridge, MA, Harvard University Press, 1994)) holds that all 'speech acts', including assertions and promises, 'alter the deontic score' (ibid 142) in a relevantly similar way. Following in Austin's footsteps, Searle proposes a revised taxonomy of 'speech acts', which, though more sensitive to the fact that only certain utterances create obligations, is framed under the vague organising principle of 'direction of fit' (J Searle, *Expression and Meaning: Studies in the Theory of Speech Acts* (Cambridge, Cambridge University Press, 1979) 3–4). It distinguishes between: assertives (which 'commit the speaker (in varying degrees) to something's being the case'), directives ('attempts (of varying degrees ...) ... to get the speaker to do something'), commissives (which 'commit the speaker (again in varying degrees) to some future course of action'), expressives (which 'express' a 'psychological state'), and declaratives (which 'brin[g] about the correspondence between the propositional content and reality') (ibid 12ff).

Procedural and Substantive Validity Criteria

For articulations of this familiar theoretical distinction, see, eg, H Kelsen, *General Theory of Law and State*, A Wedberg (tr) (New York, Russell, 1945) 124 (distinguishing way from content), 129 (distinguishing formal from material); R Guastini, 'Rules, Validity and Statutory Construction' in A Pintore and M Jori (eds), *Law and Language: The Italian Analytical School*, S Stirling, A Pirrie and Z Bankowski (tr) (Liverpool, Deborah Charles Publications, 1997) 242–43 (distinguishing formal from material); J Finnis, *Reason in Action, Collected Essays: Volume I* (Oxford, Oxford University Press, 2011) 19–20 (distinguishing form and originating fact from content); J Gardner, *Law as a Leap of Faith* (Oxford, Oxford University Press, 2012) 29 (distinguishing form from content). This rough distinction ignores finer disambiguations between the ideas of form, content, substance and procedure (amongst others), helpfully brought out by Gardner, ibid 198ff.

Section V: Valid Acts That Invoke a Legal Regime

Ross on 'Truncated Declarations'

Ross's difficulty in seeing that even '"truncated" declarations' manifest an intent to bring about the relevant result is a consequence of his more general denial that power-exercising 'declarations' are 'the expression of any intention, will or resolution'

(Ross, *On Law and Justice*, n 24, 221). For if they were, he thinks, it would be impossible to explain how my exercise of competence can ever obligate *another*. His idiosyncratic argument for this: 'My intentions can only be directed to my own course of action … I can therefore only "will" another person's course of action to the extent that I am in a position to bring it about by my own actions' (ibid 219). Here, as elsewhere, Ross overlooks that the immediate effect of my 'declaration' is a *normative change*, which (unlike the behavioural change of the person whose duties are altered) it *is* in my position to bring about. We should add that, in Ross's terminology, legal power is 'competence' (as 'power of disposition': ibid 166). He introduces the idea as part of an approving explanation of the 'second square' of Hohfeldian relationships (ibid 161ff), and it applies across public and private law (ibid 166, 202ff).

A Valid Act May Refer to the Normative Result Under a General Description

According to the early MacCormick, 'Power is conferred by a rule when the rule contains a condition which is satisfied only by an act performed with the (actual or imputed) intention of invoking the rule', where 'intention of invoking the rule' is an intention to fulfil the rule's condition and to be recognised as so intending (N MacCormick, *H.L.A. Hart*, Jurists: Profiles in Legal Theory (London, Edward Arnold, 1981) 73–74). Although this understanding of the technique of legal power captures many true considerations, it is misleading, both in that it suggests the need for detailed legal knowledge by the agent ('intention of invoking the rule') and in that it obscures that the agent's intended goal is to achieve a normative result, not to 'invoke the rule' for its own sake. It is therefore not clear enough, on MacCormick's account, that 'invoking the rule' is the *means* whereby the agent intends to achieve a normative result, and hence that this means is the *manifestation of a reflexive intention.* This point is likewise obscured in developments of MacCormick's account: see, eg, T Spaak, *The Concept of Legal Competence: An Essay in Conceptual Analysis*, R Carroll (tr) (Brookfield VT, Dartmouth, 1994) especially 121–25; J Hage, *Foundations and Building Blocks of Law* (The Hague, Eleven International Publishing, 2018) ch 10. Spaak's own rigorous account sheds much light on important aspects of legal power, but it falls short of articulating the underlying technique because it carries over some of the shortcomings of MacCormick's understanding. In particular, Spaak (*The Concept of Legal Competence*, 107–08) argues that one cannot, on pain of circularity, declare that one intends to achieve something through that very declaration of intent (relying on A Hägerström, *Inquiries into the Nature of Law and Morals*, CD Broad (tr) (Stockholm, Almquist & Wiksell, 1953) 300–01, who commits the same mistake).

Intent to be Bound in Law

In a helpful comparison of US and UK contract law, Klass ('Intent to Contract' (2009) 95 *Virginia Law Review* 1437) argues that in both regimes legal liability can generally attach to agreements regardless of a manifest intent to be bound in law. But Klass holds the view that, to the extent that rules provide for contractual liability in the absence of an intent to be bound in law, these rules are duty-imposing, not power-conferring (G Klass, 'Three Pictures of Contract: Duty, Power and Compound Rule' (2008) 83 *New York University*

Law Review 1726, especially 1743–58). According to Klass, rules governing the formation of contract are power-conferring only to the extent that they set out 'validity conditions that sort for legal purpose', such as formalities. Klass's view, unpalatably, places many contract formation rules on a par with residence-relative tax burdens. It overlooks the fact that even when contractual parties do not manifest an intent to be bound in law, they change legal positions through the special *technique* that involves manifesting a reflexive intent, an intent to do the thing the law enables them to do (though not under its legal description). Indeed, Klass insists that power-conferring and duty-imposing rules are 'structurally identical', in that they all attach certain legal consequences to the performance of certain voluntary acts, the difference between them lying exclusively in the purpose for which it is desirable that the acts be performed (ibid 1730–32, 1734–43, endorsing Raz's views on point, discussed in ch 2.IV of this book).

Law-changing Conduct Akin to Valid Action

Ross and Spaak sense that scenarios of the kind discussed in the main text are parasitic on exercises of legal power or 'acts-in the law' (Ross, *On Law and Justice*, n 24, 222; Spaak, *The Concept of Legal Competence*, 121), but they fail to appreciate that the difference lies in the absence of a manifestation of reflexive intent: whereas Ross thinks that no exercise of legal power involves a manifestation of intent (*On Law and Justice*, n 24, 218–22), Spaak suggests that those scenarios, too, involve a manifestation of intent (*The Concept of Legal Competence*, 121ff, especially 125, 126).

'Administrative Silence'

Article 24 of the main Spanish statute governing administrative procedure (Ley 39/2015, de 1 de octubre, del Procedimiento Administrativo Común de las Administraciones Públicas) provides that, with respect to certain claims addressed to the administration, the fact that the relevant deadline elapses without the administration expressly notifying a resolution 'entitles' the claimant to deem the request 'approved by administrative silence' (art 24(1)), which approval 'has for all purposes the nature of an administrative act that concludes the procedure' (art 24(2)). Although such 'administrative act' involves no use of the technique of legal power, but rather is a consequence of the law's *withdrawing* from the administration the legal power to decide (in the interests of fairness and expediency), part of the doctrine insists on the fiction that it is 'a real rights-declaring act' (JA Santamaría Pastor, *Principios de Derecho Administrativo: Volume II* (Madrid, Ramón Areces, 1999) 117). Indeed, the statute itself (art 24(4)) provides that the 'existence' of such fictitious 'administrative acts' can be proved through a 'certificate of silence' the relevant organ has a duty to issue within 15 days; the statute makes no provision for possible meta-silence.

Section VI: Valid Acts That Circulate

Valid Contracts, Wills, Enactments, etc, are Elliptical for the Validity of an Act

The act-object or process-product ambiguity of such legal concepts has been noted, for example, by Kelsen (*General Theory of Law and State*, 137), Belvedere ('Some Observations on the Language of the Italian Civil Code' in A Pintore and M Jori (eds), *Law and Language: The Italian Analytical School*, S Stirling, A Pirrie and Z Bankowski (tr) (Liverpool, Deborah Charles Publications, 1997) 373ff) and Spaak (*The Concept of Legal Competence*, 60). Non-legal uses of 'validity', despite not being wholly unrelated to the legal uses discussed in this book, do not constitute further stages in the process of abstraction. They include the logicians' highly technical use of 'validity', as well as our loose emulation thereof in ordinary conversation, when we speak of valid points, valid arguments, valid objections, etc.

Section VII: Unintentional Valid Acts

'Objective' Contractual Tests

On how part of English contract law scholarship portrays such tests as resulting from ad hoc compromises between respect for the parties' will and policy considerations, see Endicott, 'Objectivity, Subjectivity, and Incomplete Agreements', n 36. (M Chen-Wishart, *Contract Law*, 5th edn (Oxford, Oxford University Press, 2015) 44ff, provides a refreshing counter-example.) In Spanish civil law the expositional complexity is aggravated (as, eg, in JL Lacruz Berdejo et al, *Derecho de Obligaciones*, Elementos de Derecho Civil II, vol I, 3rd edn (Barcelona, Bosch, 1994) 377–78, 413–14) by the fact that the Spanish civil code defines a contract in terms of 'consent', a notion that rather closely connotes a sheer ('inner') state of mind ('A contract exists from the time one or more persons consent to being bound' (art 1254); 'There is no contract unless … there is consent of the parties' (art 1261)). The original French civil code sensibly defined a contract as 'a convention' (art 1101); the 2016 modification of this article in terms of 'a concordance of wills' represents a regression in this regard. More helpfully, the Restatement (Second) of Contract 1981 (US) defines a contract in terms of 'a manifestation of intention' (s 1, s 2(1)), with the relevant comment (comment b to s 2) clarifying that 'A promisor manifests an intention if he believes or has reason to believe that the promisee will infer that intention from his words or conduct.' On the history of 'objective' and 'subjective' theories in US contract law, see Klass, 'Intent to Contract', 1445–46.

Section IX: The Technique of Legal Validity

Exercising Legal Power does not Inherently Involve an Intention to Elicit a Response

On how a communicative account of legislation fails, inter alia, on this ground, see H Hurd, 'Sovereignty in Silence' (1990) 99 *Yale Law Journal* 945, especially 976ff. On the basis of the sound of observation that exercises of legal power do not involve manifesting an intention to elicit a response, Bach and Harnish reach the erroneous conclusion that they do not involve manifesting any intention whatsoever: success in performing these acts, say Bach and Harnish, is not 'a matter of [reflexive] intention but of what convention [the act] falls under' (*Linguistic Communication and Speech Acts* (Cambridge, MA, MIT Press, 1979) 108–34, especially 116–17, 126–27). The implied contrast between intention and 'convention' (which corresponds to the authors' contrast between 'communicative acts' and 'conventional acts') hides from view that legal 'conventions' (their vague term broadly coextensive with power-conferring rules) are *aids* to manifesting intentions, as argued in section III of this chapter. Ironically, Strawson, from whom Bach and Harnish take their cue, insists that both kinds of act involve a manifested ('overt' or 'avowed') intention (Strawson, 'Intention and Convention', n 3, 457, 459–60), the difference being that 'conventional' acts do not address a particular audience (ibid 455–56) and that the agent's overt intention cannot fail to succeed (ibid 458). Ross takes the kind of mistake committed by Bach and Harnish to a dramatic extreme: 'A promise is not in itself the expression of any intention, will or resolution. Only because the legal order invests it with "binding force" can we normally take it for granted that a person using this instrument does so because he desires the legal effect attached to a promise – just as one may similarly take it for granted that a person firing a revolver at someone does so with the intention of taking his life' (Ross, *On Law and Justice*, n 24, 221).

A Valid Act Changes Legal Positions without Further Interposition of Any Agent's Will

Henle, an early twentieth-century German private lawyer, places particular emphasis on this point in his critique of private law theories that portray the 'declarations of will' involved in transactions as mere expressions of wishes or orders for the legal system to *grant* (R Henle, *Vorstellungs- und Willenstheorie in der Lehre von der juristischen Willenserklärung* (Leipzig, A Deichert'sche Verlagsbuchhandlung Nachf (Georg Böhme), 1910) 340–59). Although it takes a legal system to bestow on us the power to mould legal positions, says Henle, the *exercise* of this power is our own doing (*Selbstbewirken*) (ibid 349). Otherwise, he notes, statutes would amount to proclamations by the legal order about its own future behaviour, in the spirit of an *album praetoris* (ibid 343). The law, as it were, says to each of us, 'I engird you with these weapons, use them as you please' (ibid 356). Because our say-so brings about the relevant normative change, rather than requesting its future occurrence, our say-so is formulated in the present tense: its legal effect occurs 'in the next temporal atom' (ibid 349, 352). (My attention was drawn to Henle's work by reading Spaak, *The Concept of Legal Competence*, 110ff.)

Communicative Utterances Reporting (Changes in) Legal Positions

The subject-matter of 'legal statements' is orthogonal to the concerns of this book. For some contributions to the study of these peculiar kinds of communicative acts, see, eg, Raz, *Practical Reason and Norms*, n 32, 170ff; J Raz, *The Authority of Law: Essays on Law and Morality* (Oxford, Oxford University Press, 1979) chs 7 and 8; HLA Hart, *The Concept of Law*, 2nd edn (Oxford, Clarendon Press, 1994) 56ff, 84ff, 102ff; Hart, *Essays on Bentham*, n 23, 144ff; K Toh, 'Raz on Detachment, Acceptance and Describability' (2007) 27 *Oxford Journal of Legal Studies* 1.

'Valid' Consent to Bodily Advances is a State of Mind, Not its Manifestation

According to section 74 of the Sexual Offences Act 2003 (UK), 'a person consents if he agrees by choice, and has the freedom and capacity to make that choice'. The idea of 'agreement' deployed in this definition is different from the idea of 'agreement' relevant to contract law (see section VII of this chapter). In explaining the objectivity of contractual agreement, Endicott ('Objectivity, Subjectivity, and Incomplete Agreements', n 36, 154) distinguishes between an 'active' and a 'stative' sense of 'agreement'. In the 'active' sense, the sense relevant to contract law, to agree is *do* something – to strike a deal. In the 'stative' sense, two people may agree, or rather *be* in agreement, simply in virtue of having similar views about an issue. The sense of 'agreement' invoked by section 74 of the Sexual Offences Act does not neatly fit into either category. Like Endicott's 'stative' sense, it is an actual rather than a manifested state of mind, but like his 'active' sense, it is circumscribed to a more or less definite point in time and relates to the (supposed) contemporaneous state of mind of another. It is therefore a mistake (committed, for example, in N MacCormick, *Institutions of Law: An Essay in Legal Theory* (Oxford, Oxford University Press, 2007) 155) to deem consent to bodily advances an exercise of legal power.

4

Justice and Convergence

THE QUERY WE raised at the start of this book has become inescapable: What is the point of legal validity? In validity's name, sensitive human interests are affected in ways that would only be justifiable if warranted by a compelling moral reason. Our social dealings assign valid decisions a place that, in truth, only just decisions deserve to occupy. The previous chapters have shown that the technique of legal validity is a facility for changing legal positions. It enables individuals and institutions – those who hold legal power – to alter, by so saying, what certain persons legally ought to do. It is a remarkable power to be able to determine how legal regulation bears on other people by expressing one's wish that this be so. But we pervasively treat valid decisions as if their power was more remarkable still. We treat them as if it was not only legal but also moral rights and duties they could craft. We treat what they provide as if it were morally due, indeed as if it *became* morally due in being validly uttered. Can the valid say-so also have *that* power?

This chapter argues that it can. Validity is a technique that makes central what certain persons chose in the past and may themselves not lastingly control. Persons may err in estimating the future, gauging the present, appreciating what is just and acting on those judgements. Their choices acquire legal validity in conforming to a set of considerably arbitrary, formal criteria. They are criteria that could reasonably have been otherwise. The resulting valid choice can be identified predominantly without opening questions about its justice. Validity is a hazardous technique. And yet legal regulation can be just. It can be just – this chapter shows – not *despite* being crafted and brought to bear on our lives through validity's hazardous toolset, but *precisely because* of it. Validity is an important part of the reason why political communities are able to make the difference to human well-being that justice requires. This chapter explains the basic logic that makes this possible.

It is the logic of *specific convergence*. Very simply put, specific convergence is convergent conduct by many persons following specific patterns. Specific convergence, I argue, is essential to securing critical aspects of human well-being all across social life, rather than only in some circumscribed or particular domains. In a context of collective convergence, specific individual conduct can become especially able, and therefore needed and due, as a means to advance endeavours we all have standing reason to support. *Generating* and sustaining needed convergence, in turn, involves publicly flagging up specific requirements, even requirements that could reasonably have been otherwise, and seeing to their general observance. Legally valid choices can saliently *mark* specific conduct as due, in a context of convergence, and thereby render it due – due morally. Sections I–III of this chapter explain why it takes specific convergence to advance justice. Sections IV–VI explain why it takes legal validity to generate specific convergence.

I. DUTIES OF JUSTICE

We have standing reason to care for the well-being of others. Sometimes we have a particularly compelling, peremptory kind of reason to perform determinate conduct for someone else's sake, a kind of reason we refer to as a duty or an obligation. We all have a moral duty not to maliciously injure or kill other persons. We all have a moral duty to single-handedly rescue others from an impending danger by taking a proportionate step that is primarily in our own hands. Those other persons have a corresponding moral right that we do. The language of rights and correlative duties is a common, convenient presentational device to articulate relationships of justice from, respectively, the end of the person *for whose sake* some conduct is due, and from the end of the person *from whom* conduct is due, who is accordingly subject to a duty – a duty of justice. The idea of justice, in its classical sense, relevant here, extends to any kind of moral duty breach of which amounts to wronging another.

The kinds of conduct that may be morally due from us for someone else's sake differ in many interesting ways. I wish to focus on one distinction, which again we can appreciate simply by reflecting on what we reasonably regard ourselves as bound to do in certain predicaments. Plainly some fundamental duties of justice hold independently of social arrangements, in the following sense. I am no less duty-bound to refrain from killing another out of revenge even if other persons do not exercise a similar kind of self-restraint. But the same logic does not apply to other familiar duties of justice. My moral duty to stop at a red light is not independent of what other drivers and pedestrians do. It is in the framework of a widely followed, operative traffic order that I am duty-bound to stop at red. But for the fact that other drivers pay heed to the light (and can be expected to continue to do so), but for the fact that they, too, stop precisely when that kind of light is or goes red, I might have no reason to do so myself; in heavy traffic, I might have a moral duty *not* to stop. Something similar applies to my moral duty to keep to speed limits and many other traffic directions. And to my moral duty to contribute to a fair revenue collection scheme by way of paying tax. And to countless other requirements of justice many of us face on a daily basis.

The curious practice-dependence of these requirements of justice is worth a closer look. Somehow, in these predicaments but not in others, a person seems to acquire a moral duty to do something *in virtue of the fact that many other persons do that same thing.* There is, in a sense, no great mystery about the reason why this is so. But spelling out that reason in full will bring out something important about the very nature of what we are calling duties of justice. Indeed it will bring out something important, and insufficiently understood, about what it takes to *realise justice*, and so foster human well-being, across many domains of social life.

A useful starting point is an understanding of the idea of duty or obligation in terms of the practical *necessity* of determinate conduct as an *especially apt* means to a valuable end.[1] Determinate conduct, whether an act or abstention, can be especially apt to serve as means to a given end by reason of a number of considerations. They include how *effective* the conduct is as a means to that end, any *burdens* or costs associated with the conduct, and *alternative* means at hand. It is easy to see that my refraining from maliciously injuring others is always an especially apt means of protecting important aspects of their well-being, aspects which for simplicity we may identify with their health. My abstention from malicious injury is especially apt as a means to the end of protecting the health of potential victims because it is effective, relatively easy to do and has no feasible alternatives. It is therefore due from me for their sake. By the same token, when a person's physical integrity is in danger, there *may* be an effective and proportionate means, perhaps uniquely in my power, to save this person. If so, my saving conduct is, here as well, especially apt to secure the person's health, and therefore needed, and therefore morally due.

But, often enough, conduct of mine only becomes especially apt to foster another person's health – to stick to this one aspect of well-being – in the context of some set of collective arrangements. This is because whether a person retains or regains his health depends in many complex ways on the behaviour of many others. A person's health can also be impaired through accidental rather than intentional bodily injury, inadequate food quality or intake, water and air pollution, or the consumption of harmful drugs. Impaired health may, in turn, call for specialist treatment and manifold forms of assistance and support. The states of affairs involved in comprehensively preventing and treating ill health can hardly be secured by persons acting each for their own part. Collective arrangements are required: for example, schemes of professional healthcare, industrial and workplace safety control, and traffic ordering, buttressed by systems of resource pooling that spread the cost of amenities in non-discriminatory fashion. The scale of these collective arrangements must be large enough to be efficient, and small enough to be manageable by means of reasonably accessible guidelines implemented through consistent and fair monitoring and compensation measures. The scale appropriate to these arrangements will tend to coincide with the scope of the kind of community we have reason to call political.

[1] Based on the formulation in J Finnis, *Natural Law and Natural Rights*, 2nd edn (Oxford, Oxford University Press, 2011) 307.

It is the presence of these collective arrangements that renders my individual conduct, performed as part of these arrangements, especially apt, and therefore needed and due, to protect the health of others. It is in the framework of an operative traffic order that my stopping here and now is an effective and proportionate means for me to safeguard the physical integrity of others. It is in the framework of a comprehensive redistribution scheme that appropriately collects and channels resources, and imposes no disproportionate or discriminatory burdens, that my contributing 16 per cent of my income by a particular date is an especially apt means to contribute to (amongst other things) the healthcare of the needy. Paying the same amount of money into a corrupt revenue collection scheme, or randomly offering it to an apparently needy stranger, would likely be a much less effective means to the same end; and any initiative I could single-handedly adopt, by way of emulating, even on a small scale, the workings of a sound redistribution scheme, would likely take a disproportionate toll on my own strengths. Note, moreover, that sound traffic and tax schemes are bound to have had reasonable alternatives prior to their adoption, not least (say) in the specific allocation of street junctions, speed limits or tax bands. But the schemes are morally binding now, once and because adopted to the exclusion of alternative schemes. They are morally binding because many people follow them, though not purely and simply because of that fact.

As these considerations suggest, a human community that can put in place such kinds of collective scheme has a unique ability to foster the health of its members. In acting as part of such a scheme, I myself share in that ability. Given the scheme, determinate conduct of mine may *become* morally due because especially apt to serve an end both serious and urgent, an end I have standing reason to strive towards but which might, in the absence of those arrangements, remain insufficiently accomplished. Somehow, in a sense to be explained, political communities have an ability to *realise* justice by *creating* requirements of justice. And key to that ability are what I have so far been loosely referring to as 'collective schemes', 'arrangements' or 'orders'. To these I now turn.

II. SPECIFIC CONVERGENCE

The forms of collective behaviour that my examples have been touching on are inherently local and variable. But they have something fundamental in common. What they have in common explains why they can systematically change what it is just to do, and wrongful not to do. What they have in common, as this section shows, is that they involve what I henceforth call specific convergence.

Specific convergence is required, as a matter of justice, where some needed state of affairs is most appropriately brought about through the convergent conduct of a large number of persons, and that conduct could in principle follow any one of several available and appropriate but incompatible patterns. The underlying means–ends relationship can be articulated as follows:

> *E* (end): As a matter of justice, some state of affairs concerning human well-being needs to be brought about.
>
> *M* (means):
>
> > *M1* (convergence). The state of affairs can most appropriately be brought about through the convergent conduct of a large number of persons.
> >
> > *M2* (specificity). The convergent conduct could in principle follow any one of several available and appropriate but incompatible patterns.

A few comments on each leg.

Proposition *E* broadly describes the end. A needed 'state of affairs concerning human well-being' may involve either the presence of something conducive to well-being, or the absence of something detrimental to it. Often enough, one and the same situation can be construed interchangeably: maintaining health, for instance, entails preventing illness and injury. 'Bringing about' accordingly extends to creating, preserving, changing, forestalling, dismantling, etc, as the case may be. 'State of affairs' covers both highly concrete targets, such as reducing waiting lists for breast cancer surgery in a particular public hospital, and ends framed more generically, such as providing timely healthcare to the poor. Indeed, often a given end will itself amount to a means to a yet further end. Perhaps limiting deductions of travel expenses is an appropriate way of raising an extra two million through corporate tax, which in turn is an appropriate means to cope with ample healthcare coverage. Means and ends are relative in life, and so they are in the above schema. But however generically framed, an end, in proposition *E*, is different from well-being as such. It is a state of affairs that instantiates or advances some aspect(s) of the well-being of some person(s), in ways determinate enough to amount to a goal attainable through determinate conduct. That is the conduct that makes up the means.

The means (*M*) is specific convergence. It is convergent conduct (*M1*) following specific patterns (*M2*). I consider each of the two component notions in turn.

Convergent conduct is characterised by three features. First, convergent conduct need not be identical or simultaneous on the part of the persons involved. Conduct that converges need not coincide in every particular. In fact, few meaningful enterprises can be sustained by identical simultaneous conduct on the part of the persons involved. Even military marches have their leaders and musicians. Where our above discussion has spoken of many people doing the 'same thing', a closer look reveals a richer picture. No income tax scheme is sound, for instance, if it exacts the same amount of money from everyone, or even the same percentage of their income. Even a single set of traffic lights directs drivers and pedestrians to perform more or less opposite kinds of conduct at any point in time: some stopping, some proceeding on their way. The diversity of efforts involved in large-scale convergence becomes most patent when we consider the extravagant range of ancillary tasks required to support any of the preceding endeavours, including tasks of monitoring and surveillance, training, licensing, and mechanisms for compensation and redress. Convergence may be of actions, tolerances, recognitions, language – all or any of these.

Secondly, convergent conduct is interdependent conduct. Where the conduct of some persons converges, what each of them has reason to do depends on the conduct of the others. It follows that people may be performing identical conduct without converging, and that they may be converging without performing identical conduct. Most people most of the time refrain from killing others. That is a simultaneous abstention. It fosters human well-being. But it is not, as such, convergent conduct. Participation in a traffic or tax scheme is convergent conduct. My reason to perform the relevant conduct depends on the scheme's being collective. Indeed, it depends on the scheme's being collective not only in design, but also in actual fact. It depends on the scheme's being actually followed by a sufficient number of persons, whether voluntarily or in response to more or less stringent incentives or threats.

This last remark highlights the third important feature of convergence. Convergence is of conduct, not of aim. Those whose conduct converges need not be motivated by the same kinds of consideration. They may not uniformly regard the conduct that is required from them as being in their best interests. They may not approve of the design of the scheme. They may not even appreciate *that* a scheme of this kind is needed, in this domain, to advance a valuable end. They may be disposed to conform only given a credible prospect of enforcement. In the extreme case, perhaps they will simply be made to conform, through someone else's more or less forceful intervention (such as a compulsory seizure to pay tax debts, or the imprisonment of a serious traffic offender). Convergence does not entail active coordination, although some needed forms of convergence will, no doubt, involve as much. Those executing a complex police raid do not *merely* converge. Convergence can even result from joint planning. But often it need not, and in many circumstances it cannot. The likely absence of shared motivations amongst the persons concerned does not affect what convergence is, although, as we shall soon see, it affects what it takes to *generate* it (section IV).

Turn now to the second leg of the means, *M2*. The necessary convergent conduct 'could in principle follow any one of several available and appropriate but incompatible patterns'. That this is so entails that the needed conduct will be considerably *specific*. Specific in two senses. First, the conduct will characteristically consist in detailed, concrete measures. Complex pursuits such as providing and funding public healthcare will not get off the ground unless the different persons and institutions involved are assigned relatively precise tasks, and the descriptions of the tasks are carefully articulated. Tasks that are specific enough in this first sense, however, will often have reasonable alternatives. They will be specific in the second sense. This second sense of specificity corresponds to what chapter 3 called arbitrariness. The organised protection of health translates into countless arbitrary particulars. Reasonable tax bands, speed limits, licence renewal periods, eligibility thresholds for assistance, service catchment areas or scales of fines – these are not arbitrary in any pejorative sense. They are arbitrary in that they embody a choice that, at least to some extent, is under-determined by reason. Those making the choice may have had no compelling reason to prefer the option they chose over some alternative option that would have likewise been appropriate and available to the same end.

Choices will sometimes be under-determined because it is genuinely a matter of *indifference* which out of a number of alternatives is picked. This often occurs at the point of fine-tuning measures by casting them in numerical or otherwise technical form – say, in setting a minimum fine at €100 rather than €110, or a deadline at 5 April or 30 June. But the technical appearance of such measures is liable to disguise that the choices leading up to them, the choices that the measures presuppose and give effect to, may not be matters of indifference in any way. They may involve high-stakes policy calls. They may adjudicate amongst *incommensurable* values and justified demands. Thus the question may be whether to set a requirement in the first place, breach of which would be fined. Thus the question may be on whom the requirement falls: say, whether income tax should be exacted officially, or whether it should be for individuals to submit a yearly declaration. Thus the question may also be whether to have a tax-funded healthcare provision, as opposed to, say, a system of private licensing coupled with subsidies or accessible insurance. Even settling on a speed limit, before a concrete figure starts to crystallise, may require a tragic compromise between various aspects of human well-being, including personal safety and the many amenities of swift transport, with beneficiaries of not wholly overlapping kinds.

Right reasoning may not take us all the way to a definite resolution to many dilemmas that arise in the life of any community – or in our own lives for that matter. Human well-being can be realised in oneself, and fostered in others, through many different kinds of avenues, vocations and projects. Part of the value of the under-determined choice lies precisely in its forging paths and making bets that, upon and because of that choosing, will deserve a special call on the chooser's attention, even though prior to that choice they were just some amongst many options reasonably open to pursuit, and even though they may eventually unravel as a mistake. Such is the challenge, the peril and the beauty of living one's own life.[2]

Then again, under-determination is not sheer indeterminacy. *M2* speaks of means 'appropriate' to the end. It may be undetermined whether healthcare should be publicly provided or publicly subsidised, but not whether to have *some* professional healthcare system accessible to the poor. It may be under-determined how many and which tax bands to use, but not whether to have

[2] On self-direction as a reason to empower, see ch 5.VII; on how self-direction grounds the moral need for law's positivity, see ch 6.I.

progressive income tax. In fact, rationally determined elements pervade even choices that appear to be perfectly indifferent on their face. It may not be at all indifferent, for instance, whether to set a speed limit at 64 or 65 mph, to the extent that evidence shows that tens and fives are easiest to understand. For that reason, in turn, 64 may be the more appropriate figure if the point of the sign is to attract attention (a strategy reportedly used in some domains). Red, as used in traffic lights, is the colour with the longest wavelength and therefore is easiest to see. Green is its opposite, and therefore is easiest to visually contrast. And where vehicles have long been driving on a certain side of the road, there is good reason, all things being equal, to stick to that arrangement – things may not have been equal, for example, when Sweden switched from left to right in 1967 in order to align with neighbouring countries. All this shows that the arbitrariness involved in specific convergence is inherently a matter of degree, as is *under*-determination by its very nature.

I have so far explained specific convergence by focusing on its ability to help communities realise justice. I have spoken of ends required by justice, and of means appropriate to fulfil these ends. It seems to follow that specific convergence is necessarily a good thing. It seems to follow, in other words, that it is specific also in the (third) sense that it is specific *to* just ends. This calls for a qualification. I do not regard the idea of specific convergence as an honorific title. There is nothing incoherent, it seems to me, in speaking of the specific convergence needed to fight an unjust war or to operate an exploitative tax system. The 'need' invoked in such cases is of a primarily instrumental or preference-based, but so far forth intelligible, kind. So are the considerations that determine how the relevant end is 'appropriately' brought about. In fact, such wider uses of the idea of specific convergence are not altogether irrelevant to our enquiry. There is an all-too-well-known continuum between just and unjust ends, and between just and unjust means. A less than fully just redistribution system departs, in some degree, from the kind of specific convergence that justice requires. But it need not for that reason be an irrational affair, even from the point of view of the rationality of justice. That justice must often remain an ideal for a community to strive *towards*, given our world as it is and persons as they are, is something the very idea of 'convergence' helpfully imports, too, through its mathematical resonance of an approach to a limit.

III. THE SCOPE OF SPECIFIC CONVERGENCE

Let us broaden our canvass. Our examples so far have been focused on the advancement of health, which is a relatively circumscribed, though pivotal, aspect of human well-being. Even so, our discussion of healthcare provision and funding has touched on forms of arrangement that are critical to fostering further, different aspects of well-being. Think of the vast network of arrangements that enable professional specialisation, recognition of qualification, and the development, transfer, attribution and protection of knowledge in any area of research. Or consider other kinds of publicly funded assistance provided to persons severally, for example in matters of housing or pensions. Or consider benefits provided to persons indistinctly, such as public transportation, security, infrastructure and generally what are known as public goods, that is, goods not perceptibly diminished by any particular person's consumption of them, and which, if provided to some, are provided to all. And consider, too, any resource pooling needed to support these arrangements, associated strategies for fair administration and control, and determinations of residence and nationality that may reasonably operate as gateways to the above entitlements.

All these arrangements plainly involve specific convergence on their own accord. They involve forms of collective convergent conduct following specific patterns that could have reasonably been different but in their effective implementation can serve as privileged means to foster well-being in ways that would otherwise not be in reach. And it bears stressing that the logic of specific convergence underlies not only the positive provision of benefits, on which our discussion has focused, but also associated patterns of mutual restraint in realms as varied as pollution and recycling, use of firearms, minimum salaries and annual leave, campaign advertising or urban planning.

These reflections suggest that specific convergence is widely called for indeed. They suggest that it is called for all across the range of domains of social life and aspects of well-being that form the subject-matter of justice in community, a subject-matter well illustrated by modern catalogues of human and constitutional rights.[3] The reflections suggest, in short, that the idea of specific convergence captures central features of what must be the case *across the board*, not only in circumscribed fields such as healthcare provision and traffic, if justice in community is to be realised.

The generalising tenor of this proposition might appear to be in tension with our earlier reference to duties of justice that hold independently of social arrangements, in that one has reason to perform the relevant conduct regardless of what others do (section I). The duty not to vengefully kill another holds independently of behavioural convergence, and its description could not reasonably be otherwise: neither *M1* nor *M2* is fulfilled in the pattern of refraining from this conduct. The duty differs in both respects from the duty to stop at a red light or to pay 16 per cent income tax. The difference between the latter kinds of duty and the duty not to vengefully kill is often expressed in terms of the contrast between *mala in se* and *mala prohibita*. Some kinds of conduct, it is said, are rightly prohibited because they are inherently wrongful (*mala in se*), whereas some other forms of conduct are wrongful because they are prohibited

[3] For a sustained argument, see G Webber et al, *Legislated Rights: Securing Human Rights through Legislation* (Cambridge, Cambridge University Press, 2018).

(*mala prohibita*). Clearly some of the forms of conduct most detrimental to human well-being are *mala in se*. It seems tempting to conclude, therefore, that specific convergence is an indispensable but relatively accessory or secondary affair when it comes to fostering human well-being as justice demands.

But that is not so. For one thing, protecting the aspects of well-being compromised by *mala in se* requires a complex range of efforts of prevention, detection, punishment and redress, which must be structured so as to involve specific convergence on their own accord. This is, amongst other things, why sound legal definitions of murder, including *mens rea*, causation and defences, as well as penalty ranges and procedural determinations for detention, investigation and trial, will be considerably more intricate than anything that could be inferred from the plain injunction 'thou shalt not kill'. Justice requires that basic elements of crimes and torts, penalties, compensation measurements, and so on, be knowable in advance, so far as possible. Just as importantly, they should be brought to bear alike in like situations. But decisions will be many, and decision-makers manifold, changing and sometimes lacking in juristic training (as in the case of jurors). Fair warning and fairness as between defendants, both of them considerations central to the requirements of justice we sum up as the Rule of Law (chapter 6.IV–VI), have little chance of being honoured in the absence of potentially highly detailed specifications envisaging fine gradations between cases, specifications that legal doctrine in the respective fields will help to systematise, and that in numerous respects may reasonably vary from jurisdiction to jurisdiction and over time. Specific provisions moreover help forestall the fruitless litigation to which needlessly vague standards might give rise in these contexts (say, on whether the sentence was 'reasonable'), thereby also minimising the unfairness of resource waste.[4]

It may be objected that these specifications, morally needed as they are, on the whole leave intact the moral duties not to commit the relevant *mala in se*. Just because the victim's death cannot causally be attributed to the defendant, or the custodial sentence is 20 years rather than 25 years, does not mean the defendant was any less obligated to refrain from killing in the first place. It is true that these specifications bear in the first instance on the normative positions of those administering the relevant processes, notably judges. But it is no less true that, through the proxy of judicial intervention, these specifications come to bear, crucially, on the normative positions of those who have breached their obligation to refrain from *mala in se* and on that account become subject to a range of new, ancillary duties: for example, duties to submit to a given penalty, pay a certain amount of compensation or provide specific redress. Such duties, when the arrangements are sound, are no less requirements of justice than the duty to abstain from *mala in se*.

[4] On the guidance and process value of precision, see T Endicott, 'The Value of Vagueness' in A Marmor and S Soames (eds), *Philosophical Foundations of Language in the Law* (Oxford, Oxford University Press, 2011).

More fundamentally though, the concern canvassed above in terms of the contrast between *mala prohibita* and *mala in se* misses its target. It misunderstands the nature of the present enquiry about the scope of specific convergence. It is not, except derivatively, an enquiry about the content of duties and rights. The modern grammar of duties and correlative rights serves to portray particular relationships of justice from the point of view of the individuals in those relationships. Specific convergence certainly adds nothing to one's duty to abstain from committing *mala in se*, and to the would-be victim's correlative right. *But specific convergence remains key to meeting the human needs for the sake of which* mala in se *must be avoided*. Once the focus is placed on what it takes to realise justice, as do propositions *E–M1–M2*, specific convergence proves to be essential also, perhaps especially, when it comes to fairly protecting the aspects of well-being impairment of which renders certain kinds of conduct inherently wrongful.

It is also worth noting that pure *mala in se* relevant to justice in community are relatively few in number. Not even most 'core' criminal offences or civil wrongs fall into this category. The duty to keep one's promises or agreements, for example, is not on a par, in this respect, with the duty not to vengefully kill. It is against a background of a standing practice, in the relevant group, of fulfilling promises and expecting them to be fulfilled, that one has genuine reason to do so oneself – indeed, that one is able to enter into 'a promise' in the first place, never mind 'a contract'. Specific convergence is involved in the very determination of what *counts* as entering into a binding contract, as section VI of this chapter shows. Contracts, furthermore, are a chief way of acquiring and transferring what we call property and other interests in things. In an important sense, the existence of such interests depends on the extent to which a community has in place collective arrangements for the non-interference with items held by some to the exclusion of the rest. There is good reason, in justice, to have and keep such arrangements. But that reason radically under-determines the countless necessary particulars to be settled in delimiting the types of holdings, forms of transfer, and related powers, entitlements and charges. Only *given* general convergence of such specifics is stealing unjust, indeed possible.

We can conclude that specific convergence is a central tool to realise justice in community. It is needed across all domains of social life that rightly fall within the community's collective jurisdiction. The presence of specific convergence in *many* domains in turn increases its effectiveness in *any* domain. All else being equal, more extensive convergence is better convergence. A scheme of resource pooling, transport or patent protection is all the more effective the greater the number of persons involved. Extensive convergence gathers additional justificatory force from providing like treatment to those in a morally comparable position (all similarly well-off, all car-drivers, etc), and in so doing it bolsters the reason each has to do his part. Whether operating in the foreground or background, directly or mediately, in channelling responses to wrongful conduct or also in shaping its description, specific convergence enables political communities to transform open-ended desiderata enshrined in rights catalogues into specific, action-guiding requirements that carry the peremptory force connoted by the vocabulary of *rights* and correlative *duties*. To the considerable extent that a person's well-being depends on the cooperation of others, specific convergence is a means of choice for us to bring about collectively what individually we deserve.

IV. MARKING AND ENFORCING

But specific convergence does not arise out of the blue. Thousands, indeed millions of persons, mostly strangers to one another, do not by happenstance find themselves converging on complex, intricate patterns of the kind that justice calls for. Somebody's more or less targeted intervention will be required in order to generate specific convergence where it is morally needed, but will not otherwise ensue.

Talk of *generating* specific convergence brings into focus a consideration that has been implicit in the preceding sections. The need to generate specific convergence is logically prior to the need for a person to undertake specific conduct *within* a convergent scheme, once adopted. Both of these needs are captured in Proposition *E*, discussed in section II, when this proposition speaks of a state of affairs that *needs* to be brought about *as a matter of justice*. Generating specific convergence is not in everybody's hands. Some persons or institutions may have a special ability to generate convergence, in some domains, and may accordingly have a moral duty to do so. Others, in turn, may have a moral duty not to interfere with or second-guess the efforts of the former. The central question of *who* should generate convergence will be left to the next chapter. We must first explain what it takes to generate it.

What it takes to generate convergence emerges from considering the kinds of obstacle that may stand in the way of its taking place. Such obstacles fall into two broad kinds. Obstacles of the first kind involve lack of information, and obstacles of the second kind involve lack of willingness to cooperate. We can therefore speak of cognitive and volitional obstacles.

Cognitive obstacles arise where persons lack information about what, if anything, they should do themselves, and about what others have done, are doing or are likely to do in the future. Insufficient warrant for expectations of future behaviour, in particular, is often a poignant obstacle to convergence, given that continuity in time is of the essence in many schemes of cooperation (chapter 6.IV). Cognitive obstacles can be paralysing even in the absence of volitional obstacles. They can be paralysing even if the persons involved understand that a collective scheme is needed in a given domain, are disposed to do their share, and appreciate that others in the group share this knowledge and disposition. Perhaps substantial segments of the population in Western Europe, for example, would be conditionally disposed to make generous contributions towards providing relief to the many innocents whom circumstances beyond their control keep stranding on our shores and near our doorsteps. Perhaps this predicament can, and in justice should, be alleviated through a Europe-wide scheme of specific convergence. Perhaps many Europeans are latently aware of all this. But in the absence of centralised guidelines, duly precise and public enough to be widely known, little progress can be expected beyond circumscribed initiatives of partly overlapping, if not conflicting, reach. From the point of view of any willing contributor, *whether* others will act, and if so *in what way*, remains disturbingly up in the air.

Volitional obstacles to convergence, needless to say, are endemic. They are especially endemic to the day-in day-out management of community affairs. Such obstacles are characteristic, for example, of patterns of mutual restraint and resource-pooling schemes. It is tempting not to do one's share if one's share involves bearing some burden one could in principle eschew, individually, without relevantly losing out. Cases in point include evading tax while benefitting from economic infrastructure and public goods, stealing but not being stolen from, or edging out business competitors by employing undocumented immigrants without paying minimum wage. This kind of predicament is different from that of drivers deciding which side of the road to drive on. In this latter, oft-rehearsed predicament, one stands to lose, not to gain, in departing from the generally followed trend. But it is the former, not the latter, predicament that is the rule, as a large and diverse community goes about channelling sensitive risks and costs, and allocating scarce fruits of common stock, in response to some demands that are no more pressing than others which must remain unattended. A predicament in which it pays to free-ride is inherently unstable, not least because the incentive to free-ride weakens *everyone's* reason to contribute, for fear of doing so pointlessly or at the mercy of those who take an unfair advantage. Even conscientious citizens may operate in the black market in the face of notoriously high evasion rates and knock-on tax rises.

Cognitive and volitional obstacles are closely related. In many practical scenarios they go hand in hand. They broadly track the elements of specific convergence picked up by propositions *M1* and *M2*. They track, respectively, the need to narrow down on *one* amongst several conceivable patterns (*M2*), and the need for *actual* convergence on it to occur (*M1*).

Generating convergence is therefore inseparable from overcoming these obstacles. Consider the second obstacle first. Willingness to cooperate in a just scheme can hardly be instilled, but it can be taught with due respect for individual conscience. Cooperation may otherwise be incentivised either by attaching benefits to performance or, often more appropriately, by increasing the cost of defection, including through threats of punishment or other forms of disadvantage. Exceptionally it may be justified to bypass altogether the relevant person's will, by rendering undue conduct impossible through forceful means. I refer to all these strategies aimed at ensuring actual convergence as *enforcement mechanisms*. The term 'enforcement' predominantly connotes mechanisms of the last-mentioned sorts, but that is consistent with their pre-eminent position. They form the background against which threats of penalty and appeals to general compliance acquire any necessary credibility. Success in enforcement builds on itself, in the same way that defection easily spreads.

Tackling the problem of lack of information, in turn, involves making the relevant information available. It must be easy to tell, for everyone concerned, what kind of conduct is to be performed or avoided. Ease of identification is audience-specific. Figuring out what is to be done must not require judgements that relevant persons cannot comfortably undertake. Arduous scrutiny or complex calculations are not generally open to persons pondering what to do in everyday settings, although they may be open to professionals whom persons may periodically consult on specialised subject-matters. Ease of identification is not only audience-specific but also other-regarding. I must have reason to assume that others will make the same identification as me, for all I know about them. And often, I do not know much. In a culturally diverse community, I can expect fellow members to have diverging skills and deeply opposed moral stances. It follows that I can only reliably identify a conduct description *as* due from me, if I can count on this same conduct description likewise standing out for others, whatever their views about its propriety, convenience or justice. What is needed, therefore, is some kind of *mark*, some grammar or method of signalling, that can be traced and spotted by many different-minded persons, across manifold domains of social life and through time.

Sound *marking mechanisms*, as I shall call them, are in an important sense self-fulfilling. To the extent they mark conduct as due, in a way apt to be convergently identified by those concerned, they contribute to *rendering* it due – due morally. Marking mechanisms needed to bring about specific convergence do not simply bear witness to something that is true independently of that marking. They do not simply inform about the fact that some specific conduct is due. They contribute to rendering it due in so marking it. Specific conduct descriptions that could have reasonably been otherwise *become* due in being flagged up within an effective convergent scheme. Marking mechanisms can render conduct obligatory, as it were, by so saying. Here moral duties, and corresponding rights, arise in being marked, highlighted, pointed up, *specified* – in yet a further sense of this term.

So both marking and enforcement mechanisms are self-reinforcing, each on their own account. It is crucial to see, however, that they are also mutually reinforcing. Marking and enforcement are interdependent to the point that, where both are needed, no question about logical priority between them can sensibly arise. On the one hand, sound enforcement presupposes marking: clear and prospective descriptions of conduct due make possible deterrence and prevention, and ensure a consistent handling of breaches in response to fair warning. On the other hand, effective marking presupposes enforcement: no mark truly *marks* in the eyes of many unless anyone can reasonably count on others paying heed to it as well. And that expectation will often be warranted precisely by the latent threat of enforcement.

In the combination of marking and enforcement lies the recipe for generating specific convergence. The joint operation of marking and enforcement renders a conduct description *salient*, and so a focus for mutual expectations. Salience is an essentially other-regarding notion.[5] When someone regards an option as salient, he regards it as the option that stands out to everyone else on those same grounds. The grounds need have nothing to do with shared goals or aims. I need have no inkling of the motivations that lead particular drivers to keep speed limits, provided I can expect *that* they will do so. A mark that is salient is a mark that can be shared by persons who share little else, not even reasons for sharing it.

V. LAW'S MARKING: LEGAL VALIDITY

Legal validity is the law's mark. It is a technique distinctly suited to devise, manifest and render salient specific conduct descriptions to a large group of persons. Along with enforcement mechanisms of the overriding strength peculiar to political communities, legal validity renders mature legal systems especially apt to generate and sustain the kind of specific convergence that justice calls for. Or so the remainder of this book will argue.

The reasons why the technique of legal validity is especially suited for marking follow from what we learned in the last chapter about the nature of this technique. At its most basic, the technique of legal validity involves expressing a choice. The choice concerns a change in legal positions. The choice becomes legally binding in being expressed – in being expressed, that is, through validity's distinct grammar. Marking, too, involves expressing a choice. The choice concerns a specific pattern of conduct. That choice can become morally binding in being expressed – in being expressed, that is, in such a way that it is salient, easy to identify, to all those concerned. Validity is a grammar that renders choices salient. Validity is not only a technique *for* changing legal positions, but it is also a signal *that* legal positions have been changed. I follow the Wills Act in making a valid will, and others shall follow it in determining *that* I made it. We saw in the last chapter why this is so: using the technique of validity involves accomplishing what one intends to accomplish *through the very manifestation of that intent*. Hence the valid act manifests not only the agent's intent, *but also the agent's success*. Ease of identification, in other words, is built right into

[5] eg T Schelling, *The Strategy of Conflict* (New York, Oxford University Press, 1963) 111ff ('focal point'); D Lewis, *Convention: A Philosophical Study* (Oxford, Basil Blackwell, 2002) 35 ('uniqueness in some conspicuous respect').

validity's technique. Validity renders a conduct description salient *in virtue of the fact that it was chosen*. It marks requirements as salient by reason of their *source*.

But there is more to the ease of identification that the technique of legal validity can provide. Beyond the basic considerations just noted, the technique of validity has additional, peculiar traits canvassed in the last chapter. Each of these traits, to different degrees, enables the technique of validity to mark in a way that is particularly sophisticated and durable. Take each of validity's four traits in turn.

The first special trait of validity is that the valid say-so can invoke a legal regime beyond what is ostensibly in the mind of the sayer (chapter 3.V). That regime may specify and supplement the agent's manifested purport, for instance by 'implying' terms or otherwise determining particulars, which terms and particulars can accordingly not be read off from the literal tenor of the valid decision. In this sense, to be sure, the valid result is harder, not easier, to identify. It may take lawyerly skill to work out its precise import. But this has a crucial flip side. The fact that one need not articulate, even know, the particulars of the normative change one's valid act introduces, makes it easier to introduce it oneself, and easier for others to recognise it as introduced. One can identify that one is performing the valid act in question, indeed that one *has* performed it, despite not being acquainted with its deeper legal ramifications.

The extent to which one can be confident that an act is valid despite not studying its particulars depends, of course, on the operation of legal presumptions favouring the validity, or at least voidability, of the act over its radical nullity for breach of validity criteria (chapter 5.V). We find such presumptions in play in numerous fields of law. What often gives rise to the presumption is the fulfilment of certain procedural requirements. Where certainty is key, a presumption of validity may even be conclusive. Compliance with certain formal steps may override any underlying substantive or procedural flaws *as a matter of law*. Under the enrolled bill doctrine, for example, the fact that legislative documents have been appropriately authenticated precludes judicial second-guessing of the procedure that led up to the enactment. Private transactions, too, may become indefeasible in virtue of being recorded in specific kinds of deed or registry. Valid decisions of countless other kinds, moreover, acquire indefeasible status upon becoming legally final.

This variegated grid of presumptions, explicit or implicit, defeasible or conclusive, goes to warrant the accustomed predicament in which it seems possible for us to tell, say, *that* a new tax statute has been enacted before reading every clause, or *that* title has passed without studying the conveyance, or *that* judgment has been validly issued before knowing which way it went. Note, by comparison, how rare it is to use such simplifications in ordinary communication. We normally understand *that* somebody said something along with *what* he said, in all its exhaustive detail. Accordingly we have a lesser need to use a tag such as 'valid' to flag up successful, meaningful communicative acts, irrespective of their truth, relevance or propriety. Someone learning a language may be grateful to be told that something is not a 'valid sentence', but this kind of concern is not ordinarily reflected in our way of talking. In everyday communicative contexts we do not need this kind of verbal stamp. But we do in legal contexts, even in everyday ones. Unreflective bus-riders, too, tend to be aware whether or not they carry a valid ticket. The complexity of legal meaning calls for particularly robust kinds of simplification. There was a time, centuries ago, when validity's mark could more or less exclusively consist in a unique seal attached to a document by way of identifying its official source. But mature legal systems have a multiplicity of official sources, and wax seals have long ceased to be forgery-proof. The shortcuts to identification both possible and operative in mature legal systems primarily involve resources at the level of legal reasoning and language. And this takes us to the second special trait of validity.

The valid say-so can endure through time and circulate as a relatively freestanding entity, referred to by placeholder terms that name configurations of legal positions ('lease contract', 'licence', 'marriage'), and often represented as such in physical supports such as deeds, passports, licence plates, marriage certificates or credit cards (chapter 3.VI). Physical proxies may themselves be iterated. The valid acceptance of an inheritance may be recorded in a valid deed, which in turn warrants a valid entry in the land registry, proof of which is supplied by a valid certificate – or by a certified copy thereof. Such physical detachment of legal positions from their originating act bolsters their normative detachment. That is to say: validity's second trait goes to buttress the *legal* rules and doctrines that prevent original flaws, or later changes of mind or circumstances, from effecting a change of established legal positions. Presumptions of validity, tightly circumscribed doctrines of frustration and rescission, limited stages of appeal and grounds thereof, and other barriers to the retroactive scope of legal changes, all in various ways reflect the principle which valid passports, certificates or licence plates *embody*, in the narrowest sense of the term.

The third peculiar trait of legal validity is that the valid say-so may accomplish effects unintentionally, not least when transactions are performed through impersonal or automated means, or when a legal regime determines particulars one had not anticipated (chapter 3.VII). The possibility of unintentional valid action entails an increased facility of identification – for others. They will be entitled to rely on what appeared to be an intentional act. Procedural safeguards such as witnessing, a two-step online confirmation process or a clearly marked 'Aye' door, may lend intentional appearance to an unintentional act, precisely because they are there to help ensure the agent consciously identifies the normative change he is making.

Validity's fourth trait, finally, is the counterpart of the third. One may fail in one's attempt to perform a valid act, however firm and manifest one's intention. A say-so will not be valid unless it complies with the valid requirements of procedure and substance (chapter 3.VIII). What looked like a valid administrative resolution may turn out to be deeply ultra vires. What looked like a binding contractual clause may be 'deemed not to have been set' by consumer legislation.[6] Presumptions of validity may be defeated, or never arise. In this respect, the fourth trait of validity compromises ease of identification. But sometimes, interestingly, it does so for the sake of ease of identification. The fact that a conveyance of land cannot be perfected orally, by saying 'this is yours', is critical to its eventual verifiability. Your interlocutor understood that by saying 'this is yours', you had every intention to perfect the conveyance then and there, but he is not the only one potentially concerned with this normative change. The reasonable observers concerned with identifying your choice may be at great temporal and geographic distance. They include subsequent owners, holders of leases, their heirs, any third parties, and ultimately judges. Here the fact that your conspicuous attempt is not valid ensures that your valid attempt will be conspicuous.

VI. TWO LEVELS OF CONVERGENCE

Our discussion in the last section has made reference to a number of different kinds of validity criteria. We have seen how, in various ways, they go to facilitate the identification of valid acts. Criteria of validity may be intricate, as can be attested to by students struggling to memorise them. Often enough, criteria of legal validity could themselves reasonably be otherwise. There is little need to labour this point, or the related point that often it is the arbitrary nature of validity criteria that facilitates the unmistakable identification of the relevant valid choice. Note, however, what this entails.

It entails that the technique of validity uses arbitrary cues to *mark* choices that are arbitrary *themselves*. It entails that both *what* is marked, and *how* it is, could often reasonably be otherwise, at least in some respects. This is a familiar experience. We need to settle on how to make statutes in order to settle on tax rates. We need to settle on how to make conveyances in order to settle on what belongs to whom. Validity is a privileged technique for marking because it can make identification turn on cues that are but one set out of countless conceivable, reasonably appropriate, arbitrary combinations. Validity is a privileged technique for marking, in other words, because *it involves specific convergence in its own right*. It is convergence on how to *identify* what is convergently do be *done*. Validity is the *salient way to generate salience*. Thus is the sophistication of law's marking portrayed in this chapter.

Law is especially apt to help communities realise justice, in the final analysis, because it can unfold specific convergence along two related though relatively independent levels. Convergence on validity criteria is a secondary level of

[6] eg in art 83 of the Spanish Real Decreto Legislativo 1/2007, de 16 de noviembre, por el que se aprueba el texto refundido de la Ley General para la Defensa de los Consumidores y Usuarios ('Abusive clauses shall be null and void, and deemed not to have been set').

convergence, which exists over and above the primary level of behavioural convergence on manifold quandaries of social life. The relative independence between the two levels of convergence is key. The relative independence of the secondary from the primary level means, amongst other things, that the way to identify a valid choice must not predominantly engage judgements about the merits, even the content, of what is chosen. By and large, the source of valid choices must be more salient than the choices' content. Convergence on identifying law is a prerequisite for convergence on the manifold patterns of conduct that justice requires. And whereas the latter kind of convergence can be intentionally *generated*, the former kind of convergence – convergence on validity criteria – in one sense cannot.

Consider, first, the sense in which it *can*. Valid statutes set validity criteria for wills. Valid regulations set validity criteria for the award of licences. Countless kinds of validity criteria can be, and are, set intentionally. Any legal system needs such targeted setting of validity criteria because, as the next chapter shows, it needs acts of empowerment. Still, relevantly for present purposes, such targeted setting of validity criteria must eventually reach an end, at the very least when it comes to the criteria identifying the highest sources of a system's law. Convergence on *them* – whether a single written constitution providing who can validly make law, or a set of institutions as makers of valid law – can only arise and endure spontaneously. 'Spontaneously' here refers to the absence of someone's choice validly selecting these sources and not others. Spontaneous convergence is non-derivative. It is convergence not generated through deliberate, targeted acts to that effect. It arises and endures in the manner of custom.

This aspect of the convergence on validity criteria is to some extent echoed in Hart's doctrine of the 'rule of recognition'.[7] Although the argument I am making stands or falls independently of the merits of Hart's puzzling doctrine, it is worth flagging up, by way of clarifying the points here advanced, how they serve to illuminate some problems that have been said to afflict Hart's analysis. I am thinking, in particular, of the accusation that Hart's account harbours a vicious circle.[8] It is true that Hart captures a reality that is self-referential.

[7] HLA Hart, *The Concept of Law*, 2nd edn (Oxford, Clarendon Press, 1994) ch 6.

[8] eg I Duncanson, 'The Strange World of English Jurisprudence' (1979) 30 *Northern Ireland Legal Quarterly* 207, 220–21; N MacCormick, *H.L.A. Hart*, Jurists: Profiles in Legal Theory (London, Edward Arnold, 1981) 108–11; N MacCormick, 'The Concept of Law and *The Concept of Law*' in RP George (ed), *The Autonomy of Law: Essays on Legal Positivism* (Oxford, Oxford University Press, 1996) 179–80; R Caracciolo, *La Noción de Sistema en la Teoría del Derecho* (Mexico, Fontamara, 1992) 76–77. Limitedly helpful proposed 'solutions' to the perceived circularity include a chronological priority of the practice over the rule (eg MacCormick, *H.L.A. Hart*, 109ff; J Coleman, 'Incorporationism, Conventionality, and the Practical Difference Thesis' in J Coleman (ed), *Hart's Postscript: Essays on the Postscript to the Concept of Law* (Oxford, Oxford University Press, 2001) 121; cf MacCormick, 'The Concept of Law and *The Concept of Law*', 179ff); a distinction between 'two distinct roles' of certain persons (J Coleman, *The Practice of Principle: In Defence of a Pragmatist Approach to Legal Theory* (Oxford, Oxford University Press, 2001) 101); and an unexplained assumption that behaviour guided by a non-existent norm creates that very norm (S Shapiro, 'On Hart's Way Out' in J Coleman (ed), *Hart's Postscript*, 153ff).

On the one hand, validity criteria are what they are because legal officials so recognise them. In this respect, legal validity presupposes the existence of an official practice. But on the other hand, Hart also explains, legal officials are what they are because valid provisions recognise them in turn. In this respect, therefore, the existence of an official practice presupposes legal validity. But this predicament can be explained without remainder in terms of the behavioural convergence on specific sets of cues or criteria that, because convergently followed to the exclusion of alternatives, are appropriate means to achieving an end (identifying law) that would otherwise not be in reach. The fact that validity both presupposes a practice of convergence, and in turn *governs* that practice, is no different, in essence, from the fact that the rules of English grammar both presuppose the convergent practice of English speakers (the rules arise from that practice) and in turn *govern* that practice (it is possible to make mistakes).[9] No more vicious circularity is involved in accounting for the ultimate convergence on legal validity than in asking when the first English spelling error was made.

In a healthy legal system, the way to identify valid decisions will be considerably independent of what these decisions provide. It will, however, not be wholly so. Sound criteria of legal validity will in several respects be responsive to the questions of justice that fall to be settled through the valid choice. It is not indifferent or otherwise under-determined, for example, whether Parliament or the Finance Minister should alter tax rates, whether a will should be executed before or after the testator's death, whether a criminal judge need give reasons for judgment, or whether a couple or their respective parents should consent to a marriage. Numerous kinds of validity criteria for which justice calls do not have reasonable alternatives. Sound criteria of validity will, on the whole, be *relatively* arbitrary only. Concerns arising at the primary level of convergence spill over onto the secondary level, as it were, and constrain what can justly serve as validity's mark.

Ease of identification, in short, must sometimes give way to other concerns. This chapter has considered validity primarily as a technique to render certain choices salient. But the point of legal validity is not only to facilitate identification. The next chapter argues that validity is also – in the same breath – a technique for allocation of power. Weighty considerations of justice bear on how legal power should be allocated, because they bear on who should make which kinds of choice. Legal systems are especially able to respond to those considerations, too. They are especially able to unfold specific convergence along two distinct yet related levels, as justice demands. They are able because of legal validity, not in spite of it.

[9] Official dictionaries or recognised cultural institutions may hold limited *marking* capacity with respect to clarifying or fine-tuning the rules of a natural language, particularly at doubtful or unstable junctures.

NOTES

Section I: Duties of Justice

Justice Concerns the Avoidance of any Wrongdoing to Another

On this classical idea of justice, see, eg, Finnis, *Natural Law and Natural Rights*, n 1, ch 7, especially section 1; J Finnis, 'Reflections and Responses' in J Keown and RP George (eds), *Reason, Morality, and Law: The Philosophy of John Finnis* (Oxford, Oxford University Press, 2013) 502–06. For a different idea of justice articulated in recent jurisprudential work, see J Gardner, *Law as a Leap of Faith* (Oxford, Oxford University Press, 2012) ch 10; J Gardner, 'Finnis on Justice' in J Keown and RP George (eds), *Reason, Morality, and Law: The Philosophy of John Finnis* (Oxford, Oxford University Press, 2013); in turn building on Hart, *The Concept of Law*, n 7, ch 8, section 1 (particularly in the first respect I go on to note). The classical idea of justice is both wider and narrower than the idea espoused by Gardner. It is wider in that it is not limited to wrongs of a primarily 'allocative' as opposed to, say, 'commutative' kind. It is narrower in two respects: it focally concerns *wrongdoing*, and so breach of duty (and rights), rather than any shortfall of conformity with reasons for action; and it focally concerns duties towards *others*, rather than also (possible) duties towards oneself. Justice's close association with rights must in turn not hide from view the important difference, obscured by the equivocal (originally Roman) understanding of justice in terms of 'giving people *their due* [or what is *due to them*]', between the person(s) *for whose sake* something must be performed (the right-holder(s)), and the person(s) *to whom* (or in respect of whom, or through engagement with whom) it must be done. Though often these two roles coincide, they need not: just punishment, inflicted on an offender for the sake of the community, is a significant case in point (J Finnis, *Human Rights and Common Good, Collected Essays: Volume III* (Oxford, Oxford University Press, 2011) 79), as are, in a somewhat different sense, contributions to a fair and operative redistribution scheme (eg via tax), which are due to the scheme's administrators but are ultimately for the sake of those whose health, housing, etc, will be assisted.

Duty Understood in Terms of the Practical Necessity of Determinate Conduct as a Means to a Valuable End

For sustained treatment, see Finnis, *Natural Law and Natural Rights*, n 1, ch 9. With special reference to human rights, Tasioulas (J Tasioulas, 'On the Foundations of Human Rights' in R Cruft, S M Liao and M Renzo (eds), *Philosophical Foundations of Human Rights* (Oxford, Oxford University Press, 2015) 51, 56–61) disaggregates several relevant factors speaking to practical necessity (duty); see also T Endicott, 'The Infant in the Snow' in T Endicott, J Getzler and E Peel (eds), *Properties of Law: Essays in Honour of Jim Harris* (Oxford, Oxford University Press, 2006) 358, 363; J Sherman, 'Unresolved Problems in the Service Conception of Authority' (2010) 30 *Oxford Journal of Legal Studies* 419, 427ff. This understanding of duty is compatible with an understanding aimed at formally representing the kind of reason one has when one has a duty, such as Raz's idea of an 'exclusionary' or 'protected' reason (J Raz, *Practical Reason and Norms* (London, Hutchinson, 1975) chs 2 and 5).

Section II: Specific Convergence

Convergence, not Coordination

Questions giving rise to the moral need for specific convergence have been variously addressed in recent bodies of legal and political theory, perhaps most prominently through the potentially misleading and distorting language and logic of game-theoretical 'coordination problems' (on which see Schelling, *The Strategy of Conflict*, n 5, especially 89ff; Lewis, *Convention*, n 5, 8ff; E Ullmann-Margalit, *The Emergence of Norms* (Oxford, Oxford University Press, 1977) ch 2; L Green, *The Authority of the State* (Oxford, Oxford University Press, 1988) ch 4). Game-theoretical 'problems' envisage a circumscribed set of 'players' who each 'face' a choice between two or more alternative courses of action. For each player, the 'outcome' will be more or less beneficial depending on how he and others choose. In a coordination game, pay-offs are maximised for all players if they each choose the same course of action: hence they all prefer convergent behaviour on one of the options, being broadly indifferent as to which. Although the choices' interdependence and the 'ambiguity' amongst the options (Ullmann-Margalit, *The Emergence of Norms*, 80; 'multiple coordination equilibria', Lewis, *Convention*, n 5, 16) echo some features of the predicament that calls for specific convergence in a political community, the game-theoretical set-up is otherwise deeply at odds with that predicament, in three respects in particular. Firstly, game theory's assumption that individual pay-offs can be exhaustively ranked along a single scale precludes an assessment of outcomes sensitive to the many-sided nature of human well-being. Indeed – secondly – it is not the (objective) well-being of the players, jointly or severally, that is registered in the pay-off scale, but their (subjective) preferences. The focus on preferences limits the scope of coordination games to situations in which persons knowingly share a disposition to converge because there is no incentive to free-ride (characteristic of 'prisoners' dilemmas'). And thirdly, the circumscription of 'problems' involving a pre-determined shortlist of 'options', with 'outcomes' being combinations of choices, forecloses consideration of an overarching end attainable *through* the collective effort (but see, eg, Ullmann-Margalit's residual reference to restrictively defined 'cooperative goals', *The Emergence of Norms*, 130ff; and the critique in C Gans, 'The Normativity of Law and its Coordinative Function' (1981) 18 *Israel Law Review* 333, 342). Adaptations of the game-theoretical model with qualifications along a few of the preceding lines have on the whole not yielded a distinctive and unequivocal framework to appropriately tackle the questions raised by this chapter, and sometimes by the authors themselves: see, notably, J Finnis, *Philosophy of Law, Collected Essays: Volume IV* (Oxford, Oxford University Press, 2011) chs 2 and 3; Finnis, *Natural Law and Natural Rights*, n 1, especially ch 9; J Raz, *The Morality of Freedom* (Oxford, Clarendon Press, 1986) 30–31, 50–51; J Raz, 'Facing Up: A Reply' (1989) 62 *Southern California Law Review* 1153, 1187ff; J Raz, 'Introduction' in J Raz (ed), *Authority*, Readings in Social and Political Theory (New York, New York University Press, 1990) 6, 15; J Raz, 'Comments and Responses' in LH Meyer, SL Paulson and TW Pogge (eds), *Rights, Culture and the Law: Themes from the Legal and Political Philosophy of Joseph Raz* (Oxford, Oxford University Press, 2003) 259; J Raz, *Between Authority and Interpretation: On the Theory of Law and Practical Reason* (Oxford, Oxford University Press, 2009) 153–54; G Postema, 'Coordination and Convention at the Foundations of Law' (1982) 11 *Journal of Legal Studies* 165; S Perry, 'Two Problems of Political Authority' (2007) 6 *American Philosophical Association Newsletter on Law and Philosophy* 31; M Köpcke, 'Positive

Law's Moral Purpose(s): Towards a New Consensus?' (2011) 56 *American Journal of Jurisprudence* 186, 193–96. For correspondingly narrow constructions of those adaptations, see L Green, 'Law, Co-ordination, and the Common Good' (1983) 3 *Oxford Journal of Legal Studies* 299; L Green, 'Positivism and Conventionalism' (1999) 12 *Canadian Journal of Law and Jurisprudence* 35; S Perry, 'Law and Obligation' (2005) 50 *American Journal of Jurisprudence* 263, 287ff; S Perry, 'Second-order Reasons, Uncertainty and Legal Theory' (1989) 62 *Southern California Law Review* 913, 930, 952; S Shapiro, 'Authority' in J Coleman and S Shapiro (eds), *The Oxford Handbook of Jurisprudence and Philosophy of Law* (Oxford, Oxford University Press, 2002) 400ff; P Soper, 'Law's Normative Claims' in RP George (ed), *The Autonomy of Law: Essays on Legal Positivism* (Oxford, Oxford University Press, 1996) 234, fn 15 at 242–43. Efforts to explain the moral need for law in terms of the bare logic of coordination games, not adapted or qualified in the ways I noted, face different problems. Waldron's and Besson's appeal to the 'partial conflict' variant of the coordination game (in which players do have a preferred option but an overriding preference to converge) assumes, implausibly, that in political communities there is broad agreement on the need to coordinate (but disagreement on how to do so): see, eg, J Waldron, *Law and Disagreement* (Oxford, Oxford University Press, 1999) ch 5; J Waldron, 'Lex Satis Iusta' (2000) 75 *Notre Dame Law Review* 1829; S Besson, *The Morality of Conflict: Reasonable Disagreement and the Law* (Oxford, Hart Publishing, 2005) ch 6. Relying more extensively on the emaciated conception of coordination, Friedman concludes, dramatically, 'that the authority of law … must float on itself' (R Friedman, 'Oakeshott on the Authority of Law' (1989) 2 *Ratio Juris* 27, 39, generally 28ff; R Friedman, 'On the Concept of Authority in Political Philosophy' in J Raz (ed), *Authority*, Readings in Social and Political Theory (New York, New York University Press, 1990) 77ff; similarly, C McMahon, 'Autonomy and Authority (1987) 16 *Philosophy and Public Affairs* 303, 312ff). Loosely in the vein of specific convergence, partly by invoking a *contrast* with 'coordination' narrowly understood, see further D Regan, 'Authority and Value: Reflections on Raz's *Morality of Freedom*' (1989) 62 *Southern California Law Review* 995, 1003ff; D Regan, 'Law's Halo' (1986) 4 *Social Philosophy and Policy* 15, 16ff; WA Edmundson, 'Social Meaning, Compliance Conditions, and Law's Claim to Authority' (2002) 15 *Canadian Journal of Law and Jurisprudence* 51; WA Edmundson, 'Political Authority, Moral Powers and the Intrinsic Value of Obedience' (2010) 30 *Oxford Journal of Legal Studies* 179; A Marmor, *Social Conventions: From Language to Law* (Princeton, NJ, Princeton University Press, 2009) especially ch 7; S Shapiro, *Legality* (Cambridge, MA, Harvard University Press, 2009) especially chs 5 and 6; R Harrison, 'The Moral Role of Conventions' in JB Murphy and A Perreau-Saussine, *The Nature of Customary Law: Legal, Historical and Philosophical Perspectives* (Cambridge, Cambridge University Press, 2007); M Greenberg, 'The Moral Impact Theory of Law' (2014) 123 *Yale Law Journal* 1288, 1310–09.

Under-determination by Reason

For helpful developments of this sound meta-ethical stance, including conceptions of incommensurability, see Raz, *The Morality of Freedom*, ch 13; Finnis, *Natural Law and Natural Rights*, n 1, 111–18; J Finnis, *Fundamentals of Ethics* (Washington, DC, Georgetown University Press, 1983) 86–94; J Finnis, *Reason in Action, Collected Essays: Volume I* (Oxford, Oxford University Press, 2011) ch 15; T Endicott, *Vagueness in Law*

(Oxford, Oxford University Press, 2000), especially chs 3 and 7; R Chang, 'Introduction' in R Chang (ed), *Incommensurability, Incomparability, and Practical Reason* (Cambridge, MA, Harvard University Press, 1997); cf R Dworkin, *Justice for Hedgehogs* (Cambridge, MA, Belknap Press, 2011) ch 5. On the self-refuting or at best implausible character of sceptical denials that rational, objective and true ('moral') judgements can be made about what is good or worthwhile in human life, see eg Finnis, *Natural Law and Natural Rights*, n 1, chs 3 and 4; Finnis, *Fundamentals of Ethics*, ch 3, especially 60 and 63–66; Finnis, *Reason in Action*, chs 3 and 4; Dworkin, *Justice for Hedgehogs*, chs 2–4. Against a broadly 'consequentialist' conception of human good as essentially amenable to being measured, aggregated and transitively ranked (and in this sense commensurable), see J Rawls, *A Theory of Justice* (Cambridge, MA, Harvard University Press, 1971) especially 19–30; Finnis, *Natural Law and Natural Rights*, n 1, 111–18; and further R Nozick, *Anarchy, State, and Utopia* (New York, Basic Books, 1974) ch 3. On the diversity of aspects of human well-being, including self-direction, see, eg, Raz, *The Morality of Freedom*, especially chs 14 and 15; Finnis, *Natural Law and Natural Rights*, n 1, especially chs 3–5.

Section III: The Scope of Specific Convergence

'Human Rights' Broadly Coextensive with Justice in Community

This sense of 'human rights' is relied on and developed in, eg, Webber et al, *Legislated Rights*, n 3; J Tasioulas, 'On the Nature of Human Rights' in G Ernst and J-C Heilinger (eds), *The Philosophy of Human Rights: Contemporary Controversies* (Berlin, Walter de Gruyter, 2012) especially 43–56; J Tasioulas, 'Human Rights, Legitimacy, and International Law' (2013) 58 *The American Journal of Jurisprudence* 1, especially 8–13; J Waldron, 'Human Rights: A Critique of the Raz/Rawls Approach' in A Etinson (ed), *Human Rights: Moral or Political?* (Oxford, Oxford University Press, 2018). For narrower or partly cross-cutting senses of 'human rights', as considerations serving distinctly 'political' roles, and/or justifying certain kinds of intervention by a state in the affairs of another, see, eg, J Rawls, *The Law of Peoples* (Cambridge, MA, Harvard University Press, 1999); C Beitz, *The Idea of Human Rights* (Oxford, Oxford University Press, 2009); J Raz, 'Human Rights Without Foundations' in S Besson and J Tasioulas (eds), *The Philosophy of International Law* (Oxford, Oxford University Press, 2010).

Mala in Se, Mala Prohibita

For arguments that fairly preventing *mala in se* calls for under-determined social arrangements, M Boardman, 'Coordination and the Moral Obligation to Obey the Law' (1987) 97 *Ethics* 546; J Penner, 'Legal Reasoning and the Authority of Law' in LH Meyer, SL Paulson and TW Pogge (eds), *Rights, Culture and the Law: Themes from the Legal and Political Philosophy of Joseph Raz* (Oxford, Oxford University Press, 2003) 73; Y Simon, *A General Theory of Authority* (Notre Dame, IN, University of Notre Dame Press, 1980) 41; and Finnis, *Natural Law and Natural Rights*, n 1, 281ff; on Aquinas' original phrasing ('*mala quia prohibita*') see ibid, fn 34 at 334. See also Besson, *The Morality of Conflict*, 200ff; Waldron, *Law and Disagreement*, 105ff: both authors speak of 'controversial' rather than underdetermined aspects. On the distinct significance, for fair warning, of an offence being *mala in se*, see J Gardner, *Offences and Defences: Selected Essays in the Philosophy of Criminal Law* (Oxford, Oxford University Press, 2007) 29; and J Gardner, J Horder and S Shute, 'Introduction: The Logic of Criminal Law' in J Gardner, J Horder and S Shute (eds), *Action and Value in Criminal Law* (Oxford, Clarendon Press, 1994) 1, 10–11.

Section IV: Marking and Enforcing

Tackling the Problem of Lack of Information

For an argument that often all that will be needed is to make the group aware *that* a commonly perceived need can be furthered through convergent conduct, see Raz, 'Facing Up', 1190; Raz, 'Introduction' in Raz (ed), *Authority*, 9; Raz, 'Comments and Responses', 259; also L Green, 'Three Themes from Raz' (2005) 25 *Oxford Journal of Legal Studies* 503, 511; L Green, 'The Duty to Govern' (2007) 13 *Legal Theory* 165, 177; unfortunately no examples are provided.

Marking and Enforcement

Ross ('On the Concepts "State" and "State Organs" in Constitutional Law' (1961) 5 *Scandinavian Studies in Law* 111, 116ff, especially 121) casts this distinction in terms of two senses of 'power' capturing, respectively, 'acts-in-law' and 'factual acts' attributed to 'the state' as part of 'the same systematic unity'. For a related distinction, Besson, *The Morality of Conflict*, 186; Waldron, *Law and Disagreement*, 104.

Section VI: Two Levels of Convergence

Two Levels of Convergence in Law

For a similar distinction, T Endicott, 'The Subsidiarity of Law and the Obligation to Obey' (2005) 50 *American Journal of Jurisprudence* 233, 237–38; for partly overlapping and intersecting distinctions, Postema, 'Coordination and Convention at the Foundations of Law'; Besson, *The Morality of Conflict*, 186ff.

Hart's 'Rule of Recognition'

This book's portrait of a secondary convergent practice of identification of law may be regarded as continuous with Hart's doctrine of the 'rule of recognition' (Hart, *The Concept of Law*, n 7, ch 6) insofar as the latter speaks of a rule whose existence is 'a matter of fact' (ibid 110), which provides the 'supreme criterion' of the validity of the system's rules (ibid 106), and which is 'appropriate for identifying law' (ibid 108, 95) precisely because (like the 'standard metre bar in Paris', ibid 109) it is widely and saliently so treated in an aggregative, *interdependent* practice: it is 'regarded … as a public, common standard of correct judicial decision, and not as something which each judge merely obeys for his part only' (ibid 115, 117). The 'rule of recognition', says Hart, provides certainty to anyone wishing to identify valid law (ibid 94); certainty being a 'social need' (ibid 130). And 'though [the rule of recognition] must exist now, [it] may in a sense be timeless in its reference' (ibid 62; also 63, 65), which distinguishes it from targeted *conferrals* of legal power that characteristically refer to future valid action. For a helpful distinction between a 'semantic' and an 'epistemic' sense of a 'rule of recognition', consistent with this book's claims about validity as a technique for marking, see J Coleman, 'Positive and Negative Positivism' in M Cohen (ed), *Ronald Dworkin and Contemporary Jurisprudence* (London, Duckworth, 1984) 29; J Coleman, 'Incorporationism, Conventionality, and the Practical Difference Thesis' in J Coleman (ed), *Hart's Postscript: Essays on the Postscript to the Concept of Law* (Oxford, Oxford University Press, 2001) 137ff; but I do not share Coleman's view about the theoretical relevance of this distinction (for criticism, S Shapiro, 'Law, Morality, and the Guidance of Conduct' (2000) 6 *Legal Theory* 127, 149ff).

Hart's 'Rule of Recognition' in the Literature

Elaborations of Hart's views that I do not wish to import into my analysis fall into four broad groups. The first group is the most extensive one. It sees in the 'rule of recognition' an (additional) *duty-imposing* character. This reading was originally proposed by Raz (*Practical Reason and Norms*, 146ff; J Raz, *The Authority of Law: Essays on Law and Morality* (Oxford, Oxford University Press, 1979) 91ff; also MacCormick, *H.L.A. Hart*, n 8, 105ff), and there is some textual support for it in Hart's original account (for one thing, his characterisation of 'social rules' suggests that they are duty-imposing (*The Concept of Law*, n 7, 54–57) and he relates the 'rule of recognition' to that analysis (ibid 57ff, 109); for another thing, he writes that '[the rule of recognition] will specify some feature or features possession of which by a suggested rule is taken as conclusive affirmative indication that it is a rule of the group *to be supported by the social pressure it exerts*' (ibid 94, emphasis added; also ibid 108, 110)). But neither Hart nor Raz spells out the nature of this duty arising from the fact of convergence. Hart arguably does not offer a complete account of 'social' duty-imposing rules (L Green, 'The Concept of Law Revisited' (1996) 94 *Michigan Law Review* 1687, 1694; Green, 'Positivism and Conventionalism', 37; J Dickson, 'Is the Rule of Recognition Really a Conventional Rule?' (2007) 27 *Oxford Journal of Legal Studies* 1, 379ff; cf Raz, *Practical Reason and Norms*, 55ff); and Raz, in turn, takes the idea that judges are under a 'duty to apply existing norms' as an unexplained premise in a range of arguments, including arguments for the centrality of 'primary' law-applying institutions (Raz, *The Authority of Law*, 87ff, 125ff), arguments for the distinction between new and existing law (ibid 90, 93, 95; Raz, *Practical Reason and Norms*, 131, 142), and arguments for characterising institutionalised normative systems as distinct from systems of absolute discretion (ibid 137ff) (in a similar spirit, MacCormick, *H.L.A. Hart*, n 8, 111ff; N MacCormick, *Legal Reasoning and Legal Theory* (Oxford, Oxford University Press, 1978) 242; N MacCormick, 'The Concept of Law and *The Concept of Law*', n 8, 179ff). It has been suggested, implausibly, that explaining how the 'rule of recognition' is duty-imposing is tantamount to explaining (the vague idea of) law's 'normativity'. A prominent line of argument, encouraged by the late Hart's claim that the 'rule of recognition' is 'conventional' (*The Concept of Law*, n 7, 255ff), holds that the convergence of official behaviour is a Lewisian 'convention'

(Lewis, *Convention*, n 5, 1969) and gives rise to obligations on its participants simply on the basis of their mutual reliance: see, eg, Postema, 'Coordination and Convention at the Foundations of Law', 179ff; Coleman, 'Incorporationism, Conventionality', 117ff; for criticism, Green, 'Positivism and Conventionalism', 40ff; Dickson, 'Is the Rule of Recognition Really a Conventional Rule?'. This argument must not be confused with the more modest claim that the fact of convergence provides 'part of the reason' for someone to join: Dickson (ibid 383ff) and Coleman ('Incorporationanism, Conventionality', 119) deny that Hart was committed even to that modest claim (cf J Gardner, 'Reasons for Teamwork' (2002) 8 *Legal Theory* 495, fn 7 at 500). The second group of elaborations regard the 'rule of recognition' as a complex pattern of (Bratmanian) cooperative activity or teamwork amongst officials that is necessary or sufficient for, or typical of, the existence of legal systems: see, eg, Coleman, *The Practice of Principle*, n 8, 90ff; S Shapiro, 'Law, Plans, and Practical Reason' (2002) 8 *Legal Theory* 387; for criticism, J Gardner, *Law as a Leap of Faith* (Oxford, Oxford University Press, 2012) 72–74. The third group of elaborations regard the 'rule of recognition' as the historically contingent set of facts and dispositions that 'constitute' a legal system as a 'social practice' different from other social practices like games, artistic genres or etiquette: see especially Marmor, *Social Conventions*, ch 2 and 7; for criticism, Köpcke, 'Positive Law's Moral Purpose(s): Towards a New Consensus?' 199–200. A fourth group of elaborations regards the 'rule of recognition' as a mere ex post facto record of regularities in official behaviour with no action-guiding force: see, eg, CE Alchourrón and E Bulygin, *Normative Systems* (New York, Springer, 1971) fn 2 at 73; Caracciolo, *La Noción de Sistema*, n 8, 75–76.

5

Reasons to Empower

TO SAY THAT *law* is capable of realising justice, in the ways charted in the previous chapter, is a somewhat elliptical way of talking.[1] Law is made and unmade, applied, invoked, altered and exploited by human beings. To say that law is, or that communities are, able to foster well-being by saliently *marking* courses of conduct required and fairly *enforcing* them is ultimately to say that persons marking and enforcing in the name of the law have that capacity, in acting within a legal system. The ability to *mark* in the law's name, in particular, is relatively widespread – at least in reasonably just communities that have no room for slavery or other perverse limitations of legal personhood. The ability to mark in the law's name is held by all those who can perform legally valid acts. We refer to that ability as a kind of power: legal power.

We noted in the previous chapter that, in many contexts, individual conduct only becomes genuinely apt to serve the well-being of others, and therefore morally due, in being part of a larger convergent scheme, such as a working traffic order indicating when and where one is to slow or stop, or an operative system of redistribution allocating benefits and burdens in specific terms. By acting as part of such a scheme, that is, by doing what the scheme requires one to do, one can foster well-being in a particularly apt, and therefore necessary, way. It could therefore also be said that, in *this* sense, a just scheme of convergence bestows on individuals power. It gives them, in certain respects, an ability they did not have before, namely an ability to advance justice through concrete forms of conduct that in the absence of the relevant scheme would be largely ineffective to that end, if not pernicious. When we speak of the ability to *mark*, we do not refer to this ability. The ability to mark is not, per se, the ability involved in discharging a specified moral duty. It is the ability to specify it in the first place. It is the ability to craft moral duties and rights, by generating morally needed convergence. In performing a valid act, for example enacting a tax statute, one is not (merely) at the receiving end of duties and rights but at the authoring end. One is able, through one's say-so, to enable others and oneself to foster well-being. One is able, by choosing soundly, to shape not only legal but also moral duties and rights. One has the power, as it were, to craft justice.

Legal power should not be unreasonably withheld or withdrawn from certain kinds of persons and institutions. But it does not follow that they should

[1] Ch 6.V explains why it is not wholly elliptical.

all have a similarly broad power to decide about similar kinds of questions. Justice requires that legal power be appropriately *allocated*, and hence that it be bestowed on certain agents for certain purposes, and limited for certain others. There are cogent considerations of justice speaking to *who* is best placed to decide about what, within the confines of a legal order. These considerations, these reasons to empower, are the subject of this chapter. They include expertise, proximity, the Rule of Law and the value of self-direction. They bear on matters as diverse as administrative structure, separation of powers, freedom of contract, prosecutorial discretion, the place of rulings, judicial review, common law and legislative modes of law-making, and democratic self-government. The remit of this chapter is not to settle all the complex questions that may surround the application of these considerations. It is to demonstrate how the technique of validity is key to settling them. The technique of validity, properly used, is a refined device for the allocation of power. Or so this chapter argues.

In so doing, this chapter pursues and deepens the argument concerning how the technique of legal validity, studied in chapters 2 and 3, can help persons and groups attain what chapter 4 has argued justice calls for.

I. EMPOWERMENT

But before we consider reasons to empower, we must home in on the very idea of *empowerment*.

We have invoked the idea of legal power from early on in the book. And yet our discussion of it so far has been simplified in focus. In particular, the last chapter's discussion of marking predominantly envisaged legally valid decisions by single persons or institutions at discrete points in time – such as legislatures enacting tax statutes, or individuals making conveyances. Validity was presented as an appropriate grammar to saliently mark the decisions in question. Possible restrictions on the agent's legal power, whether procedural or substantive, were generically put down to the governing legal regime. It is that *legal* regime of which we took account in formulating the technique of legal power, in chapter 3, in terms of a normative change brought about by *legally* manifesting one's intent, if and to the extent *the law* provides for this possibility.

We should now put a face on this legal regime. This requires turning our glance upwards rather than downwards, as it were. It requires considering not that which is rendered valid, but that which renders it so. It requires appreciating how legal power is *conferred* on one.

Legal power is a curious kind of ability. Unlike natural abilities, it is not inherent in the subject. It must be bestowed on one. One must be *em*-powered in order to exercise legal power. So legal power is a vicarious, derivative ability. What does it derive *from*? Most immediately, from an empowerment. An empowerment is a kind of act. It is an act of someone who confers legal power, typically on *another*. For example, the default speed limit for urban roads throughout the

Spanish state is 50 km/h. But the Spanish Government has empowered the City Council of Barcelona to set a reduced speed limit for certain areas in the city.[2] In exercise of this power, the Barcelona City Council has validly set the speed limit for Barcelonese residential streets at 20 km/h.[3] The empowerment by the Spanish Government is a decision in the form 'let X decide'. This decision is itself a legally valid act. It is itself an exercise of legal power. It changes legal positions. The legal positions it changes are legal powers. It changes the legal powers of city councils. They become empowered to decide by the Government's saying that they are. So the Spanish Government exercises its own legal power to regulate traffic (in turn conferred by the legislature)[4] to the effect of conferring legal power on city councils. The Government makes a choice concerning who is to choose.

The germ of the idea of empowerment lies in letting somebody's decision occupy a place it would not otherwise occupy. Occupying this place is bound up with fulfilling certain conditions. There are constraints on what the empowered decision can be *about*, and *how* it is to be taken, if it is to occupy the relevant place. The Spanish Government empowers the Barcelona City Council to set a speed limit, with the constraints (inter alia) that the 50 km/h figure is not exceeded and that the City Council acts within its territorial sphere. Only by fulfilling these constraints can the City Council's decision be legally valid. It will otherwise be ultra vires – in principle void. Fulfilling applicable constraints enables the City Council to do something it could otherwise not afford. In conferring legal power, the Spanish Government creates the possibility for the City Council to change legal duties of drivers. Note that it creates this possibility in part by limiting what the City Council can do. In this sense, the constraints, we might say, themselves are empowering.

These kinds of constraints are familiar to us by now. They are criteria of legal validity. So is the determination of *who* is to choose, and hence whom the constraints are incumbent *on*. The idea of legal empowerment is inseparable from the idea of criteria of legal validity. Legal validity is a technique for empowerment. It reflects the more or less explicit, more or less targeted, choices of certain agents concerning who is to choose about what and how.

It is worth reflecting briefly on the nature of these choices, and in particular on the nature of the fundamental *choice concerning who is to choose*. We have been looking at an ordinary example from the domain of administrative law. There are many empowerments in that domain. The modern bureaucratic state

[2] Real Decreto 1428/2003, 21 de noviembre, por el que se aprueba el Reglamento General de Circulación, art 50(1); Real Decreto Legislativo 339/1990, de 2 de marzo, por el que se aprueba el texto articulado de la Ley sobre Tráfico, Circulación de Vehículos a Motor y Seguridad Vial, art 19(3).

[3] Ordenança de Circulació de Vianants i de Vehicles, Acord del Consell Plenari de l'Ajuntament de Barcelona, de 27 de novembre de 1999, art 11(3).

[4] Ley 18/1989, de 25 de julio, de Bases sobre Tráfico, Circulación de Vehículos a Motor y Seguridad Vial.

brings many layers of executive decision-making. Some of these empowerments we can and do naturally refer to as mere *delegations*, implying that the agent who confers a power might as well have exercised the power himself. It may be under-determined, as a matter of justice, whether the central government should set mandatory speed limits for the whole state, or let regional authorities modulate them. It may be under-determined which regional authorities should be able to effect the modulation. As a matter of law, the Spanish Government certainly did have the power to set mandatory speed limits itself, but instead it chose to delegate to city councils. In this kind of case, a case of simple delegation, one transfers one's own capacity to decide about something almost in the way one transfers one's own capacity to open a door by lending a key. This kind of case has a rough equivalent in the field of private law, when an individual confers powers of attorney on another for the latter to perform, on behalf of the former, a transaction that the former was, and remains, legally qualified to effect. Morally speaking, it may well be a matter of indifference who performs the transaction.

But the nature of many choices enshrined in legal empowerments is profoundly different. It morally matters who is empowered to select the members of a legislature, as between citizens casting valid votes in general elections or government officials validly appointing legislators according to rules providing for a hereditary legislative cast. It morally matters who is empowered to issue criminal sentencing rulings, as between courts, prosecutors or administrative agencies. In these and many like scenarios, it is a question of justice who should to decide about what. Sound empowerments will allocate legal power accordingly. They will legally circumscribe what certain agents can decide about, and can in turn legally empower others to settle. Sound legal empowerments may, in important respects, be neither legally nor morally under-determined. Thus, when the legislature enacts electoral legislation specifying which categories of citizens are empowered to vote, it does not thereby confer on citizens a power that the legislature could, as a matter of law, have exercised itself (or conferred on the government) in a country with a constitutionally entrenched democratic system. Nor does the legislature, in establishing the judiciary's governing body, which will appoint judges in turn, thereby transfer to the judiciary a power it could itself exercise, as a matter of law, compatibly with the constitutional principle of separation of powers.[5] Such empowerments could not reasonably have been otherwise in the respects just noted, although no doubt there will be plenty of room left for morally under-determined choice in specifying the particulars of these empowerments, such as voting requirements, the boundaries of the criminal and administrative jurisdiction of courts, and countless procedural

[5] In Spain, the Ley Orgánica 6/1985, de 1 de julio, del Poder Judicial, empowers the Consejo General del Poder Judicial to appoint judges by issuing relevant orders (art 316(1)); in the UK, the Constitutional Reform Act 2005 (UK), pt 4, makes analogous provision concerning the Judicial Appointments Commission.

provisions – all of which may need, in justice, to be specified, but could reasonably take on different shapes.

Legal empowerments are key devices to allocate the responsibility to decide to those who, in justice, ought to bear it. An allocation of legal power can be effected in two main, complementary ways. First, valid decisions may be *postponed* where, as in the examples just mentioned, agents who are not well placed to decide empower those who are. And, secondly, once a decision has been taken by an appropriate agent, other agents may be appropriately precluded from *re-opening* that decision – so that, for instance, judges lack the power to review the content of electoral outcomes, and governments lack a general power to commute criminal sentences.

Either way, criteria of legal validity are the primary tools to make and secure allocations of legal power.[6] Criteria of validity bearing on and so shaping an allocation of legal power will often be set out in a range of different legal sources, themselves changing over time, as the next chapter brings out. Even the Barcelona City Council's exercise of legal power to set a 20 km/h speed limit is subject to an intricate set of validity criteria additional to the constraints explicitly set by the Spanish Government's regulation, including, most obviously, provisions governing general[7] and municipal[8] administrative procedure, and those determining any acts of appointment and terms of office on which the competence of all persons involved must trade.[9] Only a simplistic understanding of empowerment, associated with a narrow image of delegation, would ignore the typically manifold set of legal provisions and doctrines *in the context of which* specific acts of empowerment – determining who is to choose – genuinely acquire power-*conferring* import. Kelsen's spatial metaphor of a *hierarchy* or chain of power-conferring *norms*, made up of as many links as acts of empowerment,[10]

[6] There are other tools. They include broadly framed powers coupled with legal duties (not) to use those powers in certain ways; on the difference between invalidity and prohibition, ch 2.IV and corresponding final note; see further J Raz, *Ethics in the Public Domain: Essays in the Morality of Law and Politics*, rev edn (Oxford, Clarendon Press, 1995) 241ff on the related idea of 'directed powers'.

[7] Especially Ley 39/2015, de 1 de octubre, del Procedimiento Administrativo Común de las Administraciones Públicas.

[8] Including Ley 7/1985, de 2 de abril, Reguladora de las Bases del Régimen Local; Llei 22/1998, de 30 de desembre, de la Carta Municipal de Barcelona, especially arts 8–19; and Reglament Orgànic de l'Ajuntament de Barcelona, de 16 de febrer de 2001, especially arts 66–91.

[9] The original empowerment speaks of 'the competent organ of the municipal corporation' (Real Decreto Legislativo 339/1990, art 19(3)). In turn, Ley 1/2006, de 13 de marzo, del Régimen Especial del Municipio de Barcelona, art 18, specifies that the Barcelona City Council is competent to regulate traffic through municipal ordinances; ordinances, per Ley 7/1985, Reguladora de las Bases del Régimen Local, art 22(2)(d), are issued by city councillors in plenary session; in Barcelona, the relevant body, per Llei 22/1998, de la Carta Municipal de Barcelona, arts 10 and 11, is the Municipal Council.

[10] H Kelsen, *General Theory of Law and State*, A Wedberg (tr) (New York, Russell, 1945) 123ff; also H Kelsen, *The Pure Theory of Law*, 2nd edn, Max Knight (tr) (Berkeley, CA, University of California Press, 1967) 221ff.

still resonates in jurisprudential work and is liable to disguise the important sense in which only the *totality* of considerations that shape an agent's legal power, partly by limiting it, are aptly thought of as constituting a power-conferring *norm*, capable of relevantly guiding the agent's exercise.

For legal power is a vicarious ability not only because its exercise presupposes an act of empowerment, typically made by someone else, but also, more fundamentally still, because that immediate act of empowerment can only allocate power against the background of a wider network of criteria-setting acts and practices that jointly define the legal significance – the legal meaning – of what can validly be done. Criteria-setting acts, in turn, may specify criteria in a focally targeted fashion, by establishing binding precedent on point, or even just by adding up to a binding official custom. They may explicitly refer to a given empowerment act or be implicit in generic constraints framed, for example, in open-ended human rights language. But as between all the different kinds of act that go to shape validity criteria, and all the different kinds of criteria shaped thereby, acts of empowerment harbour and give expression to the choice central to an allocation of power, the choice that other criteria of validity inevitably presuppose and more or less latently anticipate: the choice that *someone* is to decide about something. At the end of the day, the existence of acts of empowerment is what accounts for the fact that it is *many of us, severally,* who can exercise legal power in a legal order. So criteria of validity are tools for the allocation of legal power, because and through their diverse relationships to the pivotal question of who should decide about what.

The answers to this question I call reasons to empower. They are the considerations of justice that bear on the right allocation of power, and therefore the considerations of justice that sound criteria of legal validity will reflect and advance. They represent the many respects in which criteria of legal validity are not morally under-determined and therefore do not have reasonable alternatives. They are the considerations that those setting, shaping and construing validity criteria are not morally entitled to ignore, on pain of facilitating in law what should be precluded in justice, or precluding in law what morally deserves free rein.

I group reasons to empower into four broad kinds, although this disregards some important nuances and involves a degree of overlap. This grouping has the advantage of demonstrating how analogous considerations of justice bear on uses of validity in otherwise disparate areas of law and modes of law-making, which might accordingly benefit from being brought into closer connection in relevant doctrinal and jurisprudential discussion. Needless to say, any given reason to empower is interchangeably a reason *not* to empower certain *other* kinds of agent. And sometimes one and the same reason points both ways. Different reasons, in turn, may conflict. In fact, some of these conflicts, as we shall see, poignantly illustrate the kinds of compromise one may have to take in one's stride, the kinds of dilemmas one might have to face and live with, when engaged in that cardinal but often inconspicuous enterprise of choosing who is to choose.

The four kinds of reason to empower are:

- expertise and capacity;
- proximity;
- the Rule of Law; and
- self-direction.

The following sections discuss each of these reasons in turn. I devote most attention to the third reason, not because it is weightier than the others, but because its variegated implications for questions of institutional design and law-making methods are all too often overlooked. The fourth reason, in a sense, yields the foundation for the others.

II. EXPERTISE AND CAPACITY

An habitual reason to empower is the relative expertise of certain agents, that is, their better ability to figure out certain facts in virtue of their special resources, training or skill. Expertise is an important reason to allocate power as between public authorities, and many administrative empowerments are soundly grounded on this premise. The nature, set-up and resources of administrative organs can facilitate access to specialist bodies of knowledge that are in many ways beyond the reach of the legislature and the judiciary, not least for reasons of time. A legislature may also do well to leave certain aspects of legal rules vague, thereby empowering judges to fine-tune and bring them into step with common law doctrines, seeing as the latter are the judges' tools of the trade. But broader considerations of expertise, especially non-legal expertise, may warrant judges in turn deferring to the judgement of other public authorities whose decisions the judges are called on to review.[11]

Expertise is also relevant to empowerments between private individuals. The need for legal expertise, for example, can justify the requirement that a person be represented by a lawyer in performing certain valid acts in the framework of court proceedings. Particularly in the domain of private relationships, however, relative expertise need not be great in absolute terms. And it often goes hand in hand with relative *capacity* to decide, which is the general ability to make choices unimpaired by manipulation, impulse or fear. Thus parents or guardians

[11] A Vermeule (*Law and the Limits of Reason* (Oxford, Oxford University Press, 2009)) has developed an argument for the codification of constitutional law based on, primarily, a well-working legislature's 'epistemic superiority' vis-à-vis courts.

are rightly empowered to take certain decisions on behalf of young or disabled persons. And implied contractual terms may appropriately withhold from parties the legal discretion to negotiate particulars on subject-matters regarding which one side to the deal characteristically lacks both sufficient information and bargaining power: for instance, concerning safety standards and other unwaivable rights in transport, the workplace or the sale of goods. Regulative power may be correspondingly vested in dedicated bodies or structures, such as trade unions or consumer protection agencies. Relative bargaining power may likewise be a reason *not* to empower certain kinds of market actors to enter agreements or mergers, or otherwise legally approach or seize a dominant position, as in sound antitrust regimes.

III. PROXIMITY

Persons may have privileged access to information not on grounds of special resources, training or skill, but simply on grounds of their proximity to relevant facts. Proximity is normally geographical, or otherwise such that it facilitates a privileged acquaintance with a particular environment. Social service officers of a person's neighbourhood are in a better position to tailor specific forms of assistance to a person's needs than are government bureaucrats responsible for the city, region or country at large. Not least in federal states, proximity weighs in favour of local decision-making on matters on which local considerations ought centrally to bear: this is often indistinguishable from respect for the initiative of self-government (section VII). Proximity is also a major reason supporting judicial specification of statutory standards justifiably left vague to that very end, which specification may be either for general purposes or only for the case at hand.

Can acquaintance with an environment ever be a reason *not* to empower? It can, where it could be a source of bias. Legal systems typically channel this concern through, amongst other things, a procedural split between pre-trial and trial phases of a criminal process, and appeal stages associated with different judicial ranks. A sound recusal system will moreover take account of conflicts of interest, and hence of sources of bias arising from proximity of a personal or economic kind with the parties in dispute or the disputed subject-matter (*nemo judex in sua causa*). Conflict of interest, in this sense, can recommend judicial oversight of certain decisions by parents or guardians, which would otherwise be appropriately incumbent on them on grounds of desirable proximity and relative expertise. And broader considerations of impartiality may weigh strongly in favour of review of certain kinds of executive or legislative decision by genuinely independent judicial organs, not least in human rights cases.[12]

[12] For an argument, T Endicott, 'Proportionality and Incommensurability' in G Huscroft, BW Miller and G Webber (eds), *Proportionality and the Rule of Law: Rights, Justification, Reasoning* (Cambridge, Cambridge University Press, 2014).

IV. THE RULE OF LAW: RULINGS

If empowerments were only sensitive to considerations of relative expertise and proximity, decision-making processes would be extravagantly many and disproportionately protracted. Imagine empowering local experts to validly establish, on a case-by-case basis, whether individuals are sufficiently mature and of sound mind to vote in general elections – as opposed to setting a general minimum voting age. Or imagine empowering tax collectors to calibrate our tax dues to reflect as accurately as possible the particular vicissitudes of our financial capacity – as opposed to having tax bands and other rules governing broad categories of cases. In these and countless other predicaments, a loss of bespoke tailoring is outweighed by the expediency of fewer decisions (and less potential appeals). But there is more than a sheer gain in expediency. A distinct set of requirements of justice speaks to the need for predictable and consistent legal operation on the basis of reasonably clear and stable *rules*, that is, *general* provisions, thereby minimising the extent to which a person's fate is determined by the sheer, legally uncontrolled whim of another. We sum up these requirements of justice under the heading 'the Rule of Law'.

It is well understood that the Rule of Law furnishes reasons to have general legal provisions, and to entrust the crafting of these general provisions to institutions that are capable of doing so in clear, stable, coherent, prospective and public ('promulgated') fashion. Section VI of this chapter will briefly comment on why legislatures especially, though not exclusively, are in a good position to fulfil this task. On its face, the well-known ('most complex') eighth requirement on Fuller's list, that of 'congruence between official action and declared rule',[13] complements those earlier requirements by directing that those general provisions be honoured in fact by 'official action' of a narrowly executive sort, that is, by the way the law is (in Fuller's words) 'actually administered' – so that, say, officials *do* seize our person or property, allocate resources, or otherwise facilitate or constrain our moves, and do so *only* if and as authorised by clear, stable, coherent, prospective and public general rules.

But there is implicit in the call for congruence, and in several of the other requirements, the need for distinct kinds of act that amount to particular official decisions. These particular decisions are the object of this section and the next. They are valid *decisions* as opposed to mere acts of physical enforcement. But they are decisions with a *particular* rather than a general scope: they focally concern named individuals. The Rule of Law calls for such decisions. They are not, as is sometimes assumed, a necessary evil from the point of view of the Rule of Law, an evil that the Rule of Law itself can help mitigate.[14] There is, in

[13] L Fuller, *The Morality of Law*, 2nd edn (New Haven, CT, Yale University Press, 1969) 81ff.

[14] According to Raz (*The Authority of Law: Essays on Law and Morality* (Oxford, Oxford University Press, 1979) 215–16), for example, 'particular legal orders' by 'government agencies' (such as 'a licensing authority granting a licence under certain conditions') 'are among the more ephemeral

other words, an apparent paradox in the requirements of the Rule of Law. The Rule of Law furnishes reasons to empower officials to make decisions that, being particular rather than general, appear to contravene a core desideratum of the Rule of Law.

I call these particular decisions *rulings*. The kinds of rulings needed include, of course, judicial settlements of disputes. Fuller, for one, presents the requirement of congruence as chiefly incumbent on judges. But the necessary kinds of rulings are not limited to settlements of disputes, nor indeed to decisions by judges. There are administrative rulings as well: for example planning licences, patents and social benefit awards. Some rulings concern what citizens may or may not do; other rulings concern what officials may or may not do. Some rulings authorise certain conduct ahead of its occurrence; other rulings determine whether certain past conduct was lawful or unlawful. What unites all these different kinds of decision is that their general point is to *apply* rather than to create law.

The idea of application of law is somewhat nebulous. We know what it means to apply hand cream, but it is less conspicuous just what it means to apply law. We sometimes speak of the application of law to mean its physical implementation or 'actual administration'. In this sense, officials breaking up a demonstration or arresting a suspect are applying the law. But it is more conducive to clear thinking to say that these officials are *enforcing* the law, and to pay heed to the important sense in which applying the law is equivalent to *employing* or *deploying* it.[15] The officers in our examples deploy tear gas and handcuffs, but they do not in the same sense deploy laws. They do not use laws as tools in accomplishing their endeavour. This is because, by their nature, laws – rules, propositions of law – are apt to be used as tools only in reasoning endeavours. These endeavours are judgements premised on the existence of certain laws and concluding, in light of certain facts, that the legal positions of certain persons are such-and-such. Hence applications of law are rather mundane occurrences. Your tax advisor might quite intelligibly say, 'Applying the new tax decree, your duties are as follows'. Law students may be challenged to solve a hypothetical case by applying English (or Roman, or a freshly enacted, or an imaginary …) law.

And yet not all applications of law, in this sense, are rulings. The judgements of the tax advisor and the students are not legally valid. They do not determine the application of law in a binding way. They are not official. The general point of rulings is to apply the law officially.

In saying that the general point of rulings is to *apply* the law officially I am not denying that rulings must sometimes, in fact often, supplement the law

parts of the law' and 'as such they run counter to the basic idea of the rule of law' because 'they make it difficult for people to plan ahead', though this difficulty can be 'overcome to a large extent' through a legal framework regulating their enactment.

[15] This sense of 'application' is particularly evident in the German term '*Anwendung*'.

they apply. Both judges and licensing officers may need to exercise legal discretion to the extent the law they are to apply has gaps. There are good reasons to empower judges and others makers of rulings to provide definite solutions even where the law runs out. And there are good reasons not to seek to procedurally segregate their application of law from their supplementation of it – not least because the complexity of legal meaning may frequently make it indeterminate, and at any rate controversial, *whether*, and if so to what extent, the relevant law has a gap.[16] The general point of rulings is to apply the law, and therefore sometimes to supplement it as a by-product of applying it. This distinguishes rulings from many other kinds of legally valid decision we have been discussing, in which the decision-maker may likewise exercise legal discretion. An administrative agency empowered to specify particulars of tax liability, left open by a tax statute, exercises discretion in doing so. If it issued a decree that merely replicated what is already provided in the statute, without supplementing it, this would defeat the reasons for empowering the agency. The point of empowering the agency in this way is that it supplements the law. But *there remain good reasons* to empower judges and licensing officers to issue rulings even where the applicable law has no gaps.

These reasons are chiefly reasons arising from the Rule of Law. But not all kinds of rulings are warranted by the same kinds of Rule of Law reason. There are two broadly different ways in which rulings may be called on to apply the law, and this distinction helps in appraising important aspects of the design of modern legal systems. I shall mark this distinction by speaking of declarative and constitutive rulings.[17] It is possible for either kind of ruling not to involve discretion. The general point of both kinds of ruling is to apply the law, in the above sense. But these kinds of ruling have a different specific point. The specific point of declarative rulings is to officially ascertain legal positions that exist *independently* of the ruling, whereas the specific point of constitutive rulings is to authorise or require the performance of some conduct that *but for* the ruling would not be authorised or required.

An example will help to clarify the distinction. It is perhaps best illustrated by a familiar case in which *both* kinds of rulings ought to occur in ordered sequence. A criminal judge determines that the suspect committed an offence, and sentences him to imprisonment. The determination that the crime was committed is a declarative ruling, because crimes are committed independently

[16] On the need for judicial supplementation of existing law by 'reconciling conflicts amongst incommensurable values', as a requirement of the Rule of Law, Endicott, 'Proportionality and Incommensurability', n 12; see further, J Grant, 'The Scales of Authority' (2015) 60 *The American Journal of Jurisprudence* 79; and section V of this chapter.

[17] For a similar distinction, confined to the domain of court orders in private litigation, see S Smith, 'Why Courts Make Orders (And What This Tells Us About Damages)' (2011) 64 *Current Legal Problems* 51, suggesting (fn 38 at 74) that the distinction can be traced back to the origins of the common law.

of whether they are ever detected and punished. But the determination that the defendant is sentenced to imprisonment, and hence that bailiffs are required to jail him, is a constitutive ruling. *But for* this ruling, bailiffs would not be legally required, even permitted, to put him in jail – no matter how evident the facts and how determinate the governing law. Sentencing is one important domain in which constitutive rulings are needed, and they should be preceded by declarative rulings establishing the unlawfulness of some past conduct.

But both constitutive and declarative rulings are also needed in other contexts, often in isolation from one another. Take constitutive rulings first. Constitutive rulings are required not only to authorise or require conduct by legal officials, as in the above example and other examples noted below. Constitutive rulings may also be required to authorise or require conduct *by citizens*. Constitutive rulings are characteristic of, for example, licensing schemes, patent awards, bankruptcy orders or residence permits. Even if I squarely qualify for the fishing licence for which I apply, and the licensing officer must exercise no discretion in awarding it, it is only *upon* the award that I will be legally at liberty to fish. But for this ruling, I would not be. But for the patent, others would not have an obligation to abstain from replicating my invention. But for the legal incompetence ruling, I might not lack the legal power to dispose of my property.

It may seem obvious that constitutive rulings are needed in all these domains.[18] It may be less obvious, however, *why* they are. Our habitual exposure to these types of rulings must not blind us to the fact that analogous kinds of rulings in other spheres of individual conduct would be deeply objectionable, if not practically unfeasible. Constitutive rulings to determine the right to publish certain ideas would amount to prior censorship. Constitutive rulings to determine individual tax liability would collapse the tax system. In a sound legal order we all have entitlements and duties to perform countless kinds of conduct in the absence of a prior ruling. We do not have, in all spheres of life, an army of officers at our heels, ready to rubber-stamp each of our purported moves, in the style of referees in organised sports.[19] This would be disproportionately cramping of individual self-direction (section VII) and expose us in aberrant measure to the Rule of Law pitfalls of particularised official decision-making, including

[18] Rulings that *deny* patents, licences, etc, or which *decline* to establish legal incompetence and so on, are in an important sense declarative. They are a necessary counterpart to the availability of constitutive rulings in the relevant domain. It will often be indeterminate whether, or to what extent, any given ruling is declarative or constitutive (for insightful discussion, S Smith, 'Rule-Based Rights and Court-Ordered Rights' in A Robertson and D Nolan (eds), *The Rights of Private Law* (Oxford, Hart Publishing, 2012); Smith, 'Why Courts Make Orders', n 17, 69–70). Nothing in my argument turns on this.

[19] Technically, however, goals (for example) are scored independently of the referee's pronouncement ('A goal is scored when the whole of the ball passes over the goal line, between the goalposts and under the crossbar': International Football Association Board, *Laws of the Game 2017/18*, Law 10.1.I). Hart (HLA Hart, *The Concept of Law*, 2nd edn (Oxford, Clarendon Press, 1994) 141ff) famously builds on the example of rulings by referees ('official scorers') to bring out that rules can pre-exist rulings even where the latter are final (and so may be mistaken). On final rulings, see section V of this chapter.

the risk of corruption and abuse. The important question for us, therefore, is not whether constitutive rulings are needed, but *when* (and hence why) they are.

It is here that different aspects of the Rule of Law come into play in interesting ways. An important precondition giving rise to the need for constitutive rulings, in regard to the conduct of citizens, is that the facts on which legal treatment ought to turn are potentially complex, and not amenable to being circumvented through a proxy. A professional skill, the novelty of an invention, an adult's mental incompetence or the ability to drive, all are potentially complex facts. It may take sophisticated procedures and expert knowledge to ascertain them. Moreover, there are no adequate proxies to simplify the determination of these facts. Other kinds of complex condition *do* have adequate proxies. Maturity to vote and to purchase alcoholic drinks is only approximately correlated to age, but age is, on the low end, an adequate proxy for that kind of maturity. Age alone, by contrast, would be a catastrophic proxy for the ability to drive.

It may not be enough that facts be complex and not liable to circumvention through a proxy. Constitutive rulings will typically be required when there is, in addition, a special need for predictability or certainty, notably by third parties. There are few if any purposes for which I need to know your tax duties, but it can be decisive to many of my endeavours whether you, as my trading partner, are or are not commercially disabled or entitled to conduct construction works, or whether you, as my employee, are or are not permitted to reside in this country, or whether this technological invention may or may not be replicated, or whether this company is entitled to issue stock. Valuable endeavours would not get off the ground if persons had to assess these particulars at their own peril, aware not only of the risk of mistake but also of the likelihood of divergence amongst reasonable appreciations. The needed certainty, incidentally, may also be on the part of those performing large-scale inspection tasks, such as traffic police, who cannot afford to re-open questions of qualification better ruled on earlier and by someone else. It follows that a primary Rule of Law reason calling for constitutive rulings, in regard to citizen conduct, is *predictability* concerning where other parties stand, as a matter of law. A secondary reason, of course, is *consistency* in the law's operation: trained officers will be able to follow stable patterns in deciding who is qualified to do what.[20]

Constitutive rulings authorising or requiring *official* conduct pose a different challenge. I started with the example of official conduct executing, that is, 'actually administering', a criminal punishment. There are other forms of official conduct that likewise significantly affect the interests of particular persons. Official conduct that imposes a restriction may also occur before rather than upon conclusion of a trial, by way of, for example, a preventive arrest or a home search. And some kinds of official conduct affect individual interests in

[20] Consistency amongst the decisions in turn presupposes appropriate expertise (section II) and impartiality (section III) on the part of officials making them.

a favourable fashion, for example by allocating poverty or disability support. *All* these forms of executive conduct call for constitutive rulings by default. When it comes to official conduct of this kind, as opposed to citizen conduct, rulings must be the rule, not the exception. This is because these forms of official conduct call for justification by their very nature. The defining fiduciary task of legal officials it is to serve the community, by acting on behalf of and in the name of the community as a whole. By default, therefore, officials ought not to compromise the interests of particular community members or selectively allocate resources drawn from common stock. When they do, it is critical that they can be publicly accountable for it.

Accountability is the primary Rule of Law reason to have constitutive rulings in the case of official conduct. Validly crystallising a person's liability to be treated in a certain way by state forces, ahead of the treatment's taking place, is essential to ensuring that the person's fate is not, for better or worse, determined by the sheer, legally uncontrolled whim of a discrete official ('the rule of laws, not of men').[21] This is why urgent preventive measures that must be taken without warrant, notably by police, should promptly be subject to confirmation. Grievous measures should normally be judicially authorised, and liable to review by a homogenising appeal jurisdiction. That, in turn, promotes *consistency* in the law's operation, notably where the relevant facts are complex and difficult to ascertain (as is often, for example, actual commission of an offence, or a situation of poverty).

I have so far spoken of Rule of Law reasons to have constitutive rulings. Consider now the reasons to have declarative rulings. A declarative ruling, recall, attests to the existence of legal positions that hold prior to and independently of that ruling. It says, for instance, *that* this offence was committed, or *that* this contract was breached. Declarative rulings may be issued on their own, without constitutive rulings attached. If we have agreed that you will sell me your computer for a certain price, and I have paid the price, I now have a legal right to receive the computer, and so a judge ought to hold when, if ever, called upon to pronounce. The judge's say-so is a declarative ruling.[22] Only if you fail to perform your contractual duty may the judge provide for a sanction, and in so doing issue a constitutive ruling.[23]

[21] An expression that succinctly evokes some of Aristotle's claims in, especially, Aristotle, *Politics*, CDC Reeve (tr) (Indianapolis, IN, Hackett, 1998), III.16, 1287a, 96–97 ('Thus it is more choiceworthy to have law rule than any one of the citizens', 1287a19); III.15, 1286a, 93–95; and Aristotle, *The Nicomachean Ethics*, D Ross (tr) (Oxford, Oxford University Press, 2009) V.6, 1134b1, 91 ('This is why we do not allow a *man* to rule, but *rational principle* [law], because a man behaves thus in his own interests and becomes a tyrant').

[22] Smith ('Why Courts Make Orders', n 17, 57, 66–68) draws an additional distinction between a judicial 'declaration' and a (declarative) 'order', which need not concern us. I do not share Smith's views about the nature of court orders.

[23] See Smith's argument why damages orders are constitutive ('creative') (ibid 71ff).

Declarative rulings are chiefly needed to end disputes, and to end them according to law. There is a dispute about a legal position where either relevant facts, or applicable law, or both are contested. Ending disputes entails providing resolution through adjudication – in principle by deciding in favour of one party, and so far forth against the other. Ending disputes according to law entails adjudicating in accordance with existing law as far as it goes, and otherwise supplementing it. Organs well placed to issue declarative rulings are those with personal and material capacities appropriate to what we call *judicial* roles, including adequate fact-finding methods, specialist legal knowledge, and avenues to prevent bias and ensure balanced opportunity for argumentation. In a healthy legal system, courts will be the general resort for declarative rulings.

The need to end disputes according to law speaks to all three central aspects of the Rule of Law. The law's operation is *predictable* if disputes are regularly settled in accordance with law, rather than in disregard of it. Resolutions of different disputes in application of the same general law are correspondingly *consistent*. And at least to the extent that the decision-maker applies pre-existing law, the fate of the relevant subjects is not determined by the decision-maker's sheer whim but by a general legal framework in respect of which the decision-maker is *accountable*. Note, by the way, that the Rule of Law requires that declarative rulings be generally available, not that they generally take place. One should normally be able to know one's position in law without a judicial pronouncement to that effect. Common law methods of legal education are prone to cloud the sobering truth that most of our legal dealings occur in the absence of judicial rulings, much though they may be influenced by the prospect thereof.[24] Disputes cannot be settled unless they arise. It is a measure of a community's fulfilment of the Rule of Law that disputes are, by and large, forestalled.

Constitutive rulings, as this section has shown, are key devices to forestall disputes about certain kinds of legal position in the modern state, notably by providing necessary predictability and precluding unaccountable uses of official power. We need not argue over how novel your invention is: I shall just check if you have a patent. Traffic police need not second-guess your skill to drive: they will ask if you have a driving licence. Constitutive rulings are therefore amongst the kinds of valid act most often represented in shorthand symbols or portable tokens, such as residence cards, patent references or licence plates (chapter 3.VI). In this way also, the technique of validity helps to forestall disputes. The Rule of Law requires legal validity because it requires the forestalling of disputes. But the Rule of Law also requires rulings in order to settle disputes, once arisen. The Rule of Law requires both constitutive and declarative rulings. Rulings are

[24] Dworkin's court-centred understanding of law may animate the sense that there is no law outside the courtroom: see ch 6.I.

curious kinds of valid act: they can change legal positions without involving legal discretion. A constitutive ruling creates new legal positions. A declarative ruling creates a new legal basis for the legal positions to which it attests (which is why it changes them if it attests to them erroneously).[25] The Rule of Law calls for both kinds of legally valid act, and so it calls for decisions that are particular rather than general. The apparent paradox is resolved. The Rule of Law requires rulings ultimately for the same reasons that it requires rules.

V. THE RULE OF LAW: RULINGS ABOUT VALIDITY

The need for courts as a general resort to settle legal disputes entails the need for them to settle disputes *about legal validity*, that is to say, disputes wherein the contested question includes whether a certain decision is legally valid as opposed to what particular duties, rights or powers arise under it (in conjunction with other provisions). Rulings about validity may in principle concern the validity of any exercise of legal power: for example, a contract, a ruling, a will, a governmental decree, even a piece of legislation (with some qualifications noted in the next section).

Judicial settlement of disputes about legal validity is at once especially necessary and especially intricate. It is especially necessary because legal validity is needed to furnish certainty about legal positions, by enabling many different persons to tell where they stand as a matter of law with relative ease. Disputes about validity represent a partial breakdown in the stable convergence of recognition that validity ought to help ensure (chapter 4.V–VI). Such disputes should therefore be amenable to unambiguous resolution within a reasonable time period. Here the law, reflexively, must take control of its own valid decision-making. But just that reflexive resolution may be especially intricate because it may require decisions that, in a sense, run counter to validity's logic. The Rule of Law may require that disputes about validity be settled in ways that depart from or compromise the strict logic of validity criteria. That is the logic that nothing can be valid, at any given point in time, unless *all* validity criteria are *concurrently* fulfilled.

Courts that are called on to determine whether a contract, a will or a statute is legally valid in principle have a yes-or-no question to answer. But the answer may be all but straightforward. Both its grounds and its needed specifics may be complex. Nothing is *more or less* valid as a matter of law, but it may be legally indeterminate whether it is. It may be indeterminate whether the contract fulfils a certain vaguely phrased criterion of validity ('contrary to the requirement of

[25] For a similar point, J Raz, *Practical Reason and Norms* (London, Hutchinson, 1975) 135, 145. Declarative rulings also change legal positions of a procedural sort, eg by precluding parties from obtaining a new pronouncement on the same subject, save on appeal.

good faith', 'reasonable time'). Or perhaps the facts, as known to the parties, are contestable. Or it may be indeterminate whether, *given* the obvious breach of a certain criterion of validity, the contract is, or remains, or should now be rendered, or can no longer be, or must be deemed never to have been, legally valid, and for what purposes, and vis-à-vis whom.

Respect for reasonable expectations based on an appearance of validity often justifies modulating the legal import of breaches of validity criteria. To some extent, power-conferring regimes may themselves cater for, and thereby *anticipate*, scenarios in which validity is indeterminate or in dispute (chapter 4.V). Thus it may be the law in a certain jurisdiction that regulations in breach of substantive rather than procedural criteria are valid unless and until a special court invalidates them with prospective, or limitedly retroactive, effects. Or it may be the law that the validity of enactments by regional parliaments is automatically suspended if the federal government brings a claim, until, if ever, the challenge is dismissed. Or again the law may provide that private transactions with certain impairments in consent, standing or form are *voidable*, perhaps at the aggrieved party's request, or become indefeasibly valid upon the (non)occurrence of certain facts by a certain time. Or in other ways, too, presumptions of (in)validity may be legally defeasible only by judicial pronouncement through a specified procedure, on specified grounds, and with specified temporal effects.

Such regimes empower a judge to modulate the effects of not-fully-satisfied criteria, all while reducing his discretion. But these regimes cannot reasonably, and should not seek to, replace judicial rulings altogether. However carefully drafted, power-conferring regimes cannot foresee every conceivable predicament.[26] This is so both because an act's validity criteria will often stem from a range of different legal sources, including supranational ones, and also because it is ultimately a matter of fact to what *minimum* extent validity criteria must be fulfilled (or appear to be) to warrant intelligibly calling something 'a statute', 'a contract' or 'a decree' *of which* voidability can be at issue, and *to which* a presumption of validity can feasibly apply. (What about a 'statute' voted on by MPs in a pub gathering?) Moreover, there will sometimes be good reason for law-makers to defer, more or less deliberately, to later judicial pronouncements on validity by leaving certain criteria appropriately vague, where judicial specification can be sensitive to morally relevant aspects of factual scenarios that may elude the coarse net of general rules. Therefore rulings about legal validity have a paramount closure role to play in any Rule of Law-compliant community. And that is precisely because their role is not limited to declaring what is (in)

[26] An interesting and somewhat different case is probate, the judicial process whereby a valid will is certified to be valid. It may be a precondition for administering the estate of the deceased person, even if there is no dispute about the validity of the will. The granting of probate resembles a constitutive ruling in that *but for* it, concrete duties and rights under the will may not arise. But it resembles a declarative ruling in that the point of probate is to confirm *that* a will is valid, not to so render it.

valid based on a strict, all-or-nothing logic of validity criteria, according to which *any* breach entails radical nullity.

Ending disputes *according to law* may require an iteration of rulings, including what we know as appeals, to increase the chances that a dispute is correctly settled. But the need to *end disputes* limits the scope that this iteration can reasonably take. Just as it is a mark of compliance with the Rule of Law that disputes do not arise with disruptive frequency, it is a mark of compliance with the Rule of Law that disputes do not last for a disruptively long time, or have a standing chance of being (re)launched. The reasons that call for empowering courts to settle disputes also call for circumscribing that very power. This may entail limiting the grounds of review of certain decisions, for example to questions of procedure rather than substance, or to questions of law rather than fact. And it will entail, in any case, the operation of legal doctrines of finality, with the consequent possibility of indefeasible mistakes. The Rule of Law requires that disputes be ended according to law, but the relevant law need not always be the law that governed the question in dispute. It may exceptionally be the law that governs the question of how dispute settlements acquire indefeasible status. Finality carries the potential for valid decisions that misapply pre-existing law, including criteria of legal validity. A mistaken final ruling is a decision that pre-existing law committed the judge not to give. It may not be unjust in its substance, but it was not a choice for the judge to make – perhaps it was for the legislator to modify the rule. Finality puts an end to disputes at the potential price of upsetting the allocation of legal power that validity helps to channel.

VI. THE RULE OF LAW: GENERAL LAW-MAKING

Plainly the Rule of Law requires that there be general law. This section focuses on two important further questions. First, it considers *how* that general law should be made, which in turn bears on who should make it. Second, it considers Rule of Law reasons *not* to settle certain matters by means of general law.

There are different methods to make general law. They all trade on the technique of legal validity, but do not use it in the same manner. General law can be made through the method of legislation. Legislation involves a targeted use of validity's technique. This is why we say that rules introduced by legislation have a canonical formulation. Legislatures make the rules they make by saying that they make them.[27] Case law is another way to make general law. It is an important method in common law countries. It presupposes the doctrine of *stare decisis*. Rules made by case law are made by being applied, not by

[27] This is not to suggest that the legal meaning of enactments is best understood on the model of communicative meaning: see ch 6.III–IV.

being announced.[28] The agent making them is a court with power to set precedent on point. Case law is made by a valid act, but not by so saying. The valid act is the ruling. A ruling, as we have seen, pronounces on a particular case. A ruling creates a rule by bringing it to bear on the argument leading up to the settlement of the dispute. The judge may attempt to formulate the rule he creates, but his formulation is not decisive to determining the content of the rule. It follows that case law is not a focally targeted method for making general law. A third law-making method is custom. The very doctrine of *stare decisis* has come into being as a by-product of a longstanding sequence of valid judicial rulings assigning certain prior rulings this weight. Rulings may build up to a judicial custom, just like a protracted series of valid transactions may build up to a commercial custom. Law that is made through custom is made in the least targeted way.

The legal system of a modern political community could hardly generate and sustain convergence amongst a large population in all domains of social life relevant to justice in community if it did not have a substantial body of general law, and if that general law were not in significant part crafted through the targeted method of legislation. This method is germane to the institution we know as the legislature, but it is likewise open to executive bodies, such as the government or administrative agencies to which the legislature may delegate.

The place of case law in a legal system has implications from the point of view of the Rule of Law. In a number of ways, case law is apt to compromise the predictability, consistency and accountability for which the Rule of Law calls. Case law will often not furnish a clear basis on which to *predict* the law's future operation. The rule created through case law may not be easy to identify. The judge typically applies it in the process of pronouncing on several other matters raised by parties engaged in adversarial dynamics, which are only tangentially related to a concern with setting binding precedent. The judge himself may downplay the legal change he is making. He may cast what in truth is a supplementation, if not an override, of existing law under the equivocal heading of 'interpretation'. There may be added pressure on him to do so in a cultural environment that vindicates adjudication as a purely deductive affair. But even his very role as judge naturally encourages this equivocation. For rulings, as we have seen, are at the junction between the application and the supplementation of law (section IV). Rules made through rulings may moreover be *inconsistent* with rules governing morally like cases. The court's focus is on a particular situation, which normally throws up only a small subset of the problems that those crafting the broader legal regime should have considered. Courts can only change

[28] On this contrast, and on the general distinction between law-making methods canvassed in this paragraph, see J Gardner, *Law as a Leap of Faith* (Oxford, Oxford University Press, 2012) 74–76. For an argument based on similar premises, but going as far as to deny that the doctrine of precedent bestows on courts legal power to make legal rules, see G Lamond, 'Do Precedents Create Rules?' (2005) 11 *Legal Theory* 1, especially 25–26.

law in response to cases brought before them.[29] And courts are not *accountable* in the special sense that members of a democratic legislature are: accountable politically.

On the whole, there are good reasons to bestow on courts a limited power to supplement legislative rules through the method of case law. There may be good reasons to bestow on courts a more extensive power in some respects, but the associated Rule of Law hazards must be closely attended to. For one thing, *wide* rather than limited judicial discretion must be avoided in domains in which predictability and consistency are morally key, such as the criminal law. It is inadequate, for example, that core elements of offences be moulded by courts as a matter of course, as is still substantially the case in English law. For another thing, judicial power to *override* existing legislative rules by setting incompatible precedent combines the Rule of Law pitfalls of case law with the Rule of Law pitfalls of depriving of legal force what may still appear to be a statute's legal meaning. There are more Rule of Law-friendly methods for courts to override legislative judgement. Legal systems may empower a dedicated organ to strike down legislative provisions on review. In a targeted process of review, a court can annul a legislative rule by so saying, rather than by applying an incompatible rule to a particular set of facts.[30] The problem of accountability remains, but predictability and consistency need not similarly suffer.

Sometimes, however, the question is not who should make a certain body of general law but whether to make it at all. Certain kinds of conduct are best not subject to general regulation of any kind, whether by statute, case law or otherwise. Even criminal offences are appropriately left open-ended at some junctures, where doing otherwise would fail to send out a sufficiently coherent or stringent message, or place vulnerable persons at risk. For example, a closed list of the kinds of conduct that can amount to assisting or encouraging crime, or of the kinds of injury that a person may lawfully consent to being inflicted, might unduly spur the creativity of those hoping to circumvent the prohibition and discourage valuable forms of self-restraint and care in people's relations towards one another. Such vague provisions amount to empowerments of judges to use discretion in settling particular cases. It must not be forgotten, however, that such provisions also amount to empowerments of enforcement agents, such as prosecutors and tax collectors, to exercise judgement in deciding when to validly bring charges and launch corresponding proceedings. And these latter empowerments may further the Rule of Law, or they may compromise it.

Prosecutorial and similar forms of discretion can be conducive to justice, not least by serving the Rule of Law, where this discretion is used in accordance with considerations continuous with the rationale of the stated rule, primarily

[29] In this spirit, P Yowell, 'Legislation, Common Law, and the Virtue of Clarity' in R Ekins (ed), *Modern Challenges to the Rule of Law* (Wellington, LexisNexis, 2011) 125.

[30] For an argument, see P Yowell, *Constitutional Rights and Constitutional Design: Moral and Empirical Reasoning in Judicial Review* (Oxford, Hart Publishing, 2018) 160–61.

de minimis constraints. But these empowerments, if not appropriately circumscribed, can readily degenerate into major threats to the Rule of Law or other injustices, where selective enforcement amounts to unwarranted targeting, say on racial or ideological grounds, or is used to counteract the deliberate over-inclusiveness of rules designed primarily to produce large-scale deterrent effects, or to secure political returns, rather than to be enforced. Tax laws could, for instance, attach draconian penalties to a failure to submit a formal inventory of one's foreign assets, as a relatively cheap way for the government to gather copious amounts of information and to have a legal warrant to target the few but important (or electorally convenient) cases where tax evasion or money laundering seems notorious but cannot as such be proven in law. A recent Spanish regime might be a case in point.[31]

Note that this Rule of Law threat will not be averted by having prosecution or inspection agencies announce, in more or less general or public terms, the patterns of enforcement they expect to follow. It was unjustifiable for the UK House of Lords in *Purdy v DPP* (2009)[32] to instruct the Director of Public Prosecutions to do so with respect to its enforcement of the politically controverted, but legally unconditional, offence of assisting suicide.[33] Predictability grounded on announcements that officials are not legally bound to follow, and cannot be held accountable for ignoring, is not predictability that befits government by law. Nothing short of a legally valid act can craft legal positions, and nothing other than legal positions can under the Rule of Law provide legal justification for, and reason to reckon on, official enforcement acts.

The Rule of Law can bring a community closer to realising justice, but only in the domains in which justice falls to be secured through law. These domains are vast, but they do not cover the entirety of social relationships. Countless kinds of intimate dishonesty or betrayal, for instance, ought in justice to remain outside the boundaries of the community's organised jurisdiction, at least the jurisdiction exercised through the necessarily rigid mechanisms of the criminal law. But even official executive conduct, and in that sense conduct already emerging from the operation of law, will appropriately be non-justiciable, and so immune from judicial review, where, as in the case of foreign affairs, the judicial process is not only unfit to gather relevant information (about, say, military

[31] As introduced by Ley 7/2012, de 29 de octubre, de Modificación de la Normativa Tributaria y Presupuestaria y de Adecuación de la Normativa Financiera (amending Ley 58/2003, de 17 de diciembre, General Tributaria, additional disposition 18; Ley 35/2006, de 28 de noviembre, del Impuesto sobre la Renta de las Personas Físicas, art 39(2)), the elusively drafted Spanish regime on the so-called 'Modelo 720' supports penalties exceeding confiscation for any delay in submitting one's formal inventory of foreign assets, where the subject is unable to defeat the legal presumption (!) that incumbent tax dues were not paid for the assets at the point of acquisition – a point that, as there is no prescription limit, may lie decades behind.

[32] *Purdy v DPP* [2009] UKHL 45, [2010] 1 AC 345.

[33] Suicide Act 1961 (UK), s 2(1), with s 2(4) explicitly requiring the DPP's consent as a prerequisite for validly prosecuting the offence.

risks in other countries) but would also entail a form of public accountability that could risk defeating valuable purposes of executive action best controlled managerially instead.[34] Where *law* is not a fitting tool to govern human relations, there is reason *not* to empower agents to create or apply law – not for the sake of the Rule of Law, but because the Rule of Law itself would work injustice.

VII. SELF-DIRECTION

We have now considered three broad sets of reasons to empower: expertise, proximity, and the Rule of Law. The fourth and final set of relevant reasons is the self-direction of individuals and groups.

Reasons of the fourth kind resemble reasons of the first two kinds in that they weigh in favour of certain decisions being taken by certain agents because of some special characteristics of those agents *as such*, rather than because, given the institutional position of those agents, this will secure a more predictable or consistent legal operation. But reasons of the fourth kind differ from expertise and proximity in that here what is special about the relevant agents is not their greater likelihood to *get something right*, that is, to track facts or standards of correctness existing quite independently of their decision. Here the reason to empower them is not that we *trust*[35] them to abide by certain considerations better than other agents would. To the extent the fourth kind of reason applies, there is, beyond certain limits, no criterion of correctness of a decision other than the need that it be taken *by* the agents in question. For the decision is designed to be an expression and embodiment of the agents' capacity to steer their future in a self-reliant way, as an exercise of self-directing choice.

Self-direction is the default reason for conferring private powers on individuals to mould their legal relationships with others through private transactions such as marriages, wills, incorporations or other commercial exchanges. It also supports empowering individuals to select their political representatives in general elections, and having bodies thus elected (or subject to the control of these bodies) take a lead role in shaping the community's social life. For there is value in the community's collective self-direction. A community directs itself when it is directed by agents who make reasoned choices on behalf of the collective in a way receptive and responsive to its input. 'Party politics', closed

[34] For sustained argument, see T Endicott, 'The Reason of the Law' (2003) 48 *American Journal of Jurisprudence* 83.

[35] For an articulation of the general rationale of legal empowerments in terms of an 'economy of trust' (by 'planners' of 'interpreters'), S Shapiro, *Legality* (Cambridge, MA, Harvard University Press, 2009) chs 12–13 (in light of 120ff, 195ff, 209ff); on deep ambiguities in Shapiro's argument, see M Köpcke, 'Positive Law's Moral Purpose(s): Towards a New Consensus?' (2011) 56 *American Journal of Jurisprudence* 186, 202–08.

candidate lists, subservience to lobbies, and corruption, all accordingly go to weaken the rationale of placing government in the hands of elected representatives. So does the absence of sufficiently common ties, dispositions and other marks of shared identity amongst the individuals integrating the group, whether larger or smaller than an internationally recognised 'sovereign state'.

The value of individual and collective self-direction can be traced back to the fundamental moral importance of autonomy and authenticity as aspects of human well-being (chapter 4.II). One is better off for freely embracing opportunities and for pursuing chosen paths, the treading of which will change who one is thereafter. One is better off for undertaking commitments and joining ventures that will render some aspects of the well-being of others primary objects of one's justified concern. The reasonable self-directing choice, in the face of under-determination, can *create* moral duties for oneself, and towards others, that did not exist before, or did so only in a latent and weaker, because under-specified, fashion. Choice, in this respect, involves appropriating some available options and taking responsibility for them, including responsibility for choosing unwisely or betting on what will turn out to be the wrong horse. Legal systems will therefore do well to embrace a basic principle of subsidiarity. They will do well to facilitate that, where appropriate, persons and groups, including families, associations and nations, *help themselves*.

This shows that the fourth kind of reason to empower is foundational in relation to the others. The value of self-direction is a reason to give legal clothing to a wide range of choices. But it is a reason to withhold legal validity from many other choices. It is a reason to withhold legal validity from expressed choices that were not genuinely free because not made with requisite information and capacity to choose, as per the first set of reasons to empower (expertise). It is a reason to withhold legal validity from choices that could work injustice due to bias or a failure to appreciate needs that someone closer to the situation would not overlook, as per the second set of reasons to empower (proximity). And it is a reason to withhold legal validity from choices that were not articulated in the officially ascertainable form that alone can ensure the public's reliance and a consistent treatment of what is morally alike, as per the third set of reasons to empower (the Rule of Law).

Realising justice in community involves generating patterns of large-scale convergence in many social domains. The primary responsibility to generate convergence lies with the community, and therefore with those who can act on its behalf. Sound legal regimes will express the community's commitment to *some* out of countless appropriate avenues open to pursuit. And sound legal regimes will carefully determine *who* can act on the community's behalf. One has the power to commit the community as a whole if one's say-so changes duties that the community shall exact, and if it forges rights that the community shall honour. The allocation of this power is itself a question of justice. It turns on considerations of relative expertise and proximity, respect for the Rule of Law and reasonable self-direction. The technique of validity is key to realising justice because it can bestow and limit power in response to these considerations.

NOTES

Section I: Empowerment

Empowerment is Typically of Another

But it can be of oneself. For instance, and importantly, much of the English law of judicial review of administrative decisions is case law that, rather than just considering the merits of the decisions under review, also reflexively ponders the scope of the very same judicial power of review that is being exercised, in light of the requirement of comity (see T Endicott, *Administrative Law*, 2nd edn (Oxford, Oxford University Press, 2011) 35–36); for an argument that the judges' allocation of legal power to themselves is not necessarily contrary to the Rule of Law, see T Endicott, 'Arbitrariness' (2014) 27 *Canadian Journal of Law and Jurisprudence* 49.

Empowerment is Ill-understood as Mere Delegation

When Kelsen describes the *hierarchy* of legal norms in terms of certain authorities' 'vest[ing] norm-creating power in some other authorities', he characterises this vesting as a delegation (Kelsen, *General Theory of Law and State*, n 10, 113, 123ff; also Kelsen, *Pure Theory*, n 10, 197, 221ff). In explicating the idea of delegation he unhelpfully invokes the analogy of the almighty God delegating to parents the power to issue commands to their children; Kelsen primarily has in mind, as is evident from the discussion, constitutional or legislative authorities entrusting decisions that fall within their own scope of powers to authorities of subordinate rank. There are echoes of such understanding in Bentham's insistence that all legal powers ultimately issue from the sovereign's power (J Bentham, *Of Laws in General*, HLA Hart (ed) (London, The Athlone Press, 1970) ch 2, especially 21ff, 25ff, and ch 9), a power which is accordingly 'broken into shares' (ibid 26, 80); this latter metaphor is usefully picked up and discussed in HLA Hart, *Essays on Bentham*, Studies in Jurisprudence and Political Theory (Oxford, Clarendon Press, 2001) 202–04.

Reasons to Empower

The classification proposed in the main text is not exhaustive and may cut across other conceivable ones. Consider, for instance, Harel's distinction between 'instrumental' and 'non-instrumental' (justifications for political/legal institutions and therefore) reasons to empower (A Harel, *Why Law Matters* (Oxford, Oxford University Press, 2014), or Endicott's list of four 'reasons for deference' (legal allocation of power, expertise, political responsibility and processes: Endicott, *Administrative Law*, 225ff).

Section IV: The Rule of Law: Rulings

The Rule of Law

The understanding of the Rule of Law I draw on in the text is helpfully developed in Fuller, *The Morality of Law*, n 13; Raz, *The Authority of Law*, n 14, ch 11; J Finnis, *Natural Law and Natural Rights*, 2nd edn (Oxford, Oxford University Press, 2011) 270ff; NE Simmonds, *Law as a Moral Idea* (Oxford, Oxford University Press, 2007). For a broader understanding (in terms of 'the reason of the law'), which can extend to other reasons to empower disentangled in the text, see Endicott, 'The Reason of the Law', n 34; T Endicott, *Vagueness in Law* (Oxford, Oxford University Press, 2000) ch 9.

The Rule of Law Calls for Both Generality and Particularity

For an argument, usefully disambiguating various modes of generality in law, T Endicott, 'The Generality of Law' in L Duarte d'Almeida, J Edwards and A Dolcetti (eds), *Reading HLA Hart's* The Concept of Law (Oxford, Hart Publishing, 2013).

Application of Law

The relatively few authors who discuss this idea tend to associate it with only one of the two main kinds of ruling distinguished in the main text (declarative and constitutive rulings), to the detriment of the other. Both Dan-Cohen and Kelsen, for example, downplay the presence of declarative rulings. According to Dan-Cohen (M Dan-Cohen, 'Decision Rules and Conduct Rules: On Acoustic Separation in Criminal Law' (1983) 97 *Harvard Law Review* 625, especially 626–29), 'when we loosely say that the judge, in imposing punishment on the thief, "applies" the rule forbidding stealing, we must realize that the judge is not guided or bound by that rule: he is not, in his capacity as judge, one of the rule's norm-subjects, nor does his act (that of imposing punishment) correspond to the norm-act (that is, not stealing) specified by the rule' (ibid 628). For Dan-Cohen, 'law application' involves the joint 'operation' of the rule forbidding stealing and the rule providing for punishment (ibid 629); he does not appreciate, however, that what the application *consists in* is a declarative ruling that theft was committed, not only a constitutive ruling that punishment is imposed. Kelsen, in turn, obscures the role of declarative rulings by insisting that what is legally decisive is not the mere fact that a crime was committed but the judge's opinion of it (Kelsen, *Pure Theory*, n 10, 236ff). Hence, even the judicial determination that a crime has been committed 'is constitutive in every sense', as 'it is only by this ascertainment that the fact reaches the realm of law' (ibid 239). Conversely, Raz's sound discussion of law application (*Practical Reason and Norms*, n 25, 132ff) argues that the presence of declarative rulings ('applicative determinations') is central to the existence of 'institutionalized systems' of norms. But the judge's 'orders' 'to pay damages or fines or be jailed' are swiftly bracketed from discussion as 'entirely different' matters (ibid 137).

Officials Have a Defining Fiduciary Task

Ross (A Ross, 'On the Concepts "State" and "State Organs" in Constitutional Law' (1961) 5 *Scandinavian Studies in Law* 111, 116–19; *Directives and Norms* (London,

Routledge, 1968) 132–33; *On Law and Justice* (London, Stevens & Sons Limited, 1958) 203–04) helpfully demarcates public powers (exercised by officials) from private powers in terms of, inter alia, their different 'social function': whereas private power is 'discretionary' in that there is (generally) no duty to exercise it or to exercise it in a certain way, there is a duty to exercise 'public authority' 'to serve the interests of the community' (*Directives and Norms*, 133). See further R Dworkin, *Law's Empire* (Oxford, Hart Publishing, 1998) 173–75; Bentham, *Of Laws in General*, 22. For a narrower and more technical understanding of official duties as being fiduciary, E Fox-Decent, *Sovereignty's Promise: The State as Fiduciary*, Oxford Constitutional Theory (Oxford, Oxford University Press, 2011).

Judicial Roles

On the idea of judicial power, J Finnis, 'Judicial Power: Past, Present and Future' in R Ekins (ed), *Judicial Power and the Balance of Our Constitution: Two lectures by John Finnis* (London, Policy Exchange, 2018).

Section V: The Rule of Law: Rulings About Validity

Departing from the Logic That Nothing Can be Valid Unless All Criteria are Fulfilled

Kelsen takes the law's familiar departure from that logic to the opposite extreme. 'The case of absolute nullity lies beyond the law', says Kelsen, on grounds that any decision liable to be judicially pronounced on becomes, for that reason, 'something legally existing' (*General Theory of Law and State*, n 10, 161). In order to account for this, and for legally final yet mistaken decisions, Kelsen develops his doctrine of the implicit 'alternative character' of empowerments (ibid 153ff; *Pure Theory*, n 10, 267ff; H Kelsen, *General Theory of Norms*, M Hartney (tr) (Oxford, Clarendon Press, 1991) 248–49). According to this doctrine, empowerments authorise the decision-maker to make *either* legal *or* illegal law; hence so-called void acts are legal, because authorised, unless and until avoided (ie rendered void). Since any erroneous decision has the potential of becoming final, Kelsen is committed to the view that all legal empowerments contain an implicit alternative clause – a view that, as Kelsen seems to disregard, effectively dissolves the possibility of legal reasoning. While Kelsen's original impetus for developing this doctrine surely was his general denial of the possibility of normative conflicts within a legal order (eg *Pure Theory*, n 10, 205–06), it is remarkable that he clings to that doctrine even in his final work (*General Theory of Norms*, 248–49) in which he (otherwise) openly admits that conflicts are both possible and pervasive (ibid 123ff, 211ff).

Section VI: The Rule of Law: General Law-Making

Case Law Can be Substantially Retrospective

On the associated moral hazards, distinguishing between statutory construction and a change of common law rules, B Juratowich, *Retroactivity and the Common Law*

(Oxford, Hart Publishing, 2008) especially chs 3–5; for important qualifications on the meaning and moral standing of 'retroactive' decisions by higher courts that, in giving effect to standing legal principles, contravene settled lines of precedent in lower courts, see J Finnis, *Philosophy of Law, Collected Essays: Volume IV* (Oxford, Oxford University Press, 2011) ch 20.

Some Aspects of General Legal Provisions are Best Left Vague

On how the vagueness of some standards may be in the interests of clarity, and thus of the Rule of Law, P Yowell, 'Legislation, Common Law, and the Virtue of Clarity' in R Ekins (ed), *Modern Challenges to the Rule of Law* (Wellington, LexisNexis, 2011) 116–21. On how vague rules many encourage valuable forms of private ordering, facilitate sound power allocation or enable that a rule be applied in a manner faithful to its purpose, T Endicott, 'The Value of Vagueness' in A Marmor and S Soames (eds), *Philosophical Foundations of Language in the Law* (Oxford, Oxford University Press, 2011); A Marmor, *The Language of Law* (Oxford, Oxford University Press, 2014) 92ff (distinguishing different kinds of vagueness); S Soames, 'Vagueness and the Law' in A Marmor (ed), *The Routledge Companion to Philosophy of Law* (New York, Routledge, 2012) 102.

Section VII: Self-Direction

Collective Self-direction

On the moral value of a community's self-direction through, especially, the reasoned choices of rational legislative assemblies, see, eg, R Ekins, 'How To Be a Free People' (2013) 58 *American Journal of Jurisprudence* 163.

Subsidiarity

On subsidiarity as a principle of justice, see Finnis, *Natural Law and Natural Rights*, 146–47, 159, 169ff.

6

The Systemic Character of Legal Meaning

THE PREVIOUS CHAPTER argued that there are cogent reasons bearing on which persons or institutions should settle which questions of justice. It follows from this argument that most questions of justice that fall to be settled in ordering a community's affairs could not justly be settled in a joint and one-off manner, by a reduced set of agents seeking to set the blueprint of social life once and for all. Rather, the kind of specific convergence that justice requires is one generated and moulded in the course of a process that unfolds in time and involves the choices of a great many agents with profoundly different spheres of power: wide and narrow, official and private, central and local, legislative, executive and judicial. The technique of legal validity facilitates the allocation of legal power as between them. And it facilitates that they all speak in the one legally salient voice. This is why legal validity is morally needed.

This need for legal validity presupposes the need for something that has been implicit in the previous chapters, and which academic literature has consistently failed to come to grips with. It presupposes the moral need for law's positivity and the systemic character of legal meaning. Put differently: it is morally necessary that law be *positive*, that is, crafted through human acts, which acts are nevertheless *systemically* related to one another and through time. The purpose of this chapter is to explain this.

Section I vindicates the moral need for positive law in terms of a three-part argument: communities need standards that are (i) relatively determinate, (ii) relatively easy to identify and (iii) crafted in relatively targeted fashion. The need for law's positivity is often distorted in theoretical writings. On some views, for example, law can do its morally needed job only if identifying legal requirements does not involve moral judgement to *any* degree. On some rival views, identifying the law of a just community involves moral judgement *through and through*, to the point that only expert judges may be able to pin it down correctly. On these latter views, moreover, just law is next to *fully* determinate: legal discretion is inimical to justice. Both these sets of views, I argue, capture important truths, but they exaggerate them in ways that obscure validity's supple role in crafting justice.

The remainder of the chapter spells out the systemic relationship among the legally valid acts that go to make up positive law. It is because there is reason to empower many different agents to speak in validity's voice that there is reason for legal meaning to be systemic. The systemic dimension of legal meaning, too, is mischaracterised in the literature, in either a deflationary or an inflationary way. On some conceptions, valid acts fall to be understood strictly on the model of communication, so that figuring out their meaning essentially involves ascertaining the intent manifested by a single agent on a discrete point in time. These conceptions correctly appreciate that there are similarities between the technique of validity and the technique of communication, similarities on which my own argument in chapter 3 built. But these conceptions overstate the analogy to the point of eclipsing what is distinctive about legal meaning. Alternative conceptions, by contrast, helpfully illuminate the systemic interplay of legal requirements, manifest as it is, in particular, from the perspective of the adjudicating judge. But these conceptions thereby lose sight of the fact that these requirements are and should be, themselves, the product of targeted acts of crafting, of exercises of legal power.

I. THE MORAL NEED FOR LAW'S POSITIVITY

Political communities morally need law's positivity. By law's positivity I mean the fact that the legal positions persons are in at any point are determined by the legal meaning of valid acts rather than by moral considerations that are not part of the legal meaning of valid acts.

The reasons to empower charted in the previous chapter demonstrate the need for law's positivity because they demonstrate the need for certain features of law that build on law's positivity, although they go beyond it. In order to do its morally needed job, this section explains, law must be (i) relatively determinate, (ii) relatively easy to identify, and (iii) shaped in relatively targeted fashion.

A. Determinacy

The need for determinacy, at its most basic, boils down to the need for specificity discussed in chapter 4. Justice calls for convergence on specific patterns of conduct: that is, on patterns detailed enough that very often, in some respects, they could have reasonably been otherwise. Because open-ended moral reasoning about general human needs often cannot show any particular avenue, option or project to be more choice-worthy than others, because morality, so to speak, runs out at countless junctures at which determinate guidance is morally called for, something *other than morality* must step in to provide the requisite specifics. Human choosing acts are fit to discharge this role. In this basic sense, law can furnish determinacy because it is positive. It is made by human acts.

But the determinacy that law is needed to provide has a special temporal and interpersonal dimension. This dimension comes to the fore when considering the reasons to allocate legal power, charted in the previous chapter. They show that law's determinacy can only ever be, and reasonably aspire to be, *relative*. Full determinacy (gaplessness) is technically precluded in any case, given, amongst other things, the inherent vagueness of language.[1] But there is good reason for law to be considerably less determinate than it could technically be. Law at all times needs to be determinate only to the extent that there is reason not to re-open choices of those better placed to choose. For example, if A, a legislature, is better placed to decide on tax bands than B, the tax collection agency, A should settle the question (by statute) and B should correspondingly have no discretion to ignore or override A's decision when determining the liability of particular individuals. A's decision on tax liability should be determinate to the extent that other agents are less well placed to pronounce on it than A (including judges, prosecutors and individual tax payers). But there is no kind of A who is best placed to decide exhaustively about all, or even most, questions relevant to justice that fall to be settled in crafting social relationships – questions general and particular, public and private, standing and supervened. So if law is at all times to place decisions in the hands of those who ought to take them, it cannot even *aspire* to be fully determinate at any given point in time.

Take a contract law scenario. Insofar as parties ought, in justice, to be able to design the terms of their sales agreement, the statutory and case law regime should be correspondingly vague on point. Perhaps it should reasonably set no more than some implied terms that we, as contractual parties, cannot validly exclude, along with a closure rule providing that unfair contract terms shall not be binding on one or both of us, without trying to comprehensively specify the legal meaning of 'unfair' in this context. Here it will be our agreement (B's), not the legislature's (A's) prior decision, that substantially brings determinacy into our legal relationship. Even so, we may do well to leave certain aspects of our contractual relationship open-ended. Vague contractual terms may save us bargaining time and hiccups, and may encourage greater care in our dealings than closed lists of exclusions or duties that are all too easy to work around.[2] This means that if a dispute eventually arises between us, it may be for a judge (C) to decide whether or not you are legally bound by a given term, a term that you consider unfair but I do not. In so deciding, the judge may have to exercise

[1] See generally T Endicott, *Vagueness in Law* (Oxford, Oxford University Press, 2000).

[2] In this spirit, on the value (and pitfalls) of vague determinations of responsibility, see T Endicott, 'The Value of Vagueness' in A Marmor and S Soames (eds), *Philosophical Foundations of Language in the Law* (Oxford, Oxford University Press, 2011) section 9; T Endicott, 'Objectivity, Subjectivity, and Incomplete Agreements' in J Horder (ed), *Oxford Essays in Jurisprudence Fourth Series* (Oxford, Oxford University Press, 2000) 163–70; J Waldron, 'Vagueness and the Guidance of Action' in A Marmor and S Soames (eds), *Philosophical Foundations of Language in the Law* (Oxford, Oxford University Press, 2011) 75ff.

discretion: the term may be neither clearly unfair nor clearly fair. Therefore, only once the judicial decision is final, perhaps on appeal before D, will there be something close to full determinacy in our legal relationship – but only on this particular question. Legal avenues for the final settlement of disputes, as we saw, should be generally available with respect to most types of legal position (chapter 5.V–VI). These avenues furnish a kind of determinacy that is necessarily diachronic and particularised, as opposed to synchronic and generalised.

It is worth stressing that in this contract law example, as in many analogous ones we find spread across any legal system, the judge has discretion because the constraining consideration is vague, *not because it is moral*. The provision that '[a]n unfair term … is not binding',[3] if not further specified by the legal regime,[4] is vague to the extent that the idea of an *unfair contract term* is. That extent, needless to say, is substantial. Moral ideas may be extremely vague. It is therefore indeterminate whether many kinds of slightly unfair contract term are legally binding. So if a dispute arises with respect to them, a judge will pro tanto have to exercise discretion, both legal and moral. But the provision is not empty. It certainly invalidates grossly unfair contract terms. Grossly unfair contract terms are not legally binding in this regime, and so a judge called on to pronounce has a legal duty to hold (a duty correlative to the aggrieved party's legal right that he does). If the judge holds otherwise, if (say) he rules a grossly unfair contract legally fair, he makes a mistake of law, not just a moral mistake. Vague terms introduce gaps in the law only in the measure of their vagueness. Moral terms are no exception.

Surprisingly, this view is heavily contested amongst legal theorists. A prominent line of thought, building on an understanding of authority of Razian inspiration, argues that (legally unspecified) moral terms yield legal gaps.[5] Law, it is said, cannot have practical authority unless it is possible to identify

[3] Consumer Rights Act 2015 (UK), s 62(1) ('An unfair term of a consumer contract is not binding on the consumer'). Analogous Continental regimes provide plainer examples of *invalidation* by statute in virtue of a morally circumscribed term (for a helpful comparative overview, B Häcker, 'The Impact of Illegality and Immorality on Contract and Restitution from a Civilian Angle' in S Green and A Bogg (eds), *Illegality after* Patel v Mirza (Oxford, Hart Publishing, 2018) 341–47). For example, according to § 138(1) of the German civil code, 'A legal transaction which contravenes good morals is void' (the concept of 'good morals' being only notionally specified in case law: see eg FJ Säcker et al (eds), *Münchener Kommentar zum Bürgerlichen Gesetzbuch, Band 1: Allgemeiner Teil, §§ 1–240*, 7th edn (Munich, CH Beck, 2015) § 138 para 14 (C Armbrüster)). Or again, in Spanish consumer law, 'Abusive terms shall be null and void, and be deemed not to have been set' (Real Decreto Legislativo 1/2007, de 16 de noviembre, por el que se aprueba el texto refundido de la Ley General para la Defensa de los Consumidores y Usuarios, art 83).

[4] The statutory regime of the Consumer Rights Act 2015 (UK) (especially s 62(4) and (5) and sch 2) does not substantially specify the provision.

[5] J Raz, *The Authority of Law: Essays on Law and Morality* (Oxford, Oxford University Press, 1979) 75; J Raz, *Ethics in the Public Domain: Essays in the Morality of Law and Politics*, rev edn (Oxford, Clarendon Press, 1995) 244–48; J Gardner, 'Justification under Authority' (2010) 23 *Canadian Journal of Law and Jurisprudence* 71, 71–72; L Green, 'Three Themes from Raz' (2005) 25 *Oxford Journal of Legal Studies* 503, 504ff; J Gardner, *Law as a Leap of Faith* (Oxford, Oxford University Press, 2012) 22; the understanding of authority was originally developed in, eg, Raz,

legal requirements (and so legal positions) *entirely* without resort to moral argument.[6] To have authority, on this view, is essentially to provide a service of epistemic mediation that would be of no avail if identifying the authority's directives required to *any* degree pondering the moral considerations to which the authority has privileged access, and in light of which it is therefore meant to decide. But it is part of the concept of law, the argument goes, that law *claims* to have authority; and since law claims to have authority, the argument continues, law is necessarily *capable* of having it, at least in the sense that bears on law's identification. It follows, on this view, that our statutory provision does not invalidate *any* contractual term. It must be understood elliptically, as instructing a judge, if and when the time comes, to determine the term's invalidity on the ground of its unfairness. And because the provision, on this view, does not invalidate any term, the judge does not make a mistake of law, only a moral mistake, if he rules a grossly unfair contract legally fair. Despite appearances, 'unfair' does not legally mean 'unfair'. Where the law says 'unfair' there is, in truth, a gap.

This is not the place to consider the merits of the underlying conception of authority and of its attribution to Raz, or indeed of the various 'conceptual' steps backing the above conclusion. But we should flag up some troubling implications of this view for an understanding of legal reasoning. The view entails that a legal rule, to the extent that it circumscribes legal power in moral terms ('unfair'), is primarily addressed to judges, and is not apt to *legally* guide those who are to exercise the power (eg to make the contract). They may be guided, at most, by their prediction of what the judge will decide. This is a particular instance of a mistake committed at large scale by that extreme form of Legal Realism according to which there exist no general legal standards addressed to and capable of guiding individuals and institutions before and independently of any judicial say-so,[7] standards for that reason binding on the judge. The authors who support the above authority-based argument otherwise firmly reject this Realist stance. It is consistent with their views that provisions such as '*liability-excluding* terms are invalid', or '*secret* terms are invalid' or 'terms *concerning digital content* are invalid', *do* invalidate any term that (clearly) falls within their scope. Not so, however, with morally circumscribed provisions.

This 'conceptually' based exception for moral terms, and moral terms only, strikes an embarrassing dissonance with ordinary legal reasoning (which is reasoning by those who deploy and invoke the concept of law on a daily basis), not least in light of the well-understood *constitutional* role of certain judges, higher ones in particular, in assessing the validity of exercises of legal power, including enactments, for their compliance with morally framed considerations

Ethics in the Public Domain, ch 10; J Raz, *The Morality of Freedom* (Oxford, Clarendon Press, 1986) chs 2–4.

[6] Unless, that is, '[the] tests for identifying the content of the law and determining its existence depend exclusively on facts of human behavior capable of being described in value-neutral terms, and applied without resort to moral argument' (Raz, *The Authority of Law*, n 5, 39–40).

[7] See, eg, OW Holmes, 'The Path of the Law' (1897) 10 *Harvard Law Review* 457.

(such as 'reasonableness', 'cruelty' or 'freedom of speech'). Duly radicalised, this expansive conception of gaps entails that the content of central areas of constitutional, criminal, administrative or tort law is vanishingly slight – so that, for instance, in principle no taking of alien property is wrongful in English law unless and until a judge rules it to have been 'dishonest'.[8] Or, as Gardner writes, 'Cruel punishments … do not per se violate the Eighth Amendment [of the US Constitution]. What violate the Eighth Amendment are punishments that have been authoritatively determined to be cruel.'[9]

To be sure, when courts are called on to pronounce on the validity of a transaction or an enactment, they may well annul it with prospective rather than retrospective effect. And even before the courts decide, various kinds of presumptions of validity may apply to transactions or enactments that are correct from a formal point of view (chapter 5.V; chapter 4.V). These procedural measures warranted by the Rule of Law may lend misleading plausibility to the view that moral considerations relied on by the courts in nullifying the transactions or enactments (eg 'unfair', 'freedom of speech') necessarily were *not* part of the legal regime that circumscribed the power of the parties or the law-makers in the first place. So may the standing possibility that the court's legally final judgment misapplies the relevant moral considerations. All of these predicaments, additionally, may encourage the perception, now increasingly widespread, that there cannot be more at stake in the question whether morally framed provisions create legal gaps than a theoretical quibble.[10] But none of these stances is sound. Criteria of validity, moral or non-moral, are not appropriately regarded as non-existent just because presumptions of validity and doctrines of finality can reduce, and sometimes eliminate, the legal effects of a partial breach of such criteria. Rather, the fact that by default *all* criteria of validity are relevant in law is what calls for these presumptions and doctrines, and also conditions and constrains their scope of application. Until a judicial pronouncement is final, for instance, mistakes of law can and often should bear on grounds of review – a crucial and often overlooked practical implication of theoretical debates about moral validity criteria.[11]

[8] According to s 1(1) of the Theft Act 1968 (UK), 'A person is guilty of theft if he dishonestly appropriates property belonging to another with the intention of permanently depriving the other of it'; the idea of dishonesty is only nominally specified in case law, especially after *Ivey v Genting Casinos UK Ltd t/a Crockfords* [2017] UKSC 67 (overruling *R v Ghosh* [1982] EWCA Crim 2). Morally circumscribed rules that cut across English criminal law include the very test for recklessness, which requires that the defendant foresaw a risk that it was (objectively) *unreasonable* to take (see, eg, AP Simester and others, *Simester and Sullivan's Criminal Law: Theory and Doctrine*, 6th edn (Oxford, Hart Publishing, 2016) 149).

[9] Gardner, 'Justification under Authority', n 5, 72.

[10] See, eg, S Shapiro, *Legality* (Cambridge, MA, Harvard University Press, 2011) 274.

[11] Countless legal concepts straddle the moral/non-moral divide (eg, in the criminal law, 'intent', 'consent', 'grievous bodily harm', 'use of force', 'more than merely preparatory', 'defect of reason' …). The view that moral terms create legal gaps entails that it is indeterminate whether

Of course the law could not do the morally needed job that this book advocates, the development of large-scale specific convergence, if legal provisions were *predominantly* framed in moral terms *all across* the legal system. For moral considerations are, usually, vaguer than non-moral ones, and often highly so. If legal provisions and arrangements were substantially framed in non-specified, open-ended moral terms, legal reasoning could barely furnish more determinate guidance than general moral reasoning can provide in the absence of law. Note that this constraint is a matter of degree, not an all-or-nothing one. And there is another, no less important, reason for this constraint on moral validity criteria. Moral considerations are not only comparatively vague, but they are also comparatively controversial. They are controversial as a matter of fact, even to the extent that they are rationally determined. Persons in ideologically diverse communities disagree, and are known to disagree, even about what counts as a grossly unfair contract or a grossly cruel practice. It follows that law could not warrant morally needed certainty and reliance if identifying legal positions *predominantly* required an exercise of reasoning akin to that effected by supreme courts in contentious human rights cases. Law, in other words, must not only be relatively determinate, as I have so far argued. It must also be relatively *easy to identify*. This takes us to the second argument buttressing the need for law's positivity.

B. Ease of Identification

In order for specific convergence to occur, the required patterns of conduct must be salient in the relevant group. A requirement is duly salient if many persons are able stably to converge in identifying it. Legal requirements are in principle apt to be salient, as we saw in chapter 4.V, because they are apt to be identified by reference to their source, their originating circumstances. And legal requirements are apt to be identified by reference to their source because, to begin with, they have one. Legal requirements originate in the acts of certain persons and institutions. In this basic sense, law is apt to be easy to identify because it is positive.

But law morally needs to have a rather sophisticated degree of the ease of identification. Law's positivity enables that degree of sophistication, but does not by itself guarantee it. In order for legal requirements to be appropriately salient, their identification ought sometimes to turn on special features of their source, features that are relatively easy to find out, to spot and to attribute in uncontroversial fashion. A public record is more salient, though no less 'source-based', than countless remote facts about a transaction's pedigree. Validity will

something is a mistake of law to the extent it is indeterminate whether the term applied is morally circumscribed.

therefore sometimes appropriately turn on procedural steps, such as notary attestation, witnessing or official registration, with associated valid representations or physical proofs bearing permanent witness to the existence and content of the valid act (chapter 3.VI). Moreover, in the interests of ease of identification there will sometimes be good reason to determine the legal positions persons are in through the additional means of rulings, the general point of which is to apply rules to particular cases (eg licences, work permits, judicial resolutions) (chapter 5.IV). But there is a limit to the number of rulings a healthy legal system can afford. And there is a limit, too, and an important one, on the extent to which appearances of validity deserve to be legally honoured. They must not be systematically allowed to thwart justified allocations of power, or to facilitate evasion of responsibility. There are no degrees of positivity, but ease of identification should be, and can only ever be, a matter of degree.

Here as well, one may have a skewed perception of the degree of ease of identification possible, and needed, in a legal system if one's primary focus is on adjudication by appellate courts. Dworkin's work is a magnificent illustration of that focus.[12] In his main contributions to legal theory, Dworkin chiefly conceives of law as comprising all the standards that courts have a moral duty to apply.[13] He argues that arriving at true propositions of law involves a complex all-things-considered ('interpretive') judgement, where the things to be considered include many kinds of say-so of legal officials ('past political decisions') and other facts, *as well as* (moral) principles of justice, fairness and procedural due process.[14] Correctly identifying law through an interpretive judgement, as Dworkin presents it, will not seldom be a herculean task, which even competent judges may not get right. Dworkin's overstatement of the degree to which it can take moral judgement to identify legal requirements nearly cashes out, in some central passages of his work, as a denial of law's positivity. There is, for many purposes, no general distance between (judges') legal and moral obligation, as Dworkin conceives of law.[15]

Dworkin may have done more than any other writer to bring out the systemic dimension of legal meaning canvassed later in this chapter. This dimension comes to the fore especially, though by no means only, in certain forms of judicial reasoning. Indeed adjudicative reasoning will quite naturally, and often legitimately, tend to read down legal gaps, not least under the influence of socially entrenched views of the judicial role as only ever appropriately involving law application. And higher judges with legal power to review and change

[12] For Dworkin's own statement of the limits of his focus, see, eg, R Dworkin, *Law's Empire* (Oxford, Hart Publishing, 1998) 12.

[13] A point perhaps clearest in R Dworkin, *Taking Rights Seriously* (London, Duckworth, 1978) 47.

[14] Dworkin, *Law's Empire*, n 12, especially ch 7.

[15] '[U]nless circumstances are special' (as in the case of Nazi law: ibid 101ff; Dworkin, *Taking Rights Seriously*, n 13, 344), a theory of the kind Dworkin claims to provide, if it is not 'deeply sceptical', 'must be understood as saying what judges should do in principle' (Dworkin, *Law's Empire*, n 12, 112).

settled law on moral grounds will not seldom find themselves engaging head-on with the very kinds of moral consideration that, for most ordinary purposes, the technique of legal validity does and ought to allow us to bracket away and keep outside debate. There may be good reason, for instance, to empower only a centralised judicial organ to assess the validity of certain statutory enactments on moral grounds. Even our normally useful, because simplifying, talk of discrete legal rules or norms (or principles, or standards …) may appropriately lose relevance as appellate judges enquire about the moral credentials of legal requirements in the process of reshaping the latter. In Dworkin's mature work, in fact, there is no room for talk of discrete legal standards at all.[16]

But Dworkin's court-centred account of law understates the important extent to which, outside the courtroom if not inside, legal requirements can be said to exist, can be invoked, reckoned with and relied on, quite independently of their moral merit. It understates the paramount (and very interesting!) sense in which valid bundles of legal positions must be able to circulate, to be identifiable relatively uncontroversially, in order for law to be able to tackle controversial matters in controversial ways. It understates, in short, the crucial *intermediate* step, in any kind of legal reasoning, aimed at establishing what the law is on some matter, which law may prove to have gaps and be unjust, to a greater or lesser degree, even *after* competent lawyers have correctly ascertained it. Dworkin assumes but does not sufficiently demonstrate that the law is essentially gapless, so that the 'interpretive judgement' can virtually always yield one uniquely legally and morally correct answer. Dworkin's focus obscures the important truth that law must be considerably less than fully determinate in order to fulfil its morally needed task. Indeed, according to Dworkin, the law's morally needed task is to justify the use of state coercion, which use is unjustified whenever it is not required, in virtually every detail, by pre-existing law.[17] In light of the argument defended in this book, Dworkin does not only understate the degree to which law can and should be easy to identify. He also overstates the degree to which law can and should be determinate.

C. Targeted Crafting

Dworkin's adjudicative emphasis has a further related upshot, which fails to do justice to our third argument why law's positivity is morally needed. Legally valid choices of persons and institutions, public and private, crafting legal positions to the extent their discretion allows, are next to dissolved amidst the pool

[16] Dworkin's early work (*Taking Rights Seriously*, n 13, 22ff) had famously distinguished between rules and principles.

[17] See Dworkin, *Law's Empire*, n 12, 93–94, in light of Dworkin's refutations of various forms of radical scepticism (ibid 260ff, 266ff, 412) based on the unstated premise that under-determination is not a (third) possibility.

of miscellaneous facts, 'past political decisions', states of affairs, attitudes and other events that Dworkin lumps together under the heading 'law in the preinterpretive sense', and which provide the raw input for the 'interpretive judgement'.[18] There is accordingly little room in Dworkin's account for the idea of *legal power*. There is little room, in other words, for considering the capacity of each of *many different* agents, not only judges, to *make and unmake* normative positions, not only to discover them. Law's positivity matters because it matters that certain agents get to decide about certain things. It matters because of the manifold reasons to empower, and especially the moral need for individually and collectively self-determining choice and commitment. Because law is the product of human acts, it is capable of being the product of self-directing undertaking. It is capable of being shaped in a targeted fashion.

The technique of legal validity is the central instrument facilitating targeted crafting of law. Acting validly involves doing something by manifesting one's intent to thereby do it (chapter 3.IX). A valid choice is a self-fulfilling choice, legally speaking. In a just community, legal positions will be made and unmade in a substantially targeted way. But again this requirement is a matter of degree. For one thing, choices should not be legally self-fulfilling where that would be incompatible with a just ordering of human relations. Criteria of validity can appropriately circumscribe what someone can validly choose and how (chapter 3.VIII). For example, grossly unfair contracts ought not to be legally valid, however earnestly they are intended to be. For another thing, it would not be proper for all legal positions to be shaped directly through a use of validity's technique to that effect. Chapter 5 discussed, for instance, the moral appropriateness of case law as an ancillary source of legal rules, which rules are indirect offshoots of valid rulings (chapter 5.VI).

It follows that Dworkin's adjudicative focus doubly hides from view the targeted crafting that legal powers facilitate. First, it concentrates on *one* kind of law-changing agent only, one substantially constrained by pre-existing law. Secondly, that agent's method for introducing general legal changes is itself not focally targeted. Dworkin's chain-novelists face the double handicap of lacking substantial control over *both* the general plot *and* their very own chapter. Legal positions need to be deliberately designed to an extent only, but it is an extent wider than Dworkin gives his reader reason to think.

The conclusion of this section is that communities morally need law's positivity not only because morality's under-determination calls for *something non-moral* filling in moral voids, nor only because morality's controversial character calls for relatively *uncontroversial cues* to render requirements salient. Communities morally need positive law also, and crucially, because just relations between persons can only be relations that, in significant respects, are crafted, are scripted, are imagined and ventured, by those persons themselves in

[18] ibid 65ff, 91ff.

use and exercise of their *self-directing* capacities that go to define their identity as individuals and groups.

II. THE SYSTEMIC CHARACTER OF LEGAL MEANING

If many different persons make decisions at different times on different subject-matters, those decisions may well overlap or conflict with one another. We have seen how validity makes it possible to distribute the capacity to decide, while rendering *each* of those decisions relatively easy to identify. Clearly, however, that is not enough. There must also be sufficient coherence *among* legally valid decisions. If valid decisions are not coherent with one another on the whole, they will not go to shape schemes of convergence extending to a large population and linking many different spheres of social life. It seems, therefore, as if justice placed incompatible demands on the technique of validity. Justice calls for schemes forged by different persons at different times, but this only increases the danger of inconsistent decision-making, willed or unwilled, which in turn is fatal to the prospect of conduct under the schemes converging, precisely as justice requires.

The technique of validity can accommodate both of these demands. The following pages show this. But in order to do so, our argument must undertake a shift of perspective.

The previous chapter, and the previous section, have predominantly taken a bird's-eye view in portraying the need for a diversity of valid acts all across the scenery of legal sources. It is time to consider this reality, once again, at a micro rather than a macro level. It is time to focus not on the plurality of acts but on their respective *legal meaning*. It is time to resume the perspective of an individual agent crafting legal positions – the perspective of the book's initial chapters.

It will be remembered that, in adopting this perspective, chapter 3 articulated the technique of legal validity, that is, the way one goes about performing a legally valid act. Chapter 3 showed that this technique bears some similarities to the technique of ordinary communication. But it insisted that communicating and exercising legal power are focally different forms of intentional action. The argument in chapter 3 only took note of some major differences between the two techniques, without seeking to uncover their root cause. It falls to be uncovered now.

The differences between the two techniques can be helpfully summarised by contrasting the degree of control the individual agent holds in either case over the meaning of his act. There is a sense in which we have greater control over the legal meaning of our acts than over their communicative meaning, and a sense in which the converse holds. Let us revisit the reasons why this is so.

In ordinary communication there is considerable scope for misspeaking, inadvertently insinuating, using a misleading tone or otherwise failing to express what one had hoped to convey. There are hardly any limits to what communicative acts can be *about*, including moods or feelings best expressed through subtle contextual cues that rules of language do not even purport to regulate. In law, by contrast, there is less to be said and there are fewer ways of saying it. Law pervasively limits the factors that can bear on legal meaning – so much so that any factor not foreseen by law, however indirectly, is in principle irrelevant to legal meaning. Legally speaking, it is irrelevant whether you agreed to the sale enthusiastically or reluctantly, unless there is a question of coerced consent, in which case it falls to be dealt with in accordance with the relevant regime. Legal systems, moreover, have dedicated devices to reduce the risk of unintended valid acting, including witnessing, ceremonies and warning displays. In all the preceding respects, we have greater control over legal meaning than over communicative meaning.

But in another sense the converse is true. The law places significant constraints on which positions we can validly change, and how we can do so. These constraints are criteria of legal validity. We may fail to change the legal positions we sought to change because some clauses in our draft agreement contravene a statutory regime. Or we may change legal positions we did not purport to change because case law qualifies the meaning of a term in our clause. The legal meaning of an act is co-determined by the valid acts of others that have gone to shape the applicable regime. Compare everyday conversation. However subtle the message expressed, the speaker is its single author. Establishing the communicative meaning of his act is therefore exclusively a matter of discovering the intention he reasonably manifested at a particular time.[19] In law, even legislatures and supreme courts may lack full control over the legal meaning of their acts, notably in virtue of the diverse body of law we call 'constitutional', which is not exhausted by a bare constitutional text. Although, in general, the lower the agent's rank the greater the constraints on his ability to change legal positions, institutional hierarchy is by no means always the legally relevant consideration to resolve conflicts amongst valid acts – not least because there can be no exhaustive *ranking* of institutions in a legal system that is sensitive to the many different reasons to allocate and limit power as between them (chapter 5).

One flip side of the agent's less-than-full control over the legal meaning of his act is an increased difficulty on the part of others to *identify* his act's legal meaning. This is why it can take sophisticated training to ascertain the precise legal meaning of some acts. We already noted that an act's validity may be indeterminate if it fulfils applicable validity criteria only in part (chapter 5.V). We must now stress that it is often indeterminate, or at any rate uncertain, *which* criteria bear on an act's validity, because criteria do not normally come in exhaustive lists but are scattered across different provisions of the system (chapter 5.I).

[19] Even when the speaker is a collective agent, as with 'joint statements', we look for the intent reasonably manifested on a relatively discrete occasion by that *one* (collective) source.

Law students learn quickly that 'what the law is' on many questions cannot be simply read off from the wording of a discrete statute or judicial decision. They also learn that what looked like a contract, or a will or an official resolution, may turn out not to be one. In fact, only exceptionally does the law seal off an act's wording such that it necessarily corresponds one-to-one with the act's legal meaning regardless of any breaches of substantive constraints (chapter 4.V). Such strategies are required when certainty is paramount. They include registry entries and finality doctrines. From the viewpoint of legal meaning, these are limit cases.

Legal meaning is *systemic*: whether a given act is legally valid and what its legal meaning is, at any point in time, is a function of the acts of other persons and institutions. The idea I have just expressed has two component notions. The first is that the legal meaning of an act is a function of the acts of others. The second is that legal meaning has a temporal dimension. The next two sections (sections III and IV) respectively consider these component notions. They have been repeatedly misconstrued by authors intent on fitting legal meaning into the model of communication, even where this model fails to explain what is unique and valuable about the nature of legal meaning. The comparison with communication will therefore assist us in shedding light on what this literature leaves unstated. Section V will then show why the systemic character of legal meaning, thus understood, entails that there can and will be a significant degree of coherence among legally valid acts within any legal order – among the threads that weave the fabric of law.

III. A FUNCTION OF THE ACTS OF OTHERS

The marks on this page would not mean what they mean *but for* the rules of English grammar, syntax, semantics, spelling, etc. These rules result from a recurrent and stable practice of other English-speakers using certain combinations of marks as vehicles to communicate certain messages. In this respect, the communicative meaning of my English utterances is determined by the acts of other persons. But there is a fundamental difference between this and the way in which the legal meaning of my valid acts is determined by the acts of others.

The rules of a natural language exist and endure primarily in customary form (chapter 4.VI). They are what they are as a result of loosely aggregative, sustained clusters of conduct and dispositions. By and large they are not changed by someone *saying so*, but by many persons saying many things on many different occasions using a similar, eventually shared, modus operandi. In a mature legal system, by contrast, the acts that determine legal meaning for the most part do so severally, not jointly, as the acts of legislatures, judges, contracting parties, testators, agencies and so forth. In a mature legal system, legal positions are substantially shaped in a targeted way; that is in itself, as we saw, a requirement of justice (chapter 5.VII). Moreover, the legal positions that can be shaped in targeted fashion include not only legal duties and rights, but also legal powers. That is to say: the rules on *how* to perform valid acts, unlike the rules of language, are themselves up for crafting.

An upshot of this difference is that the slow, incremental evolution of language rules in and of itself enhances both the quality and coherence of those rules. As inappropriate rules have a chance of being gradually replaced by rules that give better or simpler expression to felt communicative needs, language rules can, so to speak, 'work themselves pure' as a relatively coherent and compact set. This renders the language rules *learnable*, albeit with more or less effort needed for mastery. They can be used in largely unreflective fashion. They can substantially become second nature to a substantial number of people. This is why it makes sense to say of someone who expresses his communicative intent through the use of these rules that he *reasonably* manifests his intent, as we have been doing (chapter 3.II). Not only are these rules bound to be reasonable, typically quite good, *as* methods for effectively getting messages across, but moreover, given their essentially learnable character, it is reasonable *to assume* a working knowledge of them on the part of both speaker and audience.

No similar assumptions can comfortably be made in regard of the totality of rules of a modern legal system, which are profuse rather than compact, potentially inconsistent rather than overwhelmingly coherent, and thus hardly learnable as a comprehensive set, even for highly trained professionals. This is one of the reasons why good law schools teach the techniques of legal reasoning over and above substantive legal rules. Law is not simply a domain that involves a specialised use of language that may be inconspicuous to the layperson, a domain in this sense analogous to diplomacy, the academy and other technical contexts.[20] The sheer quantity of fresh decisions that may determine an act's legal meaning in a given jurisdiction makes it implausible to attribute a working knowledge of all of them to all those who have legal power to perform valid acts.[21] Criteria of validity, moreover, can involve potentially complex and cumbersome steps over and above the making of certain sounds or marks on a page. Our account stresses these differences between communication and legal power by distinguishing between what an agent reasonably manifests and what he *legally* manifests.

That the legal meaning of an act is a function of the acts of others does not entail that the legal meaning of every valid act is determined by the acts of others to precisely the same degree. There are good reasons, as we saw in chapter 5, to

[20] Thanks to Richard Ekins for prompting me to think about this point.

[21] It should, of course, be *possible* for anyone to ascertain the content of legal provisions, either directly or with the aid of lawyers. And in some fields of law, provisions should be articulated in such a way that facilitates understanding by the general public. Depending on these factors, amongst others, the rule that ignorance of the law is no excuse will be more or less compatible with the Rule of Law.

radically limit the discretion of certain agents on some subject-matters, while affording wide discretion to other agents. It follows that the wider an agent's discretion to shape legal positions, and the more well-versed the agent in the intricacies of the applicable regime, the closer a correspondence there will be between what the agent reasonably manifests and what he legally manifests. So much so that there is some plausibility, in this respect, in portraying the legal meaning of legislative enactments on the model of communicative meaning. In a healthy legal system, the legislature will hold the most wide-ranging power to mould legal changes relatively free from legal constraints, *and* its known legal proficiency and expertise may warrant, even as a matter of legal convention, construing the statutory text on the assumption that it was tailored by the legislature to anticipate and take effect in the regime in which it is in fact inserted. To that extent, the law-making intent that is reasonably manifested, if not by individual legislators then at least by the legislative institution, will tend to coincide with the act's legal result, and thus with the law actually made, especially at the point of inception.

Recent works of Ekins, Marmor and Raz portray legislative action as a kind of communicative action.[22] The accounts are based on a sound understanding of the technique of communication, but it is telling how they face difficulties in proportion to the extent to which they respectively make an effort to accommodate the systemic dimension of legal meaning in the communicative framework.

Consistently with his focus on the central case of legislative action, Ekins entirely brackets questions about legal constraints on the acts of a legislature assumed justifiably to have plenary law-making power.[23] Marmor, by contrast, from the outset claims to provide an account of 'law-making acts' that also extends to acts of administrative agencies and courts.[24] Despite this announcement, Marmor's actual focus throughout his discussion is on legislative enactments. Of these he says that the 'communicated content is the legal content'.[25] And he deems that content to be substantially settled through the (semantic) conventions of language.[26] He plays down possible constraints or qualifications arising from the governing legal framework, not anticipated by the legislature, as a 'rarely' occurring form of 'pragmatic enrichment' of what the legislature 'asserts'.[27] In thus placing the emphasis on the action of legislatures

[22] In the same vein, see, eg, J Goldsworthy, 'The Case for Originalism' in G Huscroft and BW Miller (eds), *The Challenge of Originalism: Theories of Constitutional Interpretation* (Cambridge, Cambridge University Press, 2011) 42–69, on the legal meaning of constitutions.

[23] R Ekins, *The Nature of Legislative Intent* (Oxford, Oxford University Press, 2012).

[24] A Marmor, *The Language of Law* (Oxford, Oxford University Press, 2014) 11; see also A Marmor, 'An Institutional Conception of Authority' (2011) 39 *Philosophy and Public Affairs* 238, wherein Marmor tentatively broaches the institutional dimension of legal power but with a focus on agents with wide discretion in exercising it.

[25] Marmor, *The Language of Law*, n 24, 12.

[26] ibid 23ff.

[27] ibid 33.

within their scope of law-making power, the account fails to make good on the opening announcement. It neglects to consider how legal constraints can and often do hinder purported changes of general legal positions by, especially, administrative agencies or courts, in ways that sit uneasily with Marmor's blanket dictum that it is 'no more than common sense' that law-making, by *any* of these agents, 'is an instance of communication'.[28]

Raz is more sensitive still to the possibility of such constraints. Up to a point, he tries to adjust the communicative model to cater for them. *Pace* Raz, however, this only demonstrates that the communicative model is not fit for purpose. According to Raz, 'we need … a way of seeing how [the law's] content is a function of various activities, and layers of activities, in continuous interaction, rather than … a function of a single act, fixed once and for all'.[29] At first blush, Raz's account of legislative action might seem not to be responsive to this concern. Raz characterises the act of legislating as an act whereby a duly authorised agent 'makes it the law … that *p* … by performing an action which expresses the intention that *p* become the law in virtue of that intention being manifestly expressed'.[30] The repetition of '*p*' entails that the act necessarily succeeds in making the legal changes it manifestly purports to make. But Raz circumspectly takes account of the fact that this might not be so. He adds, in a footnote, that the intention relevant to his definition is not 'the intention that this shall be the law of the country' but only 'the intention that the Bill be a law, ie a *prima facie* legal reason, which takes effect alongside other – sometimes competing – legal rules and doctrines'.[31]

Unfortunately this only preserves a correspondence between manifested intent and legal result at the price of distorting the very intentional form of action legislators are engaged in. An intention to make law that is only a *prima facie* legal reason, an intention to make *legally defeasible* law, is an intention that, in an important sense, anticipates its own demise. Whether or not it might occasionally be harboured by individual legislators, it is certainly not the intention that legislators manifest, qua legislators, 'in all but the most anomalous circumstances'.[32] (In the limit case, it would be roughly equivalent to: 'Be It Enacted, but only if we may.') Raz's struggle to fit the act of legislating into the model of communication may help to explain why, as we saw in chapter 3, he altogether rules out the relevance of intention to a general conception of exercises of legal power (chapter 3.VII).[33] Raz seems to resist the view that an act

[28] ibid 11.

[29] Raz, *Ethics in the Public Domain*, n 5, 300, also 310.

[30] J Raz, *Between Authority and Interpretation: On the Theory of Law and Practical Reason* (Oxford, Oxford University Press, 2009) 283.

[31] ibid fn 21 at 284.

[32] ibid 284.

[33] But again he sees (and explains) the relevance of intention to promising (see especially J Raz, 'Promises in Morality and Law' (1982) 95 *Harvard Law Review* 916, 927; J Raz, 'Promises and Obligations' in PMS Hacker and J Raz (eds), *Law, Morality, and Society: Essays in Honour of HLA Hart* (Oxford, Clarendon Press, 1977) 218).

may still be the agent's intentional act despite its legal meaning being a function of the intentional acts of others. Perhaps this is also why Raz's discussions of *law's* authority consistently portray the holder of authority as being an individual person.[34]

Other parts of Raz's work, too, are symptomatic of this neglect. His well-known 'sources thesis' asserts that the 'existence' (validity) and 'content' of a law 'depend exclusively' on its 'sources', which are 'those facts by virtue of which it is valid *and which identify its content*'.[35] Raz presents this as a truth applicable to any law, including law made by subordinate officials with little discretion. The formulation casts 'sources' as the input and 'content' as the output. In so doing, it misleadingly downplays the fact that the content of a purported law-making act, that is, what it reasonably manifests, is routinely one of the things *to be checked* in order to tell whether the act is valid and thus a legal 'source' in the first place, and a fortiori what its legal meaning is. As we have repeatedly noted, there are a number of legal devices to shield certain kinds of act from legal challenge. They include principles of institutional hierarchy (eg legislative supremacy), temporal limits on reversibility, or presumptions of validity based on certain enhanced procedural steps. Such measures go to make it the case that the act's validity depends more on *who* made it and how, than on what it is *about* – more, in this sense, on its sheer source than on its content. But this is the exception, not the standard, from the point of view of the systemic workings of validity and legal power. It is because legal meaning is systemic that there is need to seal off the manifest content of certain sources.

And it will not do to mark the difference between what an act reasonably manifests and its legal result by contrasting the act's 'communicative content' with its 'legal content'.[36] Solum, who is attentive to the possible mismatch between the two, proposes to distinguish in these terms between (say) a will 'as written' and the will's legal meaning once given a saving construction; or between a constitutional provision before and after being authoritatively construed by case law. The infelicity here lies in presenting as a communicative success what is primarily a *failed attempt* to exercise legal power. Here as well, taking seriously the idea of an exercise of legal power as a form of action involving a

[34] An authoritative directive, says Raz, must be presented as someone's view on how subjects ought to behave. The holder of authority must, amongst other things, be capable of communicating (see, eg, Raz, *Ethics in the Public Domain*, n 5, 215ff; J Raz, 'Comments and Responses' in LH Meyer, SL Paulson and TW Pogge (eds), *Rights, Culture and the Law: Themes from the Legal and Political Philosophy of Joseph Raz* (Oxford, Oxford University Press, 2003) 264).

[35] Raz, *The Authority of Law*, n 5, 39–48 (emphasis added). Raz's category of 'law' is narrower than my category of legal meaning given Raz's view that exercises of private power (eg contracts, regulations of associations) are not 'part of the legal system' (J Raz, *Practical Reason and Norms* (London, Hutchinson, 1975) 152–54); this does not affect my argument.

[36] LB Solum, 'Communicative Content and Legal Content' (2013) 89 *Notre Dame Law Review* 479 (he speaks of 'content' rather than 'meaning' because he deems the latter term ambiguous: ibid 484). Marmor, too, speaks of 'communicated content' and 'legal content' (*The Language of Law*, n 24, 12 *et passim*) but insists, focusing on legislation, that they are always identical.

self-referring or reflexive intention, as chapter 3 portrayed it, requires appreciating that, although the agent may fail to change legal positions, he manifestly *regards himself as trying to do so*.[37] Therefore, what Solum calls the 'communicative content' of legal texts is more relevantly described as their purported legal meaning – or, if the change sought was successful at one time but has later been superseded, as their former or original legal meaning.

IV. LEGAL MEANING THROUGH TIME

This last remark about the possible change in the legal meaning of an act takes us to the temporal dimension of legal meaning. The fact that it makes sense to ask whether a certain statute *remains* good law, whether in light of new case law the legal meaning of a statutory term is *still* such and such, or whether a previously defective contract has *become* valid after a court ruling, fundamentally sets apart legal meaning from the meaning of ordinary utterances in conversation.

And yet we find Marmor resolutely appealing to the idea of 'conversation' to describe a possible sequence of conflicting decisions by legislatures and courts on the same subject-matter. Such 'conversation' occurs as the legislature (say) enacts a statute, the courts 'get to hear the legislative speech' which they 'respond to' 'by the ways in which they apply the law and interpret it in doubtful cases', only to be potentially responded to in turn by the legislature's 'overruling the court's decisions' and so forth.[38] It is artificial to characterise this scenario, non-metaphorically,[39] as a 'conversation'. This is not primarily because of the fact, amply recognised by Marmor, that such 'conversation' typically leaves much less information unstated than a normal casual exchange between individuals. Nor is it because legislatures and courts, unlike ordinary conversation partners, do not stand ready to reciprocally seek and provide clarification on the spot concerning any obscurities.[40] Nor because of the inherent asymmetry between judicial and legislative contributions, insofar as the latter are not ordinarily framed as interpretations of judicial law-making acts. What renders it especially artificial to study this scenario as a conversation is that, in this peculiar exchange, *subsequent contributions are liable to alter the meaning of earlier*

[37] Marmor similarly conflates manifesting an intent with manifesting an intent *to communicate*. This leads to a sweeping statement: 'Those who have doubts that legislation is necessarily a communicative act need only consider' whether we can 'have a legislature … that fails to communicate its laws, *keeping them entirely secret*' (ibid 18, emphasis added).

[38] ibid 50; generally ch 2 et seq.

[39] As Marmor presents it, this 'conversation' is on a par with the conversation 'among the legislators themselves during the enactment process' (ibid 49–50); cf focally *metaphorical* appeals to 'conversation' or 'dialogue' as part of *normative* accounts of forms of inter-institutional interaction emphasising cooperation over incompatible determinations of law (eg, A Young, *Democratic Dialogue and the Constitution* (Oxford, Oxford University Press, 2017)).

[40] Ekins, *The Nature of Legislative Intent*, n 23, 212–13.

ones, indeed eviscerate them, so that, for example, where the legislature settles a question in a way incompatible with its prior settlement by case law, what goes on is poorly described as a quarrel between an interlocutor's saying 'This is the case' and another's responding 'I disagree, it is not'. In law, someone saying something incompatible with what you said may entail that what you said ceases to mean, now, what it meant then.

That legal meaning can change over time presupposes something more fundamental. It presupposes that it endures in time. Other acts can make changes, cancellations or qualifications because there is something there to be changed, cancelled or qualified. We are used to the lasting character of legal changes validly introduced. Present law recognises as valid today countless things that were validly made in the past, and have not expired according to their original terms. But it is important not to lose sight of the fact that that recognition itself is a matter of law. A 400-year-old conveyance is valid today not only because back then it legally manifested a transfer of title, but also because today's law has chosen to continue to recognise as legally valid what was legally manifested then.[41] This is a standing, default kind of choice made by legal orders. Legal orders do well to treat as valid today what was validly made according to sets of rules that may long be extinct, and otherwise to mitigate the onerousness of supervened legal changes. This enables legal orders to regulate the affairs of subsisting persons, in ways that respect and warrant reasonable expectations. But it remains possible, and is often fitting, for the law to choose otherwise, and to validly override or qualify prior legal changes. This choice may be explicit in targeted acts, such as an open overruling or legislative overhaul, or manifested in more implicit ways, including a gradual shift of interpretative practice that gives rise to new mandatory canons of legal construction.

This host of questions does not arise with respect to the meaning of ordinary communicative acts. Figuring out the communicative meaning of an act is a matter of determining the intent the speaker reasonably manifested, given his expected audience, on the occasion on which he spoke. Although the rules and conventions of language he used as vehicles to manifest his intent may have changed in the meantime, so that perhaps the same words uttered today in a similar context would stand for quite a different message, insofar as we are interested in the act's communicative meaning we will retrieve it by using the rules as they existed *then*.[42] Communicative acts can last in time only in the sense that they can be understood and referred to long after their making, particularly when recorded in writing or other lasting supports. We can read books the

[41] This is implicit in our formulation of the technique of legal power as changing legal positions, if and to the extent *legally* provided, by *legally* manifesting an intent to do so (ch 3.IX). The law referred to by the italicised expressions is the law existing at any given point in time at which an act's legal meaning is at stake.

[42] We speak pro tanto metaphorically when we say of a work of art that it, in and of itself, 'communicates' something independently of the artist's intentions, which we may know to have been quite different. Artistic and other kinds of meaning are not this book's subject-matter.

author has come to disown, and appraise anonymous pamphlets. But the continued presence of older books or pamphlets on our bookshelves does not diminish anybody's *ability* to contradict their claims today.

The valid acts of others can alter the legal meaning of one's act over time because, in a sense, they are the reason why one's act still has, and indeed ever had, legal meaning. It is true that such dependence of one's valid act on the valid acts of others can be disruptive from one's own point of view. Even the enduring validity of an act may be a disruption for an agent who has come to regret having performed it but is now indefeasibly bound because his legal system continuously recognises the act's legal validity. But the possibility of disruption must not obscure the fundamental *empowering* role of the acts of others, and thus of the legal system they go to make up. It is only by acting in the framework of an enduring legal system that one can wield the extraordinary power to regulate the future by acting in the present by means of validity's technique. The fact that one's valid choice can have lasting legal relevance, extending even beyond one's own lifetime, demonstrates rather than belies that in making that choice one can exercise a distinct kind of *power*. Continuity in law is a mark of power.

Here as well, Raz's account yields a different diagnosis. In law, according to Raz, 'continuity transcends and conflicts with authority';[43] they are 'forever in conflict'.[44] Raz says that, after a certain time, the continued validity of a law cannot be explained by the authority of its maker. It must instead be explained by considerations of continuity, which are independent from respect for an authority and may set limits to its power.[45] Raz's emphatic dissociation between legal authority and legal continuity is an upshot of his view that authoritative utterances are communicative acts by individual persons. Persons do not hold office or live forever, and their ability to communicate is correspondingly circumscribed. Only by taking seriously that a legally valid choice crafts normative positions within a temporally persisting legal *system*, as on our account, is it possible to appreciate, as one should, that the continuing legal validity of an act does not inherently conflict with, but is evidence of, the power exercised by its maker. It is a power to make targeted choices whose legal meaning is nevertheless systemic, because it is a function of the acts of others and lasts in time.

V. A SINGLE AUTHOR?

We can now home in on an important implication of the argument developed in the last three sections concerning the systemic character of legal meaning. The fact that an agent has less than full control over the legal meaning of his

[43] Raz, *Between Authority and Interpretation*, n 30, 233.
[44] ibid 237.
[45] ibid 233.

act, both in its inception and over time, entails that there will be a significant degree of *coherence* among legally valid acts within one and the same legal system.

Consider why this is so. To begin with, the very relation of empowerment between two acts, in and of itself, goes some way towards precluding inconsistencies (chapter 5.I). Valid acts are inconsistent with one another where they give rise to legal positions that cannot be simultaneously held, or effectively lived up to. An act that is deeply ultra vires, because in excess of the agent's substantive scope of competence, never came into existence in law: for example, when a person attempts to marry a second spouse, or a court wholly lacks jurisdiction for an order it issues. If the legal meaning of the act were the one manifestly intended by its maker, the act would be inconsistent with the empowering regime and potentially with other valid acts, including acts performed under the auspices of that regime. But legal reasoning has additional resources to preclude inconsistencies, besides empowerment. They include basic presuppositions of legal thought accepted by all legal systems, such as *lex posterior* or *lex specialis*, as well as some entrenched canons of interpretation, and countless principles germane to particular legal areas, such as the presumption of *mens rea* in criminal law. These maxims summon those engaged with legal materials to read into them reconciliations and analogies well beyond what their literal tenor might warrant. Legal systems also have devices for *eliminating* inconsistencies once they have arisen, most evident in the familiar fact that virtually all areas of legal regulation fall within the jurisdiction of some court. This may involve rulings specifically pronouncing on questions of validity, including by offering saving constructions (chapter 5.V). Finally, law-making institutions with wide-ranging powers to introduce articulate sets of legal changes can *positively forge* the kind of coherence amongst acts that can enable them to relate to one another as means to ends, or in otherwise complementary fashion, in pursuit of intelligible goals. The decisions of law-making institutions can foment coherence not least by *evincing* it, with the aid of default clauses, non-exhaustive enumerations, closure rules and other resources of legislative craft that themselves anticipate and feed into standard methods of interpretation.

All the above resources have two important things in common. The first is that the coherence they can secure, severally and jointly, is inherently incomplete and precarious. Acts that do not fully meet validity criteria, or do not meet them all, will in some cases be afforded validity (chapter 5.V; chapter 4.V). Agents who have discretion in exercising legal power may steadily use that discretion in inconsistent ways that no legal principle or procedure is there to iron out. And there is no guarantee that these resources of reasoning and procedure will in fact be used in ways conducive to coherence. This is because of the second thing they have in common. These resources *are themselves of legal making*. They are devices whereby the law, as it were, caters for its own coherence. The law cannot be fully coherent, but it aspires to become coherent. It presents itself as capable of being so rendered. Those resources are the legal expression of a deeply ingrained assumption of legal thought: the assumption that 'the law' is the single author of legal changes.

An implicit attribution of authorship to the law underlies that most accustomed lawyerly exercise aimed at establishing 'what the law requires' or 'what the law is' on some matter, in a way that largely bypasses reference to the individual contribution that discrete valid acts (a long line of case law, statutes, EU directives …) have made to the resulting legal proposition. Some official powers are explicitly exercised 'in the name of the law'.[46] The law's authorship also helps to make sense of the fact that those who exercise legal power are not fully in control of the legal meaning of their acts. Or would it be better to think of all of them as co-authors? That would be a strange kind of co-authorship: an involuntary co-authorship where the intervention of a co-author does not merely alter or complement one's contribution, but bears on it at a much earlier stage, namely, by diminishing one's ability to make it in the first place. For, recall, legal power is not on par with natural abilities: it must be conferred on us by somebody. By whom? Tracing an act's root of title will sooner or later lead us all the way back to a constitutional assembly or founding legal cast. But it is contrived to think that whenever we exercise legal power we do so 'on behalf of the founding fathers', or that whenever we reason in law we aim at establishing 'what the founding fathers require' on particular occasions. This is partly because the intentions that these persons originally manifested may have gradually lost relevance to determining the enduring legal meaning of their very own law-making acts, perhaps now subjected to extensive judicial and legislative elaboration.

In the above kinds of locution, 'the law' is intelligibly more than just elliptical shorthand for the sum of certain kinds of human act. It points to the enduring legal system, understood both as a set of meaning contents and as a set of institutions, which alone can accomplish things, for better or worse, that none of its members or constituent parts could accomplish on their own.

VI. THREADS IN A FABRIC

Given the pervasively systemic character of legal meaning, canvassed in the preceding sections, one might wonder why the communicative model has such a hold on legal theorists. The theorists I have in mind, some of whom were discussed in sections III and IV, are not on a par with the philosophers of language we considered in earlier chapters, who were led to construe exercises of legal power as linguistic phenomena partly because of their scepticism about the very idea of a normative position.[47] The idea of a normative change

[46] eg 'In the name of the Queen …' in relation to writs for commencing civil actions in the UK ('the Queen' referring to the state, the legal system).

[47] Notably JL Austin and Searle (see ch 3.IV, and ch 2.II and corresponding endnote).

in the framework of a legal order is central to the thought of the legal theorists discussed in the present chapter. But perhaps a major motivation for them to cling to the communicative model, even where it proves too rigid a mould, is the supposition that the *alternative* to understanding exercises of legal power as acts of communication is to embrace a view that barely leaves room for targeted shaping of legal positions and effectively merges legal and moral obligation – a view such as Dworkin advocates at some junctures. Dworkin himself may have animated this supposition by setting up his account of 'law as integrity' in direct opposition to the communicative model, which he criticises broadly along my lines.[48] But this supposition is false. Contrary to what Dworkin suggests, 'reject[ing] the assumption of a canonical moment at which a statute is born and has all and only the meaning it will ever have' does not necessitate 'law as integrity'.[49] The argument in this chapter demonstrates why.

Both the communicative model and its Dworkinian antagonist appreciate part of the truth about legal meaning but exaggerate it in a way that eclipses its inherently systemic character. This is true even of the accounts of Greenberg and Waldron, which have a more resolvedly systemic and institutional outlook. Greenberg's recent 'moral impact theory of law' considers the 'actions of legal institutions' in general, rather than (like Dworkin) the actions of certain adjudicative institutions.[50] And it focuses on what these institutions have decided, rather than (like Dworkin) on what they should decide. Greenberg's set-up therefore facilitates a sound appreciation of validity's role in allocating legal power and the moral need for law's positivity. But that appreciation does not come forth. Indeed, Greenberg insists that law cannot but be morally sound: 'The content of law is that part of the moral profile created by the actions of legal institutions in the legally proper way.'[51] Thus Greenberg vehemently denies what his own set-up commits him to affirming: namely, that the actions of legal institutions, as this book has shown, can only have a standing 'impact on' our moral duties (more than that: up to a point, even *craft* moral duties) because there is such thing as a *legal* impact of these actions which is so far forth not moral. It is the legal impact, indeed legal meaning, of the actions of institutions and individuals performed in the 'legally proper way' that is the technique of legal validity.

Waldron likewise makes a promising move. He does so in discussing the authority of legislation.[52] He attacks Marmor's view that intentions of particular

[48] Dworkin, *Law's Empire*, n 12, 315ff. He calls the communicative model the 'speaker's meaning' (or 'literal meaning') view of legislation.

[49] ibid 348.

[50] M Greenberg, 'The Moral Impact Theory of Law' (2014) 123 *Yale Law Journal* 1288; for Greenberg's sound assessment of some shortcomings of the communicative account, see M Greenberg, 'Legislation as Communication? Legal Interpretation, and the Study of Linguistic Communication' in A Marmor and S Soames (eds), *Philosophical Foundations of Language in the Law* (Oxford, Oxford University Press, 2011).

[51] Greenberg, 'The Moral Impact Theory of Law', n 50, 1323.

[52] J Waldron, *Law and Disagreement* (Oxford, Oxford University Press, 1999) especially ch 6.

legislators are authoritative.[53] According to Waldron, what is authoritative is the text, that is, the output of the multi-person vote. He accuses Marmor, who in turn builds on Raz, of 'forging too tight a connection between *authority* and *authorship*'.[54] And Waldron adds, 'on the Raz/Marmor account, authority cannot be systemic: it must be attributable to an author'.[55] It is to be regretted that Waldron does not expound on the notion of 'systemic authority'. He may be too rash to assume that, in law, systemic authority cannot be authority attributable to an author. He himself notes further on that '[t]o the extent that there is one author, it is the legislature considered as a body and as distinct from the individual members'.[56] Waldron could have helpfully extended this claim about the legislature's authorship to the authorship of the legal system as a whole – the system whose *single* voice lawyers are in the habit of discerning, hand in hand with engaging with datable choices by a *plurality* of different persons and bodies.

The systemic account of legal meaning, here proposed, avoids the pitfalls of the communicative model while preserving the paramount place of legally valid acts. We speak of a *system*, after all, where certain elements operate jointly within some endeavour or structure without ceasing for that reason to be distinct. A 'system' that absorbs its constituent parts to the point of blending them into one uniform whole is no longer a system. Neither is a range of wholly unconnected, disparate items. An agent that is less than fully in control of the legal meaning of his act is still an agent. Legal meaning, like communicative meaning, involves both acts and authorship. The peculiarity of legal meaning is that acts and authorship tend to *drift apart*. This is the corollary of its systemic character, and can be explained as follows.

In ordinary legal reasoning we implicitly acknowledge *both* that 'the law' is the ultimate author of normative changes *and* that valid acts are performed by individual agents. We implicitly acknowledge the law's authorship when we search for true 'propositions of law' or the 'content of the law' or 'what the law requires' on some matter, for the sake of determining what legal rights, duties and powers arise in a particular kind of *situation*. This focus is germane to any juristic effort to cast legal materials as supporting a certain conclusion, whether in court, in providing advice to a client, or by way of doctrinal reconstruction of law in textbooks or scholarly work. In this context we often speak of legal rules or norms as a way of wrapping up considerations bearing on the same kind of act-situation regardless of the sources from which they arise (as in 'the GBH rule'). But in other contexts we pervasively focus and rely on the legal validity of discrete choices and their products, not to mention their representations

[53] See A Marmor, *Interpretation and Legal Theory*, 2nd edn (Oxford, Hart Publishing, 2005) especially ch 8.

[54] Waldron, *Law and Disagreement*, n 52, 130.

[55] ibid.

[56] ibid 142.

and proofs (chapter 3.VI). Here our concern is with legal positions as bundled by reason of their *source*, rather than by reason of the situation to which they apply. This kind of source-based demarcation facilitates countless daily endeavours, as well as preparatory steps in the above forms of lawyerly and judicial reasoning.

So we have, on the one hand, the plane of the 'content of the law' and, on the other hand, the plane of discrete legally valid acts. Both planes are firmly rooted in legal thought and practice, and jurists routinely flip back and forth between them. But note their asymmetry. The more we focus on the 'content of the law', the more particular valid acts may recede into the distance. And the more we focus on particular valid acts, the more we may lose sight of the wider legal fabric. Legal validity serves to bundle units of legal meaning by reason of their source. For some purposes, we want these units of legal meaning to circulate precisely as such, because we are interested in *contributions* to the fabric of law. We are interested in things such as contracts, appointments, statutes or rulings. For other purposes, we want to grasp the legal constellation that *results* from the interplay of such sources. We are interested in legal meaning in relative isolation from its source.

This may be put more strongly. Strictly speaking, a discrete legally valid act does not have a legal meaning independently of other legally valid acts. In a sense it is inaccurate to talk of the legal meaning *of a legally valid act*. Legal meaning – the configuration of legal positions – results from the interplay amongst legally valid acts and their products. This is manifest in the accustomed observation, vindicated throughout this book, that there is no one-to-one correspondence between legally valid acts and what are intelligibly called legal norms or rules. Legal norms belong to the plane of legal meaning. They are units into which we divide legal meaning to aid our reasoning. Sometimes when we speak of a legal norm we have in mind a change in legal positions that results rather immediately from a discrete valid act, and only from it: say, a clause in a newly enacted tax statute. Everyone will understand if we say that that norm was created (or posited) by Parliament on such and such a day. It is not particularly odd to speak of that norm as 'legally valid'. But things are rarely as straightforward. When we speak of legal norms that arise from case law, we sometimes attach to them, for simplicity, the name of a case in which they were prominently developed ('the rule in *Rylands v Fletcher*'). We do this even though the cumulative mechanics of *stare decisis*, notably in some jurisdictions, rarely makes it the case that any such 'rule' results exclusively from a discrete judicial decision, especially when the line of precedents is tortuous and long. Speaking of 'the rule in *Rylands v Fletcher*' as a 'legally valid norm' may accordingly seem to some, and rightly so, a stretch of language. For even when a case lays down a rule virtually *de novo*, so that there is something approximating a one-to-one correspondence between the judge's act and the new rule, it must be remembered that case law is not a focally targeted method for crafting rules: the judge makes the rule by applying it (chapter 5.VI). This renders it even less appropriate to speak of the relevant rule as *validly made*. And finally, the asymmetry between the plane of legally valid acts and the plane of legal meaning becomes most palpable in contexts where – as sometimes in the reasoning of higher courts – individual acts that would in other contexts be regarded as validating or justifying tend to fade into a largely unfocused background, and legal meaning may be appropriately regarded as another name for the content of 'the law of the land' (in principle the whole law), consideration of which in the court's reasoning justifies the court's ruling. Legal validity, by contrast, remains a property primarily of acts.

This drifting apart of legal validity and legal meaning also explains the simplification involved, sometimes palpably so, in saying that a certain valid act has *changed the legal meaning of another*. It can sometimes be useful to think of a statute as somehow 'implying' terms *into our signed and sealed four-page agreement*. But it is no less intelligible to discuss what your legal duties are as a seller in accordance with the legal regime, a regime arising from a variety of sources – including contractual documents and statutory provisions. It can be useful to think of case law developments as somehow changing the meaning *of standing statutory clauses*, as when, for example, the term 'inflict' in the English statutory offence of malicious wounding is judicially construed to stand for 'cause'.[57] But it may be no less intelligible to discuss the legal causation requirement for the offence of malicious wounding in accordance with the legal regime, a regime arising from a combination of statutory and case law. One and the same legal reality can often be construed either way.

Whatever our focus in conducting legal reasoning, there is no escape from, although there will be differences in emphasis between, the plane of legal validity and the plane of legal meaning – the plane of legal sources and the plane of the resulting legal regime. We miss out something important about the life of legal reasoning if we define away the former or the latter plane, as this conceals the crucial relationship between the two. Legal meaning cannot come into being, never mind change, without originating valid acts. Acts cannot be legally valid unless systemically related to other acts. If 'the law of the land' can be likened to a large piece of fabric, complete with its wrinkles and mends, valid acts can be likened to the threads from which the fabric is woven.

And it is this kind of fabric for which justice calls. Large-scale convergent endeavours presuppose a degree of coherence amongst countless different threads. Validity's mark serves to handle that complexity. It facilitates the identification of distinct threads. But validity's role is not merely one of simplification. Justice requires that convergent endeavours be woven from threads introduced in targeted, self-reliant fashion by numerous different individuals and groups.

[57] Offences Against the Person Act 1861 (UK), s 20. The judicial construction is prominently made in *Ireland and Burstow* [1998] AC 147 (HL) 160–61, 164, extending the offence to non-violent and indirect means of causation such as harassment; see further *Dica* [2004] EWCA Crim 1103, [2004] QB 1257; *Konzani* [2005] EWCA Crim 706, [2005] 2 Cr App R 14, on transmissions of disease.

The technique whereby legal changes are introduced itself goes to realise the reasons for introducing them. There are good reasons to weave the fabric of law from threads of different sizes and origins, threads wide and narrow, coarse and fine, old and new. Only where that is so, can the resulting fabric of law also be a fabric of justice.

NOTES

Section I: The Moral Need for Law's Positivity

Law's Determinacy Can and Should Only Be Relative

The main text brackets out an interesting set of questions about the conceivable, perhaps inevitable, mismatch between legal and moral obligation resulting from the inability of a legal system, however just and carefully tailored, to regulate conduct in a way thoroughly consistent with an individual's moral responsibilities holding in particular circumstances. This amounts to an inability on the part of the law to be quite as determinate as morality is in the relevant respects. For an acknowledgement of this predicament, see J Finnis, *Aquinas: Moral, Political, and Legal Theory* (Oxford, Oxford University Press, 1998) 163–64; J Finnis, *Philosophy of Law, Collected Essays: Volume IV* (Oxford, Oxford University Press, 2011) 6–7, 8; on the implications for the moral claim plausibly attributed to law, see M Köpcke, 'Finnis on Legal and Moral Obligation' in J Keown and RP George (eds), *Reason, Morality, and Law: The Philosophy of John Finnis* (Oxford, Oxford University Press, 2013) 392–95. For more or less dramatic suggestions that this mismatch occasions an 'asymmetry', 'gap', 'dilemma', 'paradox' or 'moral combat' at the very heart of law, see F Schauer, 'Rules and the Rule of Law' (1991) 14 *Harvard Journal of Law and Public Policy* 645; L Alexander, 'The Gap' (1991) 14 *Harvard Journal of Law and Public Policy* 695; H Hurd, *Moral Combat*, Cambridge Studies in Philosophy and Law (Cambridge, Cambridge University Press, 1999); L Alexander, '"With Me, it's All er Nuthin": Formalism in Law and Morality' (1999) 66 *University of Chicago Law Review* 530. See further D Forte, 'The Rule of Law and the Rule of Laws' (1990) 38 *Cleveland State Law Review* 97; T Endicott, 'The Subsidiarity of Law and the Obligation to Obey' (2005) 50 *American Journal of Jurisprudence* 233; S Smith, 'Cracks in the Coordination Account? Authority and Reasons for Action' (2005) 50 *American Journal of Jurisprudence* 249; P Soper, *The Ethics of Deference: Learning from Law's Morals*, Cambridge Studies in Philosophy and Law (Cambridge, Cambridge University Press, 2002) 42ff; P Soper, 'Law's Normative Claims' in RP George (ed), *The Autonomy of Law: Essays on Legal Positivism* (Oxford, Oxford University Press, 1996) 222ff; D Regan, 'Authority and Value: Reflections on Raz's *Morality of Freedom*' (1989) 62 *Southern California Law Review* 995, 1018–19.

Identifying Legal Requirements Entirely Without Resort to Moral Argument

For arguments against the all-or-nothing character of the Razian constraint on identification, see J Coleman, *The Practice of Principle: In Defence of a Pragmatist Approach to Legal Theory* (Oxford, Oxford University Press, 2001) 143ff (and 126–27 on the distinction between evaluative considerations that are 'conditions of legality' and 'dependent reasons'); W Waluchow, *Inclusive Legal Positivism* (Oxford, Oxford University Press, 1994) especially chs 4, 5 and 8; K Himma, 'HLA Hart and the Practical Difference Thesis' (2000) 6 *Legal Theory* 1, 29ff; S Perry, 'Second-order Reasons, Uncertainty and Legal Theory' (1989) 62 *Southern California Law Review* 913, 972ff; and S Perry, 'Law and Obligation' (2005) 50 *American Journal of Jurisprudence* 263, fn 18 at 270. See further Dworkin, *Law's Empire*, n 12, 429–30; R Dworkin, *Justice in Robes* (Cambridge, MA, Belknap Press, 2006) 206ff; M Kramer, *Where Law and Morality Meet* (Oxford, Oxford University Press, 2004), part I; J Finnis, *Natural Law and Natural Rights*, 2nd edn (Oxford, Oxford University Press, 2011) 312. For sound critical discussions of the Razian view on legal gaps, which however adopt unstable intermediate stances between that view and the one defended in the main text, see T Endicott, 'Raz on Gaps – The Surprising Part' in LH Meyer, SL Paulson and TW Pogge (eds), *Rights, Culture and the Law: Themes from the Legal and Political Philosophy of Joseph Raz* (Oxford, Oxford University Press, 2003); and M Grellette, 'Legal Positivism and the Separation of Existence and Validity' (2010) 23 *Ratio Juris* 22.

Dworkin Nearly Denies Law's Positivity

A cognate but less qualified view, namely the view that extreme injustice deprives an otherwise legally valid norm of its legal validity, is defended, in recent literature, in, eg, G Radbruch, 'Gesetzliches Unrecht und übergesetzliches Recht' (1946) 1 *Süddeutsche Juristenzeitung* 105; R Alexy, *Begriff und Geltung des Rechts* (Munich, Karl Alber, 1992) 70ff; and N MacCormick, *Institutions of Law: An Essay in Legal Theory* (Oxford, Oxford University Press, 2007) ch 15. Part of the difficulty in pinning down Dworkin's position on positivity, determinacy and ease of identification lies in the elusiveness of some of his key notions ('flow from', 'threshold', 'fit', 'figure in or follow from', 'drawn directly', 'in essence factual', etc). Dworkin moreover insists that his aim is not to provide an 'algorithm for the courtroom' (*Law's Empire*, n 12, 412) but only a 'program of adjudication' (ibid 79), and that an 'experienced judge' will 'know instinctively' the correct way to identify law (ibid 245; also 231, 255ff). For an argument that Dworkin's explanation of the 'interpretive judgement' does not succeed in evading incommensurability, see Finnis, *Philosophy of Law*, ch 12, 290ff. For an argument that Dworkin understates the extent to which accounts that assign validity a more central place can reach the same conclusions about what the law requires that Dworkin defends as being legally and morally sound, see T Endicott, 'Adjudication and the Law' (2007) 27 *Oxford Journal of Legal Studies* 311, discussing Dworkin, *Justice in Robes*, ch 6.

Dworkin Leaves Little Room for the Idea of Legal Power

Kyritsis (D Kyritsis, *Shared Authority: Courts and Legislatures in Legal Theory* (Oxford, Hart Publishing, 2014) especially 107ff) proposes a partial reinterpretation of the Dworkinian project to take more conscious account of the moral need for a jurisdictionally-circumscribed interplay of various legal institutions, especially of a legislature sharing authority with courts.

Section III: A Function of the Acts of Others

Raz Portrays the Holder of Authority as an Individual Person

It has been suggested that, on Raz's account, the holder of authority need not even be human or the product of human agency. According to Perry, for example, 'it does not particularly matter whether the "advice" comes from a person or from a black box, which, for all I know, might not even be subject to the control of another person' (S Perry, 'Two Problems of Political Authority' (2007) 6 *American Philosophical Association Newsletter on Law and Philosophy* 31, 33; S Perry, 'Law and Obligation' (2005) 50 *American Journal of Jurisprudence* 263, 292). But this is a misconstruction of Raz, as it runs together questions of characterisation and questions of justification of authority, which Raz endeavours to keep apart (see, eg, Raz, *Practical Reason and Norms*, n 35, 64; J Raz, 'Facing Up: A Reply' (1989) 62 *Southern California Law Review* 1153, 1184ff). The discussions in Perry, 'Law and Obligation', 279ff; Perry, 'Two Problems of Political Authority'; J Waldron, 'Authority for Officials' in LH Meyer, SL Paulson and TW Pogge (eds), *Rights, Culture and the Law: Themes from the Legal and Political Philosophy of Joseph Raz* (Oxford, Oxford University Press, 2003) 66; S Darwall, *Morality, Authority, and Law: Essays in Second-Personal Ethics I* (Oxford, Oxford University Press, 2013) ch 8; and Soper, 'Law's Normative Claims', 238, to varying degrees ignore the fact that Raz's 'normal justification thesis' is only one of the *parts* of his theory of authority that answers to questions of justification (of a *de facto* authority independently identified); see Raz, 'Comments and Responses', n 34, 260.

The 'Sources Thesis' Downplays the Relevance of 'Content' to Identifying Law

So do cognate propositions advanced by other writers. Hart himself had written that 'the existence and content of the law can be identified by reference to the social sources' (HLA Hart, *The Concept of Law*, 2nd edn (Oxford, Clarendon Press, 1994) 269); but see Endicott, 'Adjudication and the Law', 13ff on how Hart's formulation leaves room for substantive validity criteria. According to Marmor, identifying a legal norm 'as such' is distinct from, and prior to, determining its content; the latter, he says, only exceptionally involves interpretation (Marmor, *Interpretation and Legal Theory*, n 53, 119, 90). Gardner (*Law as a Leap of Faith*, n 5), in turn, writes that 'whether a given norm is legally valid … depends on its sources, not its merits' (ibid 21), where 'sources' is defined by exclusion, as anything that is not 'merits' (ibid 20). Specifically, says Gardner, 'in any legal system, a norm is valid as a norm of that system solely in virtue of the fact that at some relevant time and place some relevant agent or agents announced it, practiced it, invoked it, enforced it, endorsed it, or otherwise engaged with it' (ibid 20). Both Marmor's and Gardner's formulations obscure, although they do not deny, the extent to which propositions of law we may intelligibly dub 'norms' do not approach the interpreter as neatly demarcated units ready to be source-checked, but are the result of a potentially complex task of reading together a number of valid acts, the validity of which may turn not merely on procedural but also on substantive considerations. Surely misled by these kinds of formulation, some critics of Hart and Raz have rendered the position of the latter authors as one that leaves no room at all for substantive validity criteria. The early Dworkin (*Taking Rights Seriously*, n 13, 17), for instance, cites as a 'key tenet' of 'legal positivism' the idea that legal 'rules … can be identified … by tests having to do not with their content but with their *pedigree* or the manner in which they were adopted or developed'. And, according to Waldron, 'The idea of positive law is the idea of a proposition … that is treated as a source of law in virtue of some fact or action that has no intrinsic connection to the content, substance, or quality of the proposition itself' (*Law and Disagreement*, n 52, 93, 96). To add to the confusion, others speak as if all substantive validity criteria involved moral judgement: eg, J Coleman, 'Incorporationism, Conventionality, and the Practical Difference Thesis' in J Coleman (ed), *Hart's Postscript: Essays on the Postscript to the Concept of Law* (Oxford, Oxford University Press, 2001) 128, 130; S Shapiro, 'On Hart's Way Out' in J Coleman (ed), *Hart's Postscript: Essays on the Postscript to the Concept of Law* (Oxford, Oxford University Press, 2001) 165; K Himma, 'Inclusive Legal Positivism' in J Coleman and S Shapiro (eds), *The Oxford Handbook of Jurisprudence and Philosophy of Law*, Oxford Handbooks Series (Oxford, Oxford University Press, 2002) 128; K Himma, 'Revisiting Raz: Inclusive Positivism and the Concept of Authority' (2007) 6 *American Philosophical Association Newsletter on Law and Philosophy* 20, 24.

Section IV: Legal Meaning Through Time

Legal Meaning Endures Until Changed or Cancelled

On how it does and should, see Finnis, *Philosophy of Law*, ch 21, 421ff. Changes in legal meaning may also, though this is less frequent, amount to valid *recoveries* of legal changes once invalid. This occurs, for instance, as a new private law regime provides for the validity of arrangements made in accordance with it but in breach of the regime in force at the time of their making: see, eg, on inheritance, transitional provision 6(2) of the law enacting the Catalan civil code (Llei 10/2008, de 10 de juliol, del Llibre Quart del Codi Civil de Catalunya, relatiu a les Successions). It likewise occurs where a change in constitutional doctrine entails that statutes declared unconstitutional under the old doctrine regain their validity and are deemed to have been 'dormant' in the meantime; on the 'dormancy theory' in US constitutional law, most clearly illustrated in the DC Court of Appeal's decision in *Jawish v Morlet*, 86 A2d 96 (DC 1952), see EF Plave, 'The Phenomenon of Antique Laws: Can a State Revive Old Abortion Laws in a New Era?' (1989) 58 *George Washington Law Review* 111; WM Treanor and GB Sperling, 'Prospective Overruling and the Revival of Unconstitutional Statutes' (1993) 93 *Columbia Law Review* 1902 (thanks to Paul Yowell for drawing my attention to this doctrinal strand).

Section V: A Single Author?

Valid Acts of One Legal System are Coherent to Some Degree

In this spirit, with an emphasis on the limits of coherence, see Raz, *Ethics in the Public Domain*, n 5, 277ff; Raz, *Between Authority and Interpretation*, n 30, ch 9; and further

J Dickson, 'Interpretation and Coherence in Legal Reasoning' in EN Zalta (ed), *The Stanford Encyclopaedia of Philosophy*, Winter 2016 Edition (online).

Basic Presuppositions of Legal Thought

Helpful articulations can be found in H Kelsen, *General Theory of Law and State*, A Wedberg (tr) (New York, Russell, 1945) 402–07 ('presuppositions of legal cognition' that go to secure that the system is 'meaningful'); A Ross, *On Law and Justice* (London, Stevens & Sons Limited, 1958) 128–34; F Schauer, *Thinking Like a Lawyer: A New Introduction to Legal Reasoning* (Cambridge, MA, Harvard University Press, 2009).

Legal Maxims That Summon Interpreters to Construe Legal Materials as if Created by a Single Author

For a searching review of existing coherence theories of legal justification, see A Amaya, *The Tapestry of Reason: An Inquiry into the Nature of Coherence and its Role in Legal Argument*, European Academy of Legal Theory Series (Oxford, Hart Publishing, 2014) ch 1. The author's own account, in ch 10, is based on a sound understanding of the moral need for coherence in law (541–44), and proposes to leave appropriate room for deference to authoritative decisions.

'The Law' as the Single Author of Legal Changes

The anthropomorphising assumption discussed in the main text, as being inherent in ordinary legal reasoning, partly overlaps with, although it is more modest than, Dworkin's personification of the community (Dworkin, *Law's Empire*, n 12, 167ff) and Kelsen's account of the state as the personification of the legal order (Kelsen, *General Theory of Law and State*, 181ff and 377: 'The State is not, like human individuals, an object of legal regulation but is the legal regulation itself'). Kelsen goes as far as to say that those who exercise legal power, public *and private*, are in one sense 'organs of the state' (ibid 192–93). The idea that legal officials act as the law's agents is espoused also by, eg, Raz (*Ethics in the Public Domain*, n 5, 215–16; J Raz, 'Hart on Moral Rights and Legal Duties' (1984) 4 *Oxford Journal of Legal Studies* 123, 131; *The Morality of Freedom*, n 5, 70), and Soper ('Law's Normative Claims', 218, 226–27).

Section VI: Threads in a Fabric

No One-to-One Correspondence Between Valid Acts and Legal Norms

See further T Honoré, 'Real Laws' in PMS Hacker and J Raz (eds), *Law, Morality, and Society: Essays in Honour of HLA Hart* (Oxford, Clarendon Press, 1977); NE Simmonds, *Law as a Moral Idea* (Oxford, Oxford University Press, 2007) 157ff; R Guastini, 'Rules, Validity and Statutory Construction' in A Pintore and M Jori (eds), *Law and Language: The Italian Analytical School*, S Stirling, A Pirrie and Z Bankowski (tr) (Liverpool, Deborah Charles Publications, 1997).

Legal Norms Belong to the Plane of Legal Meaning

For a more elaborate defence of this view, T Spaak, *The Concept of Legal Competence: An Essay in Conceptual Analysis*, R Carroll (tr) (Brookfield, VT, Dartmouth, 1994) 157–61. See further H Kelsen, *The Pure Theory of Law*, 2nd edn, Max Knight (tr) (Berkeley, CA, University of California Press, 1967) 2–10 (a norm as the 'objective meaning' of an act of will).

7

Conclusion: The Fabric of Justice

I. THE STRENGTH OF LIMITED POWER

IT IS FITTING to begin this concluding chapter by revisiting the idea of legal power. It has accompanied us throughout the course of this book's argument, and will assist us in retracing our steps. The book set itself the task of making sense of our intriguing practice of settling important questions of justice by appeal to what is legally valid. Valid things are manifold. They include statutes, passports, wills, planning licences, credit cards, mortgage assignments, patents and deportation orders. They can be made by officials or by persons in their private capacity. They can be general or particular in scope. They can be ephemeral or endure for generations. In searching for an underlying similarity amongst this colourful range of valid things, a similarity that might begin to explain why we assign them this paramount role, we turned to the idea of legal power. Legal theorists have been using this idea to loosely refer to certain kinds of act that persons perform with the aim of changing legal positions (of changing, that is, the legal duties, rights, etc, of themselves or others). We found that, properly refined, the received idea of legal power not only bears a close connection to the idea of legal validity, but it also reveals a distinct legal technique whereby valid artefacts are made. The technique consists in changing legal positions, essentially, by saying so (chapter 3.IX). Rules that govern the making of valid artefacts, says the literature, 'provide individuals with facilities for realising their wishes'.[1] They confer legal power. Our discussion showed that the valid say-so is powerful indeed. But it is not an indiscriminate capacity to give legal clothing to whatever one wishes, whenever one does. What one says one wishes to do may not crystallise as a legal result if, for example, the say-so is ultra vires or lacks requisite documentary support. Conversely, one may validly bring about results one did not wish to bring about, or wished not to bring about, if, for instance, a statute implies terms into one's transaction, or a key clause comes to be judicially construed in a way one could not anticipate. We have limited control over the legal meaning of our valid acts. This might appear to point us towards the conclusion that legal power is a limited form of

[1] HLA Hart, *The Concept of Law*, 2nd edn (Oxford, Clarendon Press, 1994) 27 (emphasis omitted).

power. Power certainly – but power curbed, diminished, in proportion to the constraints a legal system places on what we can validly accomplish and how.

But this would be a misleading conclusion. It obscures the crucial sense in which those constraints can *themselves* be empowering. They are not limits on a capacity that we could hold independently of those very kinds of constraints. They are an integral part of what confers on us power to act validly in the first place. There cannot be, in general terms, legally unlimited legal power. We have the ability to change legal positions just insofar as our act slots into an existing and enduring system made up of other valid acts, which system assigns our act a place precisely in delimiting its scope of competence. Those delimiting considerations are criteria of validity. They are characteristically set by the valid acts of other persons or institutions, for example in framing jurisdiction, determining standing or capacity, specifying timing and form, requiring or prohibiting terms, or more indirectly by helping shape the prevailing conventions of legal interpretation (chapter 5.I). A person may be nominally empowered by a decision that appoints him to a public office. But that appointment alone does not confer legal power, unless such an office has been or will be instituted by a regime determining the holder's duties and scope of jurisdiction in relation to other public powers. Electoral legislation may nominally specify which kinds of individuals are entitled to vote in general elections. But that sheer specification is not power-conferring in the absence of a regime circumscribing what the vote is about, how and when to vote, and rendering the result legally binding by restricting the possibilities or occasions of revisiting it. Ultimately, what confers legal power on us is the legal system. It confers legal power by limiting it.

In fact, the power conferred on us by law may be all the greater *precisely in being limited*. The law, for example, may constrain the procedure for validly making a transaction. Conveyancing and registration may be requirements for title to pass. This deprives me of the ability to attain the same legal result by more expedient and less expensive means. But it bestows on me the unique capacity to make an arrangement, now, that remains shielded from challenge in the future. The point of purchasing a house would be defeated if I could not reliably depend on the seller's – and his lawyers' and heirs', third parties', and ultimately judges' – recognition of my transaction and title as valid. The law may also constrain what my contractual agreements can be about. Labour law, for example, precludes me from validly signing up to exploitative work conditions, and consumer law precludes me from validly agreeing to abusive terms of sale. The law constrains my freedom to decide, but in so doing it enables me to decide freely. And there is even a more basic set of empowering constraints inherent in the law governing transactions. Contract law may hold me to my expressed commitment even when I have come to regret it. I cannot unmake a binding agreement simply to replace it with a deal I now think more advantageous. If contract law allowed me to go back on my word as a matter of course, it would be useless as a tool for me to mould my relationships with others, and for others to mould their relationships with me. Sound contract law empowers me by restraining me.

The power the last paragraph has been concerned with is more than just legal power. It is, in essence, the power we each have to steer our own life and shape our identity, as individuals and members of a group, by forging partnerships, embarking on joint ventures, and committing to others in countless ways. Amongst other things, someone's having a claim on my dedicated time and effort can decisively help us both plan and cater for our basic needs, notably those needs satisfaction of which involves specialised skill arising from division of labour. But many aspects of human well-being cannot sufficiently be provided for through piecemeal, overlapping private arrangements involving few individuals at a time. This book has argued that nothing short of large-scale efforts involving collective convergent conduct are called for in order to foster much of what persons in justice deserve (chapter 4.I–III). The presence of a framework of convergence, determining specific conduct to be followed on a community-wide scale, for example through a system of redistribution, can render a contribution of mine especially apt as a means to promoting the well-being of many persons, and thus their own ability to conduct self-reliant lives. My conduct may accordingly be needed in justice, morally due. This kind of obligation does not focally arise from a self-imposed commitment. But it arises from the very considerations that render commitments worth undertaking and keeping.

A legal system can generate and sustain just frameworks of convergence. It has resources to saliently mark specific conduct as due, and to see to its enforcement. The technique of validity renders choices salient (chapter 4.V). But in order for a legal system to design just patterns of convergence, it is important not only that the chosen patterns be salient, but also that the choices be made by those best placed to do so. In order for a legal system to design just patterns of convergence, the power to make valid choices must be allocated properly. Justice substantially determines who ought to decide about what, when and how – and who ought not (chapter 5.II–VII). Reasons to confer and withhold legal power include an agent's relative expertise, institutional capacity and proximity to relevant facts. Central to such reasons are also requirements of the Rule of Law. So is the very value of self-directing choice. The latter consideration weighs in favour of decisions being taken by those more immediately concerned by them, notably in the domain of private relationships and in the domain of a community's collective self-determination through democratic rule. The technique of legal validity is a privileged tool to allocate legal power to certain agents, and to correspondingly circumscribe the legal power of others.

Sound criteria of legal validity will reflect the reasons to empower. They will confer and constrain legal power in a way that matches those rational constraints. I am not well placed to determine next year's value added tax deduction thresholds for my country, not least because I lack the requisite information and expertise, and perhaps impartiality. Conversely, there are many things that my country's tax authorities do not have the ability morally to bind me to do. Therefore, in a just legal system I will lack the legal power to determine tax deduction thresholds, and tax authorities will lack the legal power to decide on many other aspects of my life. Note that in thus setting the bounds of legal power, sound criteria of validity do not so much limit as *delimit* our respective ability to create moral duties and rights. In a sense, sound criteria of validity render salient boundaries that justice already places on our respective authority to choose. To delimit is not to diminish or reduce. A fence that clearly demarcates the hitherto unspecified extension of your garden does not diminish that extension. Rather, it enables you and your neighbours securely to take action without treading on each other's heels. In order valuably to self-direct, as individuals and communities, we do not need unlimited freedom to turn *any* of our wishes into law, anytime. In fact we need to lack such freedom.[2]

But criteria of validity are not needed *merely* to render salient boundaries that already exist as a matter of justice. Delimiting characteristically involves drawing sharper lines. It involves making a host of more or less particular choices concerning the specific outline of the fence. Criteria of legal validity are often needed to draw lines beyond the point where morality draws them. Settling on sound patterns of convergence pervasively calls for under-determined choices, that is, choices that could reasonably have been otherwise. Sound law-making decisions, and other legally valid choices, very often do not merely reflect what morally ought to be done quite independently of those choices. They are able to *craft* new moral duties and rights. They can render conduct due, also morally speaking, by marking it as due. The creative element in this crafting does not amount simply to fine-tuning particulars, say by specifying a tax deduction threshold from within a reasonable range. In the absence of an operative system of resource pooling, which effectively collects and channels resources, I might have little reason to pay value added tax in the first place. My standing reason to contribute to my community's expenses crystallises into a moral duty to make a specific contribution given the presence of a sound scheme of collective convergence rendering salient and enforcing chosen patterns of conduct. It is in the context of this scheme, and in furtherance thereof, that the valid specifications of legislative and tax authorities can craft requirements of justice as if by so saying.

The technique of legal validity can confer on us the power to craft justice. It can *confer* it, not in the sense of bestowing on us an ability we could otherwise

[2] As Endicott shows, even that most self-consciously comprehensive form of community that is a sovereign state, including its legislature, will be appropriately subject to legal constraints arising from its own prior commitments, such as binding treaties, and from internationally proclaimed demands of human rights (T Endicott, 'The Logic of Freedom and Power' in S Besson and J Tasioulas (eds), *The Philosophy of International Law* (Oxford, Oxford University Press, 2010)).

not hold and exercise to any degree. It can confer it in the sense of *facilitating* its exercise. A legal system has remarkable tools to help a political community realise justice, not least by helping persons carve their life path and build up relationships in the framework of supportive community arrangements and a congenial environment in which to dwell. We do not prosper alone. Even achievements that are focally ours crucially capitalise on the achievements of others, and on their cooperation, perseverance and support. The technique of validity empowers us to rally the power of others.

It is therefore sound to liken legal power to the ability to open and close a water gate. This pertinent image is suggested by Rudolf Henle, an early-twentieth-century German private law scholar, writing shortly after Germany had adopted its civil code – a piece of valid law that confers legal power on individuals. Legal power, says Henle, is 'power … to engage foreign power'.[3] For 'a man can open the gate through which the water flows down, but he cannot generate the force of the stream'.[4] The man may have relatively small discretion in modulating the size and direction of the opening. Certain private transactions afford much discretion to design one's relationships; others comparatively little. But one may still exercise power even if one lacks substantial freedom to determine the terms of its exercise. We noted at the end of chapter 2 (section V) that the power a person can be said to wield is not only a function of his targeted control over the specifics of what he can bring about. It is also a function of the importance or significance of what he can bring about, relative to the ease with which he can do so. Legislatures should have broad discretion in designing legal relationships. Spouses should have much less discretion in shaping the legal terms of the marital regime to which they subject themselves. But even spouses bring about legal changes in targeted fashion – by so saying. And even the legislature engages foreign power – the power of the legal system, within which the mere say-so of a group of MPs acquires its distinct legal meaning as a statutory enactment.

This book has shown why legal power is power to engage foreign power, both from a legal and from a moral point of view. In law, a discrete valid say-so can invoke a complex legal regime beyond what is in the mind of the sayer (chapter 3.V). Across public and private law, legal reasoning attends *both* to valid acts, as acts that individually modulate the legal stream of rights, duties and powers, *and* to the stream preceding and jointly resulting from such modulations (chapter 6.VI). It is that stream we look to in seeking to pinpoint 'what the law is' on some matter. It takes valid acts to craft law, but it takes law for any act to be legally valid.

[3] R Henle, *Vorstellungs- und Willenstheorie in der Lehre von der juristischen Willenserklärung* (Leipzig, A Deichert'sche Verlagsbuchhandlung Nachf (Georg Böhme), 1910) 356 ('Macht … fremde Macht anzurufen').

[4] ibid 345 ('Der Mensch kann die Schleuse öffnen, durch die das Wasser herniederströmt, aber er kann nicht die Wasserkraft schaffen').

Morally speaking, too, legal power is power to engage foreign power. It is so not only in the vein of the harmless juristic fiction that personifies 'the law'. It is power to engage the power of other persons – carpenters, nurses, students, fathers, writers, entrepreneurs, neighbours, farmers, engineers, those who hold resources and those who can administer them, those who will not cooperate in the absence of reciprocal reassurance, those who have grown to expect little from the world, and any and each of us in these and countless other capacities. And it is power to engage not only their sheer manual or intellectual power, but also their power to craft further moral duties and rights through their relatively targeted, legally constrained say-so. As the etymology of the term 'craft' invites us to appreciate, in the absence of the requisite *strength*, which was a primary meaning of the old English term '*cræft*' (and is the focal sense of the German '*Kraft*' or the Swedish '*kraft*'), little can and will be crafted. Control of the legal water gate is the strength of limited power.

II. VALIDITY'S SPELL

Validity could not serve as a technique for operating the legal water gate, and therefore as a technique to craft justice, if identifying valid decisions predominantly turned on moral judgement. Valid choices can craft justice because it is relatively inessential to their validity whether they do (chapter 6.I). For one thing, generating salience amongst members of a large and diverse group, in settling controversial moral questions, requires relying on cues that even persons with different ideologies and skills can convergently identify. For another thing, valid choices are called on to devise strategies even in the face of rational under-determination, and so in the absence of uniquely preferable solutions to quandaries that need addressing, perhaps through a tragic compromise. Finally, the technique of validity can be a channel for one's self-direction to the extent that one's valid choices are not liable to being second-guessed in light of what other people think it would have been fairer or wiser to choose. The argument from controversy, the argument from under-determination and the argument from self-direction require that it be possible, by and large, to recognise and engage with what is legally valid while setting morally sensitive questions aside – assumed, silenced, perhaps unknown.

Ordinary engagement with legal validity, by lawyers and laypersons, routinely leaves moral questions outside debate. We confidently appeal to and rely on what is legally valid almost *as if* legal validity required no additional explanation, no further backing to warrant what it is used to warrant. We do this so pervasively that one may legitimately wonder whether there is some spell at work. This is the predicament canvassed in the opening pages of this book (chapter 1.I). We undertook to unravel the point of this spell. It is now in plain sight.

It is the genius of validity's mark that it can be invoked and referred to in countless contexts under countless descriptions. One may look out for validity's mark to turn back troubling legal challenges. One may treat it as a reliable predictor of what other persons will do, perhaps in order to do the same and not collide on the highway. One may see in validity's mark the august expression of the people's will. One may simply care to know what is the done thing. One may do any and all of these things unreflectively. Validity's technique provides shortcuts for identifying the existence of valid decisions, and even the gist of their content (chapter 4.V). It is possible, and frequent, to sign up to a transaction without grasping all its particulars. Few people read the terms and conditions of the *apps* they install. And perhaps only conscientious MPs are versed in the details of the bills on which they vote. Validity's mark can be relevant in many different trains of reasoning. It can form a premise in many different kinds of judgement. Here belongs the full catalogue of judgements, of grounds for 'accepting' legal rules, which Hart was keen on brandishing in *The Concept of Law*, in an effort to dissociate his account of law, and of the 'internal viewpoint', from a normative exercise in political philosophy.[5] Ironically, as Hart perhaps did not appreciate, the availability of those miscellaneous judgements, enabling a broad convergence of identification (chapter 4.VI), is a crucial precondition for a legal system to accomplish what any sound political philosophy will urge it should.

So it is possible, by and large, to engage with legal validity without engaging in moral judgement. But it is not *necessary* to eschew moral judgement to engage with legal validity. The argument in this book illustrates how both things are compatible. In fact, it is in contemplation of the need for large-scale convergent efforts that one may have the most robust kind of moral reason to care about validity's positive, procedural, non-moral mark. Moreover, sometimes moral judgement will be called for, as a matter of law, to determine whether a decision is legally valid (chapter 6.I). And there are many other contexts in which one ought, morally, to second-guess the justice of decisions bearing validity's mark. The danger of injustice is inherent in law, because it is inherent in anything man-made, and it can materialise owing to as many factors as may hinder sound choice in any sphere of life – some of them looming all the larger the greater the stakes of choices entrusted to relatively few persons' hands, as they are often in law.

Validity's technique can do much to reduce the danger of legal injustice, especially by means of an appropriate allocation of legal power, with associated procedural guarantees, evidential burdens and presumptions, and avenues of legal accountability, including institutional checks and mechanisms for review and appeal (chapter 5.V). But validity cannot eliminate every form of error, bias and abuse, consistently with the requirements of justice that validity is meant to advance. It may sometimes be just to fail to remedy an injustice created by a

[5] eg Hart, *The Concept of Law*, n 1, 115, 203.

valid decision. Deference and finality are essential to just government. But law may also fail to remedy injustices it is wrongful *not* to remedy. Valid decisions may create injustices that could and should be avoided. In some ways, the technique of legal validity can pave the way for such injustices to arise and endure. In some ways, validity can increase, rather than reduce, the danger of legal injustice. There are moral hazards inherent in validity's technique. The very features of validity that help us bypass moral questions may discourage us from tackling these questions head-on, when they should be. In that case, validity's spell can be perverse.

These moral hazards of legal validity are but a sombre counterpart of its morally valuable capacities, and should be keenly kept in view in assessing the prospects of justly putting to use validity's resources. Central to the technique of validity is a self-fulfilling say-so. In engaging with legally valid things, we systematically treat somebody's expressed purport as being, itself, the purported accomplishment. Operating with legal sources is operating with the views of others, in a context that renders those views true almost in virtue of the fact that they are expressed. Here the fact that a relevant person says something, as a matter of law, makes it true. By an apparently innocuous extension of validity's logic, one can come to treat as just what the relevant person claims to be just, in virtue of the fact that he claims it. Morally flavoured legal language does not help forestall this slip. Neither do validity's resources geared towards precluding moral second-guessing. Validity can perpetuate injustice precisely by rendering it invisible, unaddressed, condoned.

Law's systemic dimension aggravates the danger. 'What the law is' on some matter often does not correspond to the view of a single person or group, manifested on a discrete occasion. It may represent the views of a number of agents, complemented and qualified by the views of yet others. In reading together legal materials, we inevitably lose sight of their individual makers, with their strengths and weaknesses, personal and institutional, whose choices have gone to shape, in mostly unstated ways, the propositions we now attribute to a faceless entity (chapter 6.V). Modern state administration gives rise to numerous chains of decision-making in distributing legal power, sometimes as between supra-national and local institutions. In many domains it is critical that general legal provisions, as may be set out in constitutions, treaties or framework legislation, be gradually individuated by being brought to bear on increasingly specific scenarios by a sequence of decisions of different agents – think of migration control, environmental protection or the promotion and assessment of research. But protracted chains of empowerment can entrench and perpetuate mistakes in providing a breeding ground for careless outsourcing of responsibility. A valid act in a sense *reiterates*, it bears renewed witness to the validity of, the more general provisions it uses as a legal warrant. For in performing the valid act, the agent professes not only that he wishes to make a certain legal change, but also that he has the ability to do so. And the proximate source of that ability is the say-so of someone else. So the valid act presents itself, often explicitly, and implicitly otherwise, as a continuation, as a concretising implementation, of a legal effort initiated by others, an effort whose validity the act does not reconsider, and whose justice it is not for the act to question. And with every new empowerment, that question may sink ever deeper into the largely unexplored background of considerations that technical legal argument sidesteps.

Legal education has a paramount role to play in counteracting these hazards of legal validity. It is therefore troubling to find that certain kinds of legal education, particularly in some legal cultures, are designed to grant scarce opportunity to look beyond validity's spell, if only in order to appreciate its existence. A legal education that systematically teaches students to eschew the kinds of question that legal argument leaves unstated may encourage the perception, by no means rare amongst law students, that their legal system already addresses all that it needs to address. The sequential exposure of students to problems for which legal regimes are a fix, subject after subject, fix after fix, may distract attention away from the sobering and empowering truth that needed segments of the law's fabric, at any point of time, remain to be woven.

Because woven of legal validity, the fabric of law can also be a fabric of justice. Validity makes it possible to craft just relations between persons by dressing these relations in clothing that hides their justice from view. This is why injustice, too, can bear validity's mark. The law's fabric, like any fabric, can be put to wicked uses. There is more to validity than justice. And there is also more to justice than validity. There are some forms of injustice that legal regulation would only compound, for example by undermining valuable forms of trust or expression in family, friendship and other spheres of personal or community life that may have greater incidence on the well-being of persons, for better or worse, than anything liable to legal scrutiny and validation. Legal systems make an implicit claim to comprehensiveness, given ringing expression in the universalising moral language of constitutional documents, and manifested in the wide, often unspecified, scope of legal competence of law-making institutions. But that ought not to blind one to the fact that legal validity cannot set the agenda of all there is cause to seek and serve, to wish for and work for. Each of us has moral business that ought never show up in a government gazette, and that is fundamental for this very reason. In many ways, that moral business starts where legal validity ends.

Bibliography

Alchourrón, CE and Bulygin, E, *Normative Systems* (New York, Springer, 1971)

Alexander, L, 'The Gap' (1991) 14 *Harvard Journal of Law and Public Policy* 695

——, '"With Me, it's All er Nuthin": Formalism in Law and Morality' (1999) 66 *University of Chicago Law Review* 530

Alexy, R, *Theorie der Grundrechte* (Frankfurt am Main, Suhrkamp, 1986)

——, *Begriff und Geltung des Rechts* (München, Karl Alber, 1992)

Amaya, A, *The Tapestry of Reason: An Inquiry into the Nature of Coherence and its Role in Legal Argument*, European Academy of Legal Theory Series (Oxford, Hart Publishing, 2014)

Aristotle, *The Nicomachean Ethics*, D Ross (tr) (Oxford, Oxford University Press, 2009)

——, *Politics*, CDC Reeve (tr) (Indianapolis, IN, Hackett, 1998)

Atienza, M and Ruiz Manero, J, *Las piezas del Derecho: Teoría de los enunciados jurídicos* (Barcelona, Ariel, 1996)

Austin, JL, 'Other Minds' in JL Austin, *Philosophical Papers*, JO Urmson and GJ Warnock (eds) (Oxford, Clarendon Press, 1961) 44–84

——, *How To Do Things With Words*, 2nd edn, JO Urmson and M Sbisà (eds) (Cambridge, MA, Harvard University Press, 1975)

Bach, K and Harnish, RM, *Linguistic Communication and Speech Acts* (Cambridge, MA, MIT Press, 1979)

Beitz, C, *The Idea of Human Rights* (Oxford, Oxford University Press, 2009)

Belvedere, A, 'Some Observations on the Language of the Italian Civil Code' in A Pintore and M Jori (eds), *Law and Language: The Italian Analytical School*, S Stirling, A Pirrie and Z Bankowski (tr) (Liverpool, Deborah Charles Publications, 1997) 339–418

Bentham, J, *Of Laws in General*, HLA Hart (ed) (London, The Athlone Press, 1970)

Besson, S, *The Morality of Conflict: Reasonable Disagreement and the Law* (Oxford, Hart Publishing, 2005)

Boardman, M, 'Coordination and the Moral Obligation to Obey the Law' (1987) 97 *Ethics* 546

Bobbio, N, 'Kelsen and Legal Power' in SL Paulson and B Litschewski-Paulson (eds), *Normativity and Norms: Critical Perspectives on Kelsenian Themes* (Oxford, Clarendon Press, 1998) 435–49

Brandom, RB, *Making it Explicit: Reasoning, Representing, and Discursive Commitment* (Cambridge, MA, Harvard University Press, 1994)

Bulygin, E, 'Tiempo y Validez' in CE Alchourrón and E Bulygin, *Análisis lógico y Derecho* (Madrid, Centro de Estudios Constitucionales, 1991) 195–214

——, 'Sobre las normas de competencia' in CE Alchourrón and E Bulygin, *Análisis lógico y Derecho* (Madrid, Centro de Estudios Constitucionales, 1991) 485–97

Caracciolo, R, *La Noción de Sistema en la Teoría del Derecho* (Mexico, Fontamara, 1992)

Chang, R, 'Introduction' in R Chang (ed), *Incommensurability, Incomparability, and Practical Reason* (Cambridge, MA, Harvard University Press, 1997) 1–34

Chen-Wishart, M, *Contract Law*, 5th edn (Oxford, Oxford University Press, 2015)

Cohen, LJ, 'Critical Notice' (1962) 71 *Mind* 395

——, 'Do Illocutionary Forces Exist?' (1964) 14 *The Philosophical Quarterly* 118

Coleman, J, 'Positive and Negative Positivism' in M Cohen (ed), *Ronald Dworkin and Contemporary Jurisprudence* (London, Duckworth, 1984) 28–48

——, 'Incorporationism, Conventionality, and the Practical Difference Thesis' in J Coleman (ed), *Hart's Postscript: Essays on the Postscript to the* Concept of Law (Oxford, Oxford University Press, 2001) 99–147

——, *The Practice of Principle: In Defence of a Pragmatist Approach to Legal Theory* (Oxford, Oxford University Press, 2001)

Conte, AG, 'Eidetic-Constitutive Rules' in A Pintore and M Jori (eds), *Law and Language: The Italian Analytical School*, S Stirling, A Pirrie and Z Bankowski (tr) (Liverpool, Deborah Charles Publications, 1997) 133–46

Dan-Cohen, M, 'Decision Rules and Conduct Rules: On Acoustic Separation in Criminal Law' (1983) 97 *Harvard Law Review* 625

Darwall, S, *The Second-Person Standpoint: Morality, Respect, and Accountability* (Cambridge, MA, Harvard University Press, 2006)

——, *Morality, Authority, and Law: Essays in Second-Personal Ethics I* (Oxford, Oxford University Press, 2013)

Davies, WH, *The Autobiography of a Super-Tramp* (London, Fifield, 1908)

Dickson, J, 'Is the Rule of Recognition Really a Conventional Rule?' (2007) 27 *Oxford Journal of Legal Studies* 1

——, 'Interpretation and Coherence in Legal Reasoning' in EN Zalta (ed), *The Stanford Encyclopaedia of Philosophy*, Winter 2016 Edition (online)

Duncanson, I, 'The Strange World of English Jurisprudence' (1979) 30 *Northern Ireland Legal Quarterly* 207

Dworkin, R, *Taking Rights Seriously* (London, Duckworth, 1978)

——, *Law's Empire* (Oxford, Hart Publishing, 1998)

——, *Justice in Robes* (Cambridge, MA, Belknap Press, 2006)

——, *Justice for Hedgehogs* (Cambridge, MA, Belknap Press, 2011)

Edmundson, WA, 'Social Meaning, Compliance Conditions, and Law's Claim to Authority' (2002) 15 *Canadian Journal of Law and Jurisprudence* 51

——, 'Political Authority, Moral Powers and the Intrinsic Value of Obedience' (2010) 30 *Oxford Journal of Legal Studies* 179

Ekins, R, *The Nature of Legislative Intent* (Oxford, Oxford University Press, 2012)

——, 'How To Be a Free People' (2013) 58 *American Journal of Jurisprudence* 163

Endicott, T, 'Objectivity, Subjectivity, and Incomplete Agreements' in J Horder (ed), *Oxford Essays in Jurisprudence Fourth Series* (Oxford, Oxford University Press, 2000) 151–71

——, *Vagueness in Law* (Oxford, Oxford University Press, 2000)

——, 'Raz on Gaps – The Surprising Part' in LH Meyer, SL Paulson and TW Pogge (eds), *Rights, Culture and the Law: Themes from the Legal and Political Philosophy of Joseph Raz* (Oxford, Oxford University Press, 2003) 99–115

——, 'The Reason of the Law' (2003) 48 *American Journal of Jurisprudence* 83

——, 'The Value of Vagueness' in A Marmor and S Soames (eds), *Philosophical Foundations of Language in the Law* (Oxford, Oxford University Press, 2011) 14–30

——, 'The Subsidiarity of Law and the Obligation to Obey' (2005) 50 *American Journal of Jurisprudence* 233

——, 'The Infant in the Snow' in T Endicott, J Getzler and E Peel (eds), *Properties of Law: Essays in Honour of Jim Harris* (Oxford, Oxford University Press, 2006) 348–66

——, 'Adjudication and the Law' (2007) 27 *Oxford Journal of Legal Studies* 311

——, 'The Logic of Freedom and Power' in S Besson and J Tasioulas (eds), *The Philosophy of International Law* (Oxford, Oxford University Press, 2010) 245–60

——, *Administrative Law*, 2nd edn (Oxford, Oxford University Press, 2011)

——, 'Proportionality and Incommensurability' in G Huscroft, BW Miller and G Webber (eds), *Proportionality and the Rule of Law: Rights, Justification, Reasoning* (Cambridge, Cambridge University Press, 2014) 311–42

——, 'The Generality of Law' in L Duarte d'Almeida, J Edwards and A Dolcetti (eds), *Reading HLA Hart's* The Concept of Law (Oxford, Hart Publishing, 2013) 15–36

——, 'Arbitrariness' (2014) 27 *Canadian Journal of Law and Jurisprudence* 49

Ferrer, J, *Las normas de competencia: Un aspecto de la dinámica jurídica* (Madrid, BOE/Centro de Estudios Políticos y Constitucionales, 2000)

Finnis, J, *Fundamentals of Ethics* (Washington, DC, Georgetown University Press, 1983)
——, *Aquinas: Moral, Political, and Legal Theory* (Oxford, Oxford University Press, 1998)
——, *Natural Law and Natural Rights*, 2nd edn (Oxford, Oxford University Press, 2011)
——, *Reason in Action, Collected Essays: Volume I* (Oxford, Oxford University Press, 2011)
——, *Human Rights and Common Good, Collected Essays: Volume III* (Oxford, Oxford University Press, 2011)
——, *Philosophy of Law, Collected Essays: Volume IV* (Oxford, Oxford University Press, 2011)
——, 'Reflections and Responses' in J Keown and RP George (eds), *Reason, Morality, and Law: The Philosophy of John Finnis* (Oxford, Oxford University Press, 2013) 459–582
——, 'Judicial Power: Past, Present and Future' in R Ekins (ed), *Judicial Power and the Balance of Our Constitution: Two lectures by John Finnis* (London, Policy Exchange, 2018) 26–61
Forte, D, 'The Rule of Law and the Rule of Laws' (1990) 38 *Cleveland State Law Review* 97
Fox-Decent, E, *Sovereignty's Promise: The State as Fiduciary*, Oxford Constitutional Theory (Oxford, Oxford University Press, 2011)
Friedman, R, 'Oakeshott on the Authority of Law' (1989) 2 *Ratio Juris* 27
——, 'On the Concept of Authority in Political Philosophy' in J Raz (ed), *Authority, Readings in Social and Political Theory* (New York, New York University Press, 1990) 56–91
Fuller, L, *The Morality of Law*, 2nd edn (New Haven, CT, Yale University Press, 1969)
Gans, C, 'The Normativity of Law and its Coordinative Function' (1981) 18 *Israel Law Review* 333
Gardner, J, 'Reasons for Teamwork' (2002) 8 *Legal Theory* 495
——, *Offences and Defences: Selected Essays in the Philosophy of Criminal Law* (Oxford, Oxford University Press, 2007)
——, 'Justification under Authority' (2010) 23 *Canadian Journal of Law and Jurisprudence* 71
——, *Law as a Leap of Faith* (Oxford, Oxford University Press, 2012)
——, 'Finnis on Justice' in J Keown and RP George (eds), *Reason, Morality, and Law: The Philosophy of John Finnis* (Oxford, Oxford University Press, 2013) 151–66
——, Horder, J and Shute, S, 'Introduction: The Logic of Criminal Law' in J Gardner, J Horder and S Shute (eds), *Action and Value in Criminal Law* (Oxford, Clarendon Press, 1994) 1–20
Garzón Valdés, E, 'Two Models of Legal Validity: Hans Kelsen and Francisco Suárez' in SL Paulson and B Litschewski-Paulson (eds), *Normativity and Norms: Critical Perspectives on Kelsenian Themes* (Oxford, Clarendon Press, 1998) 263–71
Goldsworthy, J, 'The Case for Originalism' in G Huscroft and BW Miller (eds), *The Challenge of Originalism: Theories of Constitutional Interpretation* (Cambridge, Cambridge University Press, 2011) 42–69
Grant, J, 'The Scales of Authority' (2015) 60 *American Journal of Jurisprudence* 79
Green, L, 'Law, Co-ordination, and the Common Good' (1983) 3 *Oxford Journal of Legal Studies* 299
——, *The Authority of the State* (Oxford, Oxford University Press, 1988)
——, 'The Concept of Law Revisited' (1996) 94 *Michigan Law Review* 1687
——, 'Positivism and Conventionalism' (1999) 12 *Canadian Journal of Law and Jurisprudence* 35
——, 'Three Themes from Raz' (2005) 25 *Oxford Journal of Legal Studies* 503
——, 'The Duty to Govern' (2007) 13 *Legal Theory* 165
Greenberg, M, 'Legislation as Communication? Legal Interpretation, and the Study of Linguistic Communication' in A Marmor and S Soames (eds), *Philosophical Foundations of Language in the Law* (Oxford, Oxford University Press, 2011) 217–56
——, 'The Moral Impact Theory of Law' (2014) 123 *Yale Law Journal* 1288
Grellette, M, 'Legal Positivism and the Separation of Existence and Validity' (2010) 23 *Ratio Juris* 22
Grice, P, 'Meaning' (1957) 66 *The Philosophical Review* 377
——, *Studies in the Way of Words* (Cambridge, MA, Harvard University Press, 1989)
Guastini, R, 'Invalidity' (1994) 7 *Ratio Juris* 212
——, 'Rules, Validity and Statutory Construction' in A Pintore and M Jori (eds), *Law and Language: The Italian Analytical School*, S Stirling, A Pirrie and Z Bankowski (tr) (Liverpool, Deborah Charles Publications, 1997) 229–47

Häcker, B, 'The Impact of Illegality and Immorality on Contract and Restitution from a Civilian Angle' in S Green and A Bogg (eds), *Illegality after* Patel v Mirza (Oxford, Hart Publishing, 2018) 329–68

Hage, J, *Foundations and Building Blocks of Law* (The Hague, Eleven International Publishing, 2018)

Hägerström, A, *Inquiries into the Nature of Law and Morals*, CD Broad (tr) (Stockholm, Almquist & Wiksell, 1953)

Halpin, A, 'The Concept of a Legal Power' (1996) 16 *Oxford Journal of Legal Studies* 129

Hare, RM, *The Language of Morals*, 2nd edn (Oxford, Oxford University Press, 1961)

——, 'Meaning and Speech Acts' (1970) 79 *The Philosophical Review* 3

Harel, A, *Why Law Matters* (Oxford, Oxford University Press, 2014)

Harris, JW, *Legal Philosophies* (London, Butterworths, 1980)

Harrison, R, 'The Moral Role of Conventions' in JB Murphy and A Perreau-Saussine, *The Nature of Customary Law: Legal, Historical and Philosophical Perspectives* (Cambridge, Cambridge University Press, 2007) 35–52

Hart, HLA, *Essays on Bentham*, Studies in Jurisprudence and Political Theory (Oxford, Clarendon Press, 2001)

——, *Essays in Jurisprudence and Philosophy* (Oxford, Oxford University Press, 1983)

——, *The Concept of Law*, 2nd edn (Oxford, Clarendon Press, 1994)

Henle, R, *Vorstellungs- und Willenstheorie in der Lehre von der juristischen Willenserklärung* (Leipzig, A Deichert'sche Verlagsbuchhandlung Nachf (Georg Böhme), 1910)

Henry, O, 'The Cop and the Anthem' in O Henry, *100 Selected Stories* (Ware, Wordsworth Editions, 1995) 32–36

Himma, K, 'HLA Hart and the Practical Difference Thesis' (2000) 6 *Legal Theory* 1

——, 'Inclusive Legal Positivism' in J Coleman and S Shapiro (eds), *The Oxford Handbook of Jurisprudence and Philosophy of Law*, Oxford Handbooks Series (Oxford, Oxford University Press, 2002) 125–65

——, 'Revisiting Raz: Inclusive Positivism and the Concept of Authority' (2007) 6 *American Philosophical Association Newsletter on Law and Philosophy* 20

Hohfeld, WN, 'Some Fundamental Legal Conceptions as Applied in Judicial Reasoning' (1913) 23 *Yale Law Journal* 16

Holmes, OW, 'The Path of the Law' (1897) 10 *Harvard Law Review* 457

Honoré, T, 'Real Laws' in PMS Hacker and J Raz (eds), *Law, Morality, and Society: Essays in Honour of HLA Hart* (Oxford, Clarendon Press, 1977) 99–118

Hurd, H, 'Sovereignty in Silence' (1990) 99 *Yale Law Journal* 945

——, *Moral Combat*, Cambridge Studies in Philosophy and Law (Cambridge, Cambridge University Press, 1999)

Juratowich, B, *Retroactivity and the Common Law* (Oxford, Hart Publishing, 2008)

Kelsen, H, *General Theory of Law and State*, A Wedberg (tr) (New York, Russell, 1945)

——, *Reine Rechtslehre*, 2nd edn (Vienna, Österreichische Staatsdruckerei, 1960)

——, *The Pure Theory of Law*, 2nd edn, Max Knight (tr) (Berkeley, CA, University of California Press, 1967)

——, *General Theory of Norms*, M Hartney (tr) (Oxford, Clarendon Press, 1991)

Klass, G, 'Three Pictures of Contract: Duty, Power and Compound Rule' (2008) 83 *New York University Law Review* 1726

——, 'Intent to Contract' (2009) 95 *Virginia Law Review* 1437

Köpcke, M, 'Positive Law's Moral Purpose(s): Towards a New Consensus?' (2011) 56 *American Journal of Jurisprudence* 186

——, 'Finnis on Legal and Moral Obligation' in J Keown and RP George (eds), *Reason, Morality, and Law: The Philosophy of John Finnis* (Oxford, Oxford University Press, 2013) 379–95

——, *A Short History of Validity and Invalidity: Foundations of Private and Public Law* (Cambridge, Intersentia, forthcoming)

Korta, K and Perry, J, 'Pragmatics' in EN Zalta (ed), *The Stanford Encyclopedia of Philosophy*, Winter 2015 Edition (online)
Kramer, M, *Where Law and Morality Meet* (Oxford, Oxford University Press, 2004)
Kyritsis, D, *Shared Authority: Courts and Legislatures in Legal Theory* (Oxford, Hart Publishing, 2014)
Lacruz Berdejo, JL et al, *Derecho de Obligaciones, Elementos de Derecho Civil II*, vol I, 3rd edn (Barcelona, Bosch, 1994)
Lamond, G, 'The Coerciveness of Law' (2000) 20 *Oxford Journal of Legal Studies* 39
——, 'Do Precedents Create Rules?' (2005) 11 *Legal Theory* 1
Lewis, D, *Convention: A Philosophical Study* (Oxford, Basil Blackwell, 2002)
MacCormick, N, *Legal Reasoning and Legal Theory* (Oxford, Oxford University Press, 1978)
——, *H.L.A. Hart*, Jurists: *Profiles in Legal Theory* (London, Edward Arnold, 1981)
——, 'The Concept of Law and The Concept of Law' in RP George (ed), *The Autonomy of Law: Essays on Legal Positivism* (Oxford, Oxford University Press, 1996) 163–94
——, 'Powers and Power-Conferring Norms' in SL Paulson and B Litschewski-Paulson (eds), *Normativity and Norms: Critical Perspectives on Kelsenian Themes* (Oxford, Clarendon Press, 1998) 493–506
——, *Institutions of Law: An Essay in Legal Theory* (Oxford, Oxford University Press, 2007)
—— and Bankowski, Z, 'Speech Acts, Legal Institutions and Real Laws' in P Birks and N MacCormick (eds), *The Legal Mind: Essays for Tony Honoré* (Oxford, Clarendon Press, 1986) 121–33
Marmor, A, *Interpretation and Legal Theory*, 2nd edn (Oxford, Hart Publishing, 2005)
——, *Social Conventions: From Language to Law* (Princeton, NJ, Princeton University Press, 2009)
——, 'An Institutional Conception of Authority' (2011) 39 *Philosophy and Public Affairs* 238
——, *The Language of Law* (Oxford, Oxford University Press, 2014)
McMahon, C, 'Autonomy and Authority' (1987) 16 *Philosophy and Public Affairs* 303
Munzer, S, *Legal Validity* (The Hague, Martinus Nijhoff, 1972)
Nino, CS, *Introducción al Análisis del Derecho* (Barcelona, Ariel, 1983)
Nozick, R, *Anarchy, State, and Utopia* (New York, Basic Books, 1974)
Paulson, S, 'An Empowerment Theory of Norms' (1988) 1 *Ratio Juris* 58
Penner, J, 'Legal Reasoning and the Authority of Law' in LH Meyer, SL Paulson and TW Pogge (eds), *Rights, Culture and the Law: Themes from the Legal and Political Philosophy of Joseph Raz* (Oxford, Oxford University Press, 2003) 71–98
Perry, S, 'Second-order Reasons, Uncertainty and Legal Theory' (1989) 62 *Southern California Law Review* 913
——, 'Law and Obligation' (2005) 50 *American Journal of Jurisprudence* 263
——, 'Two Problems of Political Authority' (2007) 6 *American Philosophical Association Newsletter on Law and Philosophy* 31
Pfordten, D von der, 'Validity in Positive Law – A Mere Summary Concept' in P Westerman et al (eds), *Legal Validity and Soft Law* (Dortrecht, Springer, 2018) 1–18
Plave, EF, 'The Phenomenon of Antique Laws: Can a State Revive Old Abortion Laws in a New Era?' (1989) 58 *George Washington Law Review* 111
Postema, G, 'Coordination and Convention at the Foundations of Law' (1982) 11 *Journal of Legal Studies* 165
Radbruch, G, 'Gesetzliches Unrecht und übergesetzliches Recht' (1946) 1 *Süddeutsche Juristenzeitung* 105
Ransdell, J, 'Constitutive Rules and Speech-Act Analysis' (1971) 68 *The Journal of Philosophy* 385
Rawls, J, *A Theory of Justice* (Cambridge, MA, Harvard University Press, 1971)
——, *The Law of Peoples* (Cambridge, MA, Harvard University Press, 1999)
Raz, J, *Practical Reason and Norms* (London, Hutchinson, 1975)
——, *The Authority of Law: Essays on Law and Morality* (Oxford, Oxford University Press, 1979)
——, *The Concept of a Legal System*, 2nd edn (Oxford, Oxford University Press, 1980)
——, 'Promises in Morality and Law' (1982) 95 *Harvard Law Review* 916

——, 'Hart on Moral Rights and Legal Duties' (1984) 4 *Oxford Journal of Legal Studies* 123
——, *The Morality of Freedom* (Oxford, Clarendon Press, 1986)
——, 'Facing Up: A Reply' (1989) 62 *Southern California Law Review* 1153
——, 'Introduction' in J Raz (ed), *Authority*, Readings in Social and Political Theory (New York, New York University Press, 1990) 1–19
——, *Ethics in the Public Domain: Essays in the Morality of Law and Politics*, rev edn (Oxford, Clarendon Press, 1995)
——, 'Voluntary Obligations and Normative Powers' in SL Paulson and B Litschewski-Paulson (eds), *Normativity and Norms: Critical Perspectives on Kelsenian Themes* (Oxford, Clarendon Press, 1998) 451–70
——, 'Comments and Responses' in LH Meyer, SL Paulson and TW Pogge (eds), *Rights, Culture and the Law: Themes from the Legal and Political Philosophy of Joseph Raz* (Oxford, Oxford University Press, 2003) 253–73
——, *Between Authority and Interpretation: On the Theory of Law and Practical Reason* (Oxford, Oxford University Press, 2009)
——, 'Human Rights Without Foundations' in S Besson and J Tasioulas (eds), *The Philosophy of International Law* (Oxford, Oxford University Press, 2010) 321–37
Regan, D, 'Law's Halo' (1986) 4 *Social Philosophy and Policy* 15
——, 'Authority and Value: Reflections on Raz's Morality of Freedom' (1989) 62 *Southern California Law Review* 995
Ross, A, 'Book Review: Kelsen, "What is Justice?"' (1957) 45 *California Law Review* 564
——, 'Tû-Tû' (1958) 70 *Harvard Law Review* 812
——, *On Law and Justice* (London, Stevens & Sons Limited, 1958)
——, 'On the Concepts "State" and "State Organs" in Constitutional Law' (1961) 5 *Scandinavian Studies in Law* 111
——, *Directives and Norms* (London, Routledge, 1968)
——, 'Rise and Fall of the Doctrine of Performatives' in RE Olson and AM Paul (eds), *Contemporary Philosophy in Scandinavia* (Baltimore, MD, The Johns Hopkins Press, 1972) 197–212
——, 'Validity and the Conflict between Legal Positivism and Natural Law' in SL Paulson and B Litschewski-Paulson (eds), *Normativity and Norms: Critical Perspectives on Kelsenian Themes* (Oxford, Clarendon Press, 1998) 147–63
Ruiter, DWP, *Institutional Legal Facts: Legal Powers and Their Effects* (Dortrecht, Kluwer, 1993)
Säcker, FJ et al (eds), *Münchener Kommentar zum Bürgerlichen Gesetzbuch, Band 1: Allgemeiner Teil, §§ 1–240*, 7th edn (Munich, CH Beck, 2015)
Sandro, P, 'Unlocking Legal Validity: Some Remarks on the Artificial Ontology of Law' in P Westerman et al (eds), *Legal Validity and Soft Law* (Dortrecht, Springer, 2018) 99–124
Santamaría Pastor, JA, *Principios de Derecho Administrativo: Volume II* (Madrid, Ramón Areces, 1999)
Sartor, G, 'Legal Validity: An Inferential Analysis' (2008) 21 *Ratio Juris* 212
Saussure de, F, *Course in General Linguistics*, C Bally and A Sechehaye (eds), W Baskin (tr) (New York, McGraw Hill, 1960)
Scanlon, TM, *What We Owe to Each Other* (Cambridge, MA, Harvard University Press, 1998)
Schauer, F, 'Rules and the Rule of Law' (1991) 14 *Harvard Journal of Law and Public Policy* 645
——, *Thinking Like a Lawyer: A New Introduction to Legal Reasoning* (Cambridge, MA, Harvard University Press, 2009)
Schelling, T, *The Strategy of Conflict* (New York, Oxford University Press, 1963)
Searle, J, 'How to Derive "Ought" from "Is"' (1964) 73 *The Philosophical Review* 43
——, 'Austin on Locutionary and Illocutionary Acts' (1968) 77 *The Philosophical Review* 405
——, *Speech Acts: An Essay in the Philosophy of Language* (Cambridge, Cambridge University Press, 1969)
——, *Expression and Meaning: Studies in the Theory of Speech Acts* (Cambridge, Cambridge University Press, 1979)
——, *The Construction of Social Reality* (New York, Free Press, 1995)

Shapiro, S, 'Law, Morality, and the Guidance of Conduct' (2000) 6 *Legal Theory* 127
——, 'On Hart's Way Out' in J Coleman (ed), *Hart's Postscript: Essays on the Postscript to the* Concept of Law (Oxford, Oxford University Press, 2001) 149–91
——, 'Law, Plans, and Practical Reason' (2002) 8 *Legal Theory* 387
——, 'Authority' in J Coleman and S Shapiro (eds), *The Oxford Handbook of Jurisprudence and Philosophy of Law*, Oxford Handbooks Series (Oxford, Oxford University Press, 2002) 382–439
——, *Legality* (Cambridge, MA, Harvard University Press, 2009)
Sherman, J, 'Unresolved Problems in the Service Conception of Authority' (2010) 30 *Oxford Journal of Legal Studies* 419
Simester, AP et al, *Simester and Sullivan's Criminal Law: Theory and Doctrine*, 6th edn (Oxford, Hart Publishing, 2016)
Simmonds, NE, *Law as a Moral Idea* (Oxford, Oxford University Press, 2007)
Simon, Y, *A General Theory of Authority* (Notre Dame, IN, University of Notre Dame Press, 1980)
Smith, S, 'Cracks in the Coordination Account? Authority and Reasons for Action' (2005) 50 *American Journal of Jurisprudence* 249
——, 'Why Courts Make Orders (And What This Tells Us About Damages)' (2011) 64 *Current Legal Problems* 51
——, 'Rule-Based Rights and Court-Ordered Rights' in A Robertson and D Nolan (eds), *The Rights of Private Law* (Oxford, Hart Publishing, 2012)
Soames, S, 'Vagueness and the Law' in A Marmor (ed), *The Routledge Companion to Philosophy of Law* (New York, Routledge, 2012) 95–108
Solum, LB, 'Communicative Content and Legal Content' (2013) 89 *Notre Dame Law Review* 479
Soper, P, 'Law's Normative Claims', in RP George (ed), *The Autonomy of Law: Essays on Legal Positivism* (Oxford, Oxford University Press, 1996)
——, *The Ethics of Deference: Learning from Law's Morals*, Cambridge Studies in Philosophy and Law (Cambridge, Cambridge University Press, 2002)
Spaak, T, *The Concept of Legal Competence: An Essay in Conceptual Analysis*, R Carroll (tr) (Brookfield, VT, Dartmouth, 1994)
——, 'Norms that Confer Competence' (2003) 16 *Ratio Juris* 89
——, 'Explicating the Concept of Legal Competence' in JC Hage and D von der Pfordten (eds), *Concepts in Law* (Dortrecht, Springer, 2009) 67–80
Strawson, PF, 'Intention and Convention in Speech Acts' (1964) 73 *The Philosophical Review* 439
Summers, RS, 'Toward a Better General Theory of Legal Validity' (1985) 16 *Rechtstheorie* 65
Tasioulas, J, 'On the Nature of Human Rights' in G Ernst and J-C Heilinger (eds), *The Philosophy of Human Rights: Contemporary Controversies* (Berlin, Walter de Gruyter, 2012) 17–59
——, 'Human Rights, Legitimacy, and International Law' (2013) 58 *The American Journal of Jurisprudence* 1
——, 'On the Foundations of Human Rights' in R Cruft, SM Liao and M Renzo (eds), *Philosophical Foundations of Human Rights* (Oxford, Oxford University Press, 2015) 45–70
Toh, K, 'Raz on Detachment, Acceptance and Describability' (2007) 27 *Oxford Journal of Legal Studies* 1
Treanor, WM and Sperling, GB, 'Prospective Overruling and the Revival of Unconstitutional Statutes' (1993) 93 *Columbia Law Review* 1902
Ullmann-Margalit, E, *The Emergence of Norms* (Oxford, Oxford University Press, 1977)
Vermeule, A, *Law and the Limits of Reason* (Oxford, Oxford University Press, 2009)
Waldron, J, *Law and Disagreement* (Oxford, Oxford University Press, 1999)
——, 'Lex Satis Iusta' (2000) 75 *Notre Dame Law Review* 1829
——, 'Authority for Officials' in LH Meyer, SL Paulson and TW Pogge (eds), *Rights, Culture and the Law: Themes from the Legal and Political Philosophy of Joseph Raz* (Oxford, Oxford University Press, 2003) 45–70
——, 'Vagueness and the Guidance of Action' in A Marmor and S Soames (eds), *Philosophical Foundations of Language in the Law* (Oxford, Oxford University Press, 2011) 59–83

——, 'Human Rights: A Critique of the Raz/Rawls Approach' in A Etinson (ed), *Human Rights: Moral or Political?* (Oxford, Oxford University Press, 2018)
Waluchow, W, *Inclusive Legal Positivism* (Oxford, Oxford University Press, 1994)
Watson, G, 'Asserting and Promising' (2004) 117 *Philosophical Studies* 57
Webber, G et al, *Legislated Rights: Securing Human Rights Through Legislation* (Cambridge, Cambridge University Press, 2018)
Wright, GH von, *Norm and Action: A Logical Enquiry* (London, Routledge & Kegan Paul, 1963)
Young, A, *Democratic Dialogue and the Constitution* (Oxford, Oxford University Press, 2017)
Yowell, P, 'Legislation, Common Law, and the Virtue of Clarity' in R Ekins (ed), *Modern Challenges to the Rule of Law* (Wellington, LexisNexis, 2011)
——, *Constitutional Rights and Constitutional Design: Moral and Empirical Reasoning in Judicial Review* (Oxford, Hart Publishing, 2018)

Index

www.ingramcontent.com/pod-product-compliance
Lightning Source LLC
LaVergne TN
LVHW052326200926
848481LV00002B/682

* 9 7 8 1 5 0 9 9 4 5 2 4 5 *